INADVERTENT NUCLEAR WAR

The Implications of the Changing Global Order

Titles of Related Interest

INADVERTENT NUCLEAR WAR

The Implications of the Changing Global Order

Edited by

HÅKAN WIBERG,
IB DAMGAARD PETERSEN AND PAUL SMOKER

247007

PERGAMON PRESS
OXFORD • NEW YORK • SEOUL • TOKYO

UK	Pergamon Press Ltd, Headington Hill Hall, Oxford OX3 0BW, England
USA	Pergamon Press Inc., 660 White Plains Road, Tarrytown, New York 10591-5153, USA
KOREA	Pergamon Press Korea, KPO Box 315, Seoul 110-603, Korea
JAPAN	Pergamon Press Japan, Tsunashima Building Annex, 3-20-12 Yushima, Bunkyo-ku, Tokyo 113, Japan

First edition 1993

Library of Congress Cataloging-in-Publication Data
Inadvertent nuclear war : the implications of the changing global order / editors: Håkan Wiberg, Ib Damgaard Petersen, and Paul Smoker. -- 1st ed.
p. cm.
Includes bibliographical references.
1. Nuclear warfare. 2. Nuclear crisis control. 3. World politics--1989- I. Wiberg, Håkan, 1942- . II. Petersen, Ib Damgaard. III. Smoker, Paul.
U263. I53 1993
355.02'17--dc20 93-33126

ISBN 0-08-041380-3

Printed in Great Britain by BPCC Wheatons, Ltd, Exeter

Contents

v

Preface

The concept of this volume stems from a symposium, 'Accidental Nuclear War' that was held in Copenhagen on June 29 - July 1, 1990, arranged in collaboration by the Institute for Political Science, University of Copenhagen and the Centre for Peace and Conflict Research in Copenhagen, with additional financial support from *Sikkerheds-og Nedrustningspolitisk Udvalg* and *Dansk Udenrigspolitisk Institut*. The contributions were finalized in May-June 1993.

We are grateful to the Board of the *Swedish Initiative for the Prevention of Accidental Nuclear War* for permission to reprint Appendix B.

We would also like to record our gratitude to Mr. Jens Mathiesen at the Centre for Peace and Conflict Research, who has been indispensable in getting the files organized, cleaned up and edited into a Camera Ready Copy.

The editors

Copenhagen and Yellow Springs, July 1993.

About the Authors

Herbert L. Abrams is Professor of Radiology at Stanford University and Member-in-Residence at the Center for International Security and Arms Control, Stanford University.

Ingemar Ahlstrand is a Doctor of Engineering (Stockholm University of Technology); Master of Economics and is president of the executive committee of *The Swedish Initiative for the Prevention of Accidental Nuclear War.*

Vladimir Belous is a Doctor of History and a retired Major General. He is also active in the *Committee of Soviet Scientists for Peace against Nuclear War.*

Paul Bracken is Professor of Public Policy and Political Science at Yale University and a member of the *International Institute for Strategic Studies* and of the *Council on Foreign Relations.*

Morris Bradley (Doctor of Psychology, University of Strathclyde) is Director of the *Richardson Institute for Peace Studies* at the University of Lancaster.

Dagobert L. Brito is the Peterkin Professor of Political Economy at Rice University. His research interests include arms races and war, topics in public economics, and economic theory.

Francesco Calogero is Professor of Theoretical Physics at the University of Rome 'La Sapienza' and Secretary-General of the *Pugwash Conferences on Science and World Affairs* and a Board Member of the *Stockholm International Peace Research Institute* (SIPRI).

Marta Cullberg-Weston (Doctor of Psychology and Psychoanalyst IPA) is a Board Member of *Transnational Foundation for Peace and Futures Studies* and former Vice President of *Swedish Psychologists against Nuclear War.*

ix

Michael D. Intriligator is Professor of Economics and Political Science at the University of California, Los Angeles. His research interests include strategy and arms control, econometrics, and economic theory.

Tapio Kanninen (Master of Economics and Doctor of Political Science) is Political Affairs Officer at the *Office for Research and the Collection of Information* (ORCI) in the offices of the UN Secretary-General in New York.

Alexander K. Kislov is a Professor and Director of *Peace Research Institute Moscow* at the USSR Academy of Sciences.

Lloyd R. Leavitt (Lieutentant General (ret.), United States Air Force and Former Vice Commander of *Strategic Air Command*) is a Visiting Scholar at Cornell University.

Bent Natvig is Professor in Mathematical Statistics and Dean of the Faculty of Sciences at the University of Oslo. He is also President of the *Norwegian Statistical Association*, and of the association *Science and Responsibility in the Nuclear Age*.

Ib Damgaard Petersen is Associate Professor of Political Science at the University of Copenhagen.

Boris Raushenbach is a Professor of Physics and active on the *Committee on Automatic Control*, Moscow and *Committee of Soviet Scientists for Peace against Nuclear War*.

Karl K. Rebane is Professor of Theoretical and Mathematical Physics and Solid State Physics at the University of Tallinn; Academician, at the *Estonian Academy of Sciences* and the *USSR Academy of Sciences;* and member of the *Committee of Soviet Scientists for Peace Against Nuclear War*.

Frederick L. Shiels is Professor of Government at Mercy College.

Paul Smoker is Lloyd Professor of Peace Studies and World Law at Antioch University; Director emeritus of the *Richardson Institute for Peace Studies*, University of Lancaster and Secretary General of the *International Peace Research Association* (IPRA).

Håkan Wiberg is Professor of Sociology at Lund University; Director of the *Centre for Peace and Conflict Research* Copenhagen and President of the *European Peace Research Association* (EuPRA).

PART I

Introduction

Chapter 1

Accidental Nuclear War: The Problematique

Håkan Wiberg

1. Introduction

Since Hiroshima and Nagasaki, there has always been a danger of explosions of nuclear weapons. When fears were first voiced, e.g. by Niels Bohr (Christmas-Møller, 1985), they were primarily concerned with the risk that a political crisis and a military confrontation might escalate into a 'calculated' nuclear war. The term 'calculated' might be understood in a narrow sense, covering, e.g. exercises in escalation described by Kahn (1965) - or it might allow for misperceptions, mis-understandings and, for that matter, miscalculations. These fears were increased by several incidents during the first two postwar decades when Nuclear Powers engaged in nuclear sabre-rattling, culminating in the Cuban crisis. (After that, and definitely after 1973, demonstrations have been more subtle, better described as 'body language' than 'sabre-rattling.')

Another type of scenario pictured a new Hitler commanding a state with nuclear weapons and prepared to use them entirely 'irrationally'; in some versions, this might spark off a 'catalytic' nuclear war between major Nuclear Powers.

In later decades, attention has increasingly been given to what can more genuinely be called *accidental* nuclear war. There is now a controversy as to whether 'calculated' or 'accidental' nuclear war - however the semantical boundary is drawn between them - constitutes the worst danger. Several authors in the present volume see the accidental case as the most threatening one; the opinion of other authors ranges between agreement with this assessment and seeing accidental nuclear war as 'a more remote possibility'. After the recent rapid détente, fears of intentional or miscalculated nuclear war between major Nuclear Powers have clearly diminished. While some categories of nuclear weapons have been eliminated, reduced or removed by agreements or reciprocated unilateral actions, the bulk of strategic nuclear weapons are still there. The START I and

START II agreements are not yet ratified by all parties, and even when they become effective, they only define reductions by a few percent per year; and like always, it is anybody's guess what new technologies may emerge that are not covered by the treaties.

It therefore appears that the *relative* importance of the primarily accidental type of nuclear war has increased. To what extent can we also say anything well-founded about the *absolute* risk under various conditions, as earlier authors (Frei & Catrina, 1983) have attempted to do?

That depends on what we intend to use the answer for: a debate on the permissibility of nuclear deterrence, an argument on détente measures among Nuclear Powers, a concrete proposal for improving the safety of specific components in the systems, and so on. How comprehensive, how precise and how well-confirmed an estimate must be varies with these things. Let us look at why.

No known technical construction, human being or social organization is absolutely failsafe. Possible errors in one component thus cannot be restlessly eliminated by substituting other components of other kinds for it.

These remarks are intended to be trivial, 'absolutely failsafe' to be understood so strictly as to make them verge on tautology. They apply to nuclear weapons as well as to dishwashers, but there is a fundamental difference between these. We can get a clear picture of what may possibly go wrong with a dishwasher, who is legally responsible if anything does go wrong and what the costs would then be for whoever is liable. Producers and consumers will have access to the data required for rational decisions about whether and how to produce one and about which, if any, to buy. Nobody wants a dishwasher that is even close to being absolutely failsafe: it would be prohibitively costly to build and probably too cumbersome to operate to save much time. Normal dishwashers will do for those who want one. They are *expendable*: if there were convincing reasons for banning them, we could do without them with little harm (although most owners would not want to). At the same time, they are *defensible*, in the sense that (except, perhaps, for some very strict environmentalists) nobody sees the harm they may create as a sufficient cause for banning them.

In both respects, nuclear weapons are far more controversial. To some antagonists the problem whether *anything* can justify the possession of nuclear weapons is raised by the magnitude of the costs of anything going wrong. As against that, some protagonists argue, e.g. in deterrence terms, that the potential costs for abolishing them - if this is ever possible - would also be unacceptable. Each of these positions is held by wide sectors of public opinion as well as of scholarly opinion. There is no agreement on them among the authors of this volume; nor is such agreement needed in order to see the problems of accidental nuclear war as extremely important. This introduction is not meant to take a stand between these positions; it merely attempts to sort out and formulate the moral, logical, theoretical and empirical problems that are involved in taking any such stand.

2. Moral aspects: the role of probability

Assume, for the sake of argument, that nuclear deterrence prevents or reduces some risks of war. Is that enough to make the *use* of nuclear weapons morally defensible? Is it enough to make the *threat* to use nuclear weapons defensible?

Moral philosophers of various persuasions (Russell, 1959; Lewy, 1970; Goodwin, 1982; Blake & Pole, 1983 & 1984; Dougherty, 1984; Fox & Groarke, 1985; Child, 1986) have discussed these issues, in some cases with quite different conclusions. This introduction is no place to go into *ethical* arguments. We need, however, consider a couple of *metaethical* ones, dealing with issues on the validity of various *ways of arguing*, but leaving the validity of specific *arguments* aside.

Among several types of moral thinking, there are two that predominate, at least in Western thinking: *deontological ethics*, arguing in terms of duties, and *teleological ethics*, thinking in terms of means and ends.

Let us first look at the logic of deontological ethics. If *Thou shalt not kill* is accepted as a duty, whether derived from a religious or a secular moral system, an argument about the validity of this norm can concern two main issues. One of them is whether the norm has been deduced from that moral system by correct logic; and this is precisely a matter of logic, not a matter of facts. The other issue concerns the validity of the underlying system, where the debaters may agree or disagree. Here, too, arguments about *intended effects* or about *consequences* are irrelevant. Two persons may disagree in their choice of moral systems; and then the discussion stops there (at least for the sake of the present argument). They may also share the same moral system, but disagree on whether the deduction of the norm is logically binding, e.g. on whether it must be seen as absolute or conditional. While nuclear weapons and deterrence have been discussed by adherents of varieties of deontological ethics, the aspect of accidental nuclear war is of limited relevance there.

If the moral discussion takes place within a framework of teleological ethics, on the other hand, information about possible consequences of an action *is* often relevant, in particular in utilitarian versions of teleological ethics, where the anticipated consequences (or their relative probability) are decisive for the moral status of a contemplated action. Even within utilitarian ethics, however, we find different - and non-equivalent - versions, depending on *how* they are seen to decide it. It is important what logic of decision is employed. When making (ethical or pragmatic) decisions, there are essentially two types of logic to choose between: *minimax* and *expected utility*. (I disregard some others of lesser importance.) When we have two or more essential decision-makers involved, we may also have to resort to *game theory*.

2.1 Minimax logic
Stripped of mathematics, the essence of minimax logic is as follows: if the worst possible consequence of action A is worse than the worst possible consequence of action B, then B is to be preferred to A. This holds even if the *best* possible consequences of action A are better than the best possible consequences of B. Minimax logic is, as it were, one for pessimists, not for optimists.

In our concrete example, if thought of in minimax terms, the gist of the argument *against* nuclear deterrence is that since a nuclear war is worse than anything else, actions that have a nuclear war as one *possible* consequence, however unlikely, must be avoided.

There are some logical problems with this kind of argument against nuclear deterrence. First, it presupposes that there *are* actions that do not have nuclear war as a possible consequence. This is disputed by deterrence protagonists who argue that reducing or abolishing nuclear deterrence would increase the risk of conventional war, which would in turn increase the risk for nuclear war. Obviously, there can be no nuclear war without nuclear weapons, and an instantaneous abolition of *all of them* would eliminate any risk of an - accidental or calculated - nuclear war. The crux of the matter is rather whether there is *any* road from the present situation to a hypothetical state of total nuclear disarmament that does not include parts where the risk is higher than at present. Intriligator & Brito (1990b) present a theoretical argument, based on strategic logic, why the last part of the road would contain such a danger, whereas Natvig (Ch. 4), discussing system reliability, argues that the first part of the road would mean a reduction of risks. There is no necessary contradiction between these two positions, but taken together they yield an important question: if both are right, where on the road does the increase in risk due to strategic logic outweigh the reduction we expect on the basis of reliability considerations?

Second, the argument crucially presupposes a normative premise: that a nuclear war is worse than anything else - which has also been disputed (the 'dead versus red' issue). There is nothing remarkable about this: *any* moral argument presupposes at least some normative premises, and for clarity's sake it is better to have them explicit and clearly visible than hidden under a cloak of 'science.'

Third, the argument hinges on how we define 'possible' in this context: is the opposite of something being 'possible' that it is 'absolutely and completely excluded', or merely that it is 'for all practical purposes negligible'? In the second case, it is crucial for the argument into what category we put inadvertent nuclear war. This is where further study comes in - at the same time as we should remember that there are also some normative assumptions hidden in the phrase 'for all practical purposes'.

2.2 Expected utility
Utilitarian ethics may also use as its adjunct a logic of decision with *expected utility* as its criterion. Whereas minimax logic only requires us to be able to distinguish 'possible' from 'impossible', expected utility logic makes stronger demands. In essence, it presupposes that for each option an actor has, he can estimate the probability of each possible outcome of that option. For option number j, having non-zero probability for at least some among the n possible outcomes, the expected utility is defined as

$$EU(j) = \sum_{i=1}^{n} P(i/j) \times v(i)$$

where $P(i/j)$ is the probability of outcome i occurring if j is chosen, and $v(i)$ is the value, or utility, of this outcome. The criterion says that it is rational to choose action alternative number k, if and only if its expected utility is *no less than* that of any other alternative.

Cast in this logic, the simplest argument against any possession of nuclear weapons is that since the negative utility of a nuclear war is so much greater than anything else that we can put it at *minus infinity*, and since the probability that such a possession will lead to a nuclear war differs from exactly zero, the expected utility of the existence of nuclear weapons is also minus infinity, for which reason they should be abolished.

If the argument is given in this form, however, the price for simplicity is that there remain two crucial questions to answer. Is it permissible to represent the utility of a nuclear war at *minus infinity*? And is it the *only* event for which this is appropriate? Again, it should be remembered that the questions themselves, as well as any answer to them, presuppose normative premises.

If the answer to the first question is No, then nuclear war has to be treated like any other event: even if its negative utility is very great, an extremely low probability for its resulting from an action may make that action preferable to others that have greater probabilities for lesser evils. If the answer to both questions is Yes, then *any* non-zero probability for nuclear war is sufficient to conclude that nuclear weapons are impermissible. If the answer to the first question is Yes and to the second No, then *indecision* is a possible conclusion, since minus infinity is neither greater nor less than minus infinity.

Second, this logic assumes probabilities to be calculable and possible to express in cardinal numbers. For accidental nuclear war, this leads to the logical problem whether that is possible for a unique future event. (The reply can be Yes or No, depending on exactly how you interpret 'probability' in 'subjective probability' or 'relative frequency' terms.) It also presupposes that we deal with *events*: something that *happens*, the probability for which can be calculated (if other conditions are met). The discourse on accidental nuclear war, however, deals with two broad types of dangers, with different logics: *events* (things happening) and *actions* (somebody doing something).

A central problem in the debate on accidental nuclear war is precisely in what context, in what *decision logic*, it should be seen. The logics outlined here are the major - but not the only - ones, and there is no agreement on which one is applicable, perhaps not even on whether this is a logical or a moral question. One important difference between the logics lies in how they reason about acceptability of risks. This always has a normative component; but we can investigate the underlying logic as well as the methods of making estimates (Council for Science and Society, 1977).

A parallel may be found in the debate on nuclear *energy*, where protagonists and antagonists, even highly qualified ones, have clearly tended to use different logics. Advocates for nuclear energy tend to see the issue as one of expected utility, arguing that the expected negative utility of using nuclear power for energy production (a small probability times great damage) is not as bad as the alternatives: for example, burning fossil fuels means a high probability for loss of many human lives due to mining, pollution, etc. The antagonists, on the other hand, often implicitly use minimax logic, e.g. when they argue that a worst case accident is such a great catastrophe that *any* non-zero probability should exclude the use of nuclear power. Whereas there are often largely consensual scientific methods for deciding at least some of the differences about facts and consequences, the choice of decision logic does not belong there. You cannot *prove* that one is better than the other, at least not without introducing some normative assumption in the premises.

Since this may be difficult to accept - it flies in the face of 'common sense' that there can be varieties of logic - it may also account for an interesting feature in the debate on nuclear energy. When highly qualified scholars (pros and antis) are asked about the grounds for their own position, they systematically ascribe it to rational arguments. When they are asked, however, how it comes that equally qualified experts with the same access to information have arrived at the opposite conclusion, they invariably ascribe that to irrational motives: personality traits, group pressure, economic or political interests, etc. (Brante, 1989). I am afraid that a closer analysis of the debate on nuclear weapons would reveal a similar picture. Put in more general terms, this also indicates one contributing risk factor concerning accidental nuclear war: we have a strong tendency to overestimate our own rationality - and this is a dangerous thing to do.

2.3 Game theory

The consequences of my actions often depend on what other people do. In some cases, these people can be regarded as belonging to 'Nature', meaning that I can estimate probabilities for their doing one thing or the other, or at least classify them as 'possible' or 'impossible.' After that I am back in minimax logic or expected utility logic, whether my problem is ethical or pragmatic.

In other cases, however, such estimates are meaningless, because the situation is *strategic*, in the sense that we both calculate with what the other one will try to achieve. Game theory was invented (Von Neumann & Morgenstern, 1944; Luce & Raiffa, 1957) to analyze what is 'rational' behavior in such situations, but was soon also discovered to be an important instrument in ethical analyses of such concepts as 'fairness' and 'justice'. (Braithwaite, 1955). As a tool for analysing nuclear strategy and related topics, it had a first wave in the 1960s (Rapoport, 1960, 1964; Schelling, 1963); in the latest wave, Brams (1985) has been a major author.

Game theory can tell us little about the 'events' end of accidental nuclear war. Its contributions to the 'actions' end, however, include a better understanding of why dilemmas may force opposing decision-makers to make decisions landing them both in a worse situation than if they had made other decisions. As usual, the most interesting results are the 'counterintuitive' ones, e.g. Brams's demonstration of why it may be rational to call for less than perfect verification of arms control treaties. I would also hold that a game theoretical analysis is necessary in ethical analyses of nuclear weapons and doctrines.

2.4 No total picture

With regard to accidental nuclear war, the most ambitious intellectual goals have to be abandoned. There is no known way of piecing the logically different analyses of events and of actions together into some total 'probability of accidental nuclear war'. Nor, for that matter, is this possible in the case of different kinds of events. Too many assumptions have to be made, too many kinds of interaction taken into account, for any meaningful numbers to be produced - if numbers are what we want. For some of the calculations referred to above, however, we have to want them; and the conclusion from that is that we have to revert to arguments and calculations that pose more modest demands on overall quantifiability.

This observation is not, and should not be, the end of the debate on accidental war. We can - and should - still assess a number of more specific risks and uncertainties that surround the handling of nuclear weapons, try to piece them together into an overall picture and indicate ways and means of reducing some risks, perhaps even eliminating some others. Even if absolute safety is unattainable and very precise estimation impossible, there are many cases where it is possible to say that one (technical, organizational or political) arrangement is safer than another and therefore to be preferred - at least as long as avoiding an inadvertent nuclear war is the foremost criterion.

3. Empirical aspects: what can go wrong?

Some of the risks and uncertainties concerning nuclear weapons fall within the competence of already existing fields of enquiry; others call for interdisciplinary integration of approaches and results from two or more fields. The analytical distinctions between different types of dangers made below do not express any belief that they can be so neatly compartmentalized in practice. Categorizations can also be made in several different ways, as we can see in the long list provided by Shiels (Ch. 8). The points below are merely a crude summary:

1. The hardware parts of the C^3I systems surrounding nuclear weapons. (Example: Burnout of a diode.)

2. Program errors in these systems. (Example: An exercise program being put in by mistake.)

3. Errors in interpretation of the information emerging from them. (Example: Radar images of wild geese or civilian airplanes being mistaken for hostile aircraft or missiles.)

4. Mistakes made by authorized decision-makers, whether due to the structure of the decision situation, the structure of the decision-making process, situational factors or insanity. (Tuchman, 1984, overflows with historical examples of decision-makers creating catastrophes for themselves by acting against their own interests. While some sources indicate that decision-makers have

been dangerously close to it in crisis situations (cf. Petersen & Smoker, Ch. 11), no use of nuclear weapons appears to have been authorized since Nagasaki.)

5. Accidental launching or explosions of nuclear weapons. (There have been a few cases described in open sources (Leitenberg, 1977; Gregory & Edwards, 1989) of bombs being accidentally dropped - Glassboro, Spanish coast - or missiles accidentally launched - if we count the Titan case into that category. For all we know, there has been no case of accidental explosion; certainly not outside the territory of the owner.)

6. Unauthorized launching of nuclear weapons. (One crucial issue here is who is authorized, or how far the authority to authorize is delegated. In all Nuclear Powers, this information is highly classified. There have been indications in older literature of such authorization having been erroneously assumed to exist. Procedures have changed since then; exactly how is only known to a limited extent (Blair 1993), and today we have to rely entirely on scenarios for examples.)

3.1 Events: technology
In some cases, especially those of 'pure technology', the 'event' label obviously applies, and probabilities can be assessed by the means already existing for investigating the reliability of complex technical and/or computer systems. Even without access to classified information, we must assume that the Nuclear Powers have invested very much in making these types of errors more and more unlikely by means of technical improvements. One crucial question here is whether there is any theoretically definable limit to how far security can be improved.

Another technology-engendered source of risk has to do with 'the time factor' discussed by Calogero (Ch. 9) and others. The momentous technological development, past and anticipated, gives decision-makers less and less time, in the worst cases just a few minutes, to go through all the moves of cross-checking, consulting others, weighing alternatives, etc., before making irrevocable decisions with unprecedented consequences. Abrams (Ch. 3) points out that the SDI plans, if implemented, would reduce this available time even further. That will, by necessity, hand much of interpretation - and even of decisions - over to computers. Raushenbach (Ch. 5) argues that it is just as possible for two opposing computer systems as for two groups of human decision-makers to misinterpret and misunderstand each other, with catastrophic consequences.

3.2 Events: human beings

The 'event' label may also be attached to some types of 'human errors', e.g. due to situational or permanent mental deficiencies in persons taking part in the handling of nuclear weapons on the 'cog-in-the-wheel' level. The likelihood of such deficiencies in a given population can be assessed on a statistical basis; it is less easy to assess the risk of their leading to an accident. This is also a factor that decision-makers are obviously aware of and have tried to eliminate.

One way is of doing this is by psychological screening; but Abrams (Ch. 6) demonstrates that many persons with grave mental deficiences nevertheless slip past the screening and that others develop them after the screening without being detected until, e.g., committing murder.

Another way is to construct operational procedures to make the entire system minimally sensitive to the possibility of a single person going insane, e.g. by requiring that two or more persons do something simultaneously in order for a nuclear weapon to be activated. The essential logic is that if the likelihood for one given person to go insane is small but 'non-negligible', the likelihood for *two* given persons do so at the same time will be so very small that it is - rightly or wrongly - regarded as 'negligible'. The logic presupposes that the probabilities are statistically independent, in which case the likelihood for a double mistake of this kind is the square of the likelihood for a single mistake - and the square of something small is something extremely small. On the other hand, Cullberg-Weston (Ch. 7) and others argue that if one person can influence another, or if both are exposed to the same extreme stress, this makes the double-check assumption illusory. If so, the likelihood is higher than the square and may well be in the magnitude of that for a single person.

3.3 Events: organizations

Dealing with human frailty by technical or organizational solutions has the weakness that they are not infallible either. What this weakness means depends on whether we focus on the system being able to do what it is supposed to or on its being able to avoid what it is supposed not to do. Major reviews of the US system of nuclear weapons, such as Bracken (1983) and Blair (1985), focus primarily on the former, concluding, *inter alia*, that it is unlikely that the command and control system will function as intended in a hot war. Perceived weaknesses in these respects may also have effects for the second problem, for example in the case of the submarine commander who believes that the system has been struck out by hostile action and that this is why he does not get expected signals, etc. The main problem concerning accidental nuclear war, however, is the latter: being sure that things will *not* happen.

Some aspects are, of course, technological. The vital problem, however, is not. There is so much redundancy built into the systems that scenarios of accidental nuclear war due to a single technical failure are among the least likely. In order to be fatal, technical failures either have to come simultaneously in an unpredictable pattern - or they have to be compounded by organizational failures. Natvig (Ch. 4) analyzes what this has meant in case of other types of systems and what general conclusions can be drawn of relevance for accidental nuclear war.

To get more understanding of organizational failures, we may turn to the sociology of organizations. One main point offered there is - if we strip it of sociologese - that people very often do not act according to the book. They invent simplifications and shortcuts that make their work less time-consuming, less boring, less alienating or less stressful; and they learn to hide that by reverting to the book when there is any superior around, relaxing again when (s)he leaves. The postmortems of a number of major 'technological' catastrophes like Challenger, Chernobyl, Bhopal - not to speak of lost battles in war - indicate that such behavior was one crucial factor: people did not do what the rules required them to do. As for warfare, Luttwak (1987) makes the point that excessive trust in one's own ability to carry out tactics according to instructions is a recipe for defeat - unless the adversary has even more of it.

People do not behave by the book - although in some kinds of organizations, like military ones in peacetime, one may be able to bring them rather close to it. In addition, many organizations would just break down if everybody *did* behave by the book - as witnessed by the successes that policemen, customs officers and other groups can achieve by work-to-rule strikes. We must always assume that the actual probability for a catastrophe to emerge in an organization is greater, sometimes far greater, than it would be if everybody behaved according to instructions and organizational rules.

An empirical assessment must therefore be based on how the organizations *actually* function, rather than on their organizational charts. It will also be difficult to carry out such studies in a reliable way: organizations tend to 'defend' themselves against them. There has also been the apparently paradoxical observation (Freudenberg, 1988) that the longer a system has worked without an accident, the higher the risk of an accident, various security measures being eroded by being increasingly seen as superfluous. This is related to the empirical results presented by Bradley (Ch. 10) to the effect that there appears to be a 'risk-compensation effect' in some categories of people, making them drive less carefully when the road has been improved.

Some of these types of errors do not derive from any mental deficiencies, and will therefore be hard to eliminate by psychological screening. They *may* be possible to reduce or even eliminate in other ways. Inside an organization, the main possibility for keeping their effects under control appears to lie in intense and multi-level surveillance - which in turn is likely to create new problems and risks, e.g. by increasing stress factors. An alternative is to have two or more organizations that are independent of each other, and require that information from one has to be confirmed by another in order to serve as basis for action. This is the essential logic of 'dual phenomenology'; that the logic is sound means that it can *improve* safety, but not that it can make it *absolute*.

For the above reasons, the leadership of an organization may be less aware of what goes on in the organization than it believes. It has no monopoly on that: entire organizations may delude themselves as to how they operate and what factors they are affected by. For example, according to the ethos of the organization, the collection and processing of information on possible nuclear attacks is (self-) assumed to be 'purely professional', not making political evaluations; these are assumed to enter the process higher up when the critical information has been passed on. Yet, Petersen and Smoker (see Ch. 11) reveal a strong statistical relationship between international political tension and warning indicators, thus casting some doubt over this assumption of 'politics-free' assessment.

3.4 Non-events: decision-making

The 'event' label becomes more problematic as we consider actors higher up the ladder of authority, where decision-makers have conditional or absolute authority to act according to discretion. This discretion will be exercised under various pressures and in many cases when the decision-maker is in comparatively bad shape, e.g. heavily fatigued, woken up in the middle of the night, or working under unprecedented mental stress. Decisions will often have to be taken under extreme time pressure when heavy information overload is combined with lack of some types of vital information. Cullberg-Weston (Ch. 6) shows that these things are known to make for more simplified, stereotyped and inflexible perceptions of the situation, the number of perceived action alternatives shrinking rapidly.

This is not only a matter of how a single person functions, but also of how small groups function. Studies of earlier crisis situations indicate that the small group of - formally or informally appointed - advisors that have access to such decision-makers as presidents or submarine commanders, tends to be selected in such a way that much of the alleged critical functions of the group vanish. Potential dissenters have been screened out in advance - or get marginalized in the process - and the group is affected by the perceptual distortions known as 'groupthink' (Janis, 1972), 'error of attribution' (Heradstveit, 1981), etc.; the list of technical terms is steadily growing.

The reason for using the term 'non-events' is that as we move up the organizational ladder, the type of risk assessments that can be expressed by probabilistic calculi becomes decreasingly relevant: we are no longer dealing with the law of averages. True, decision-makers at any level are human beings belonging to organizations of human beings, with the implications already hinted at, and there is quite a literature about leaders of states with severe mental deficiencies and problems (Abrams, 1990). In order to understand what may happen at this level, however, psychological and sociological generalizations will not suffice. The element of decision-making is crucial, and we have to get an understanding of its context: the strategic situation, the available options of both adversaries, the expected outcomes of various combinations of choices, etc. (To that we have to add, of course, their perceptions of these factors, perceptions of each others' perceptions, and so forth - but that is the part that brings us back to psychology and social sciences.) This means that we need more of the instruments for analysis of decision-making, such as game theory, in assessing what can go wrong. In some cases, such analyses may indicate ways of improving unilateral decision-making so as to reduce the risks of accidental nuclear war.

In many cases, however, the diagnosis is rather that (no matter how rational the individual decision-makers) it is the *situation* that presents problems to rational decisions - or that may make rational decisions have even worse consequences that less rational ones. If the combination of two adversary systems provides an advantage for one or both of them in striking first, or that irreparable harm is suffered by being struck first, this will in itself increase the risks of an inadvertent nuclear war.

Several scenarios have elaborated different variations of this type of dilemma. MAD (for Mutually Assured Destruction) has traditionally been seen as the only feasible way to obviate it: if both participants will be annihilated, there is no longer any advantage in striking first, and both parties need worry less about the other side being thus tempted. Whether we regard it as a state of affairs (which is clearly there) or as a doctrine (which it is not), it suffers from weaknesses.

Seen as a state of affairs, MAD suffers from an inherent instability due to the risk for sudden technological breakthroughs. If one of the adversaries develops the means of protecting itself against a strike from the other, mutual deterrence would no longer be there, the other side would be likely to read it as a preparation for a first strike and to do things that would lock them into a vicious circle of tension. This was an argument against extended civil defense measures in the 1960s, it was crucial for getting the ABM treaty in the 1970s, and it has been a main argument against SDI/Star Wars in the 1980s (at least the version presented in President Reagan's vision of it). Yet this risk of technological breakthrough will always be there, so MAD can never become completely stable.

As a doctrine candidate, MAD also has this weakness: it is sensitive to this type of technological breakthroughs (and to the other type: drastic improvements in the capability of incapacitating the nuclear weapons on the other side). This means that it will be very difficult to get even close to the theoretically ideal version of it: Minimal Deterrence, since both sides will insist on having many times more than this to have some buffer against technological breakthroughs on the other side - and this vast redundancy increases the risks for *accidental* nuclear war. Another weakness is psychological, rather than logical: MAD militates against traditional thinking by having as an essential premise that it is good to be vulnerable (because that will reduce the other side's incentive to strike first). In particular, this flies in the face of standard military thinking anywhere. While MAD remained a main part of the declaratory doctrine of the USA and - in a different language - of the USSR since the 1960s, decreasing warning times and increasing uncertainty as to whether they would be able to deliver retaliatory strikes gradually moved their actual postures towards 'launch on warning' as first options, even moving dangerously close to preemption (Blair 1993).

When the *problem* consists in technological creativity, we cannot expect technological *solutions* to it; especially not when these solutions would be required to take care of a maximally difficult task: verifying treaties about abstaining from future technological breakthroughs. Nor will it help much to try to unilaterally ensure more 'rational' decision-making procedures when the decision-makers are prisoners of precisely the rational solution to some mixed-motive games (Prisoner's Dilemma is just one out of many). Solutions will have to include some form of grand restructuring to help the potential adversaries escape an 'irrational' situation where it is precisely rational behavior that may be most dangerous; and this they can only do by common efforts.

4. Nuclear weapons and deterrence: two dilemmas and a certainty

4.1 Dilemmas of reliability and legitimacy
Let us now consider two dilemmas at the most abstract level. The first is the reliability dilemma that we have in many situations where different demands for reliability counteract each other. In the case of nuclear weapons systems, its essence is as follows: on the one hand, it is seen as imperative that no nuclear weapons are launched without proper authorization - and on the other hand, the systems are built to ensure that they are actually launched when authorized. The dilemma derives from the fact that the more certain it is that one of these demands will be fulfilled, the less certain is the other one. Simplifying greatly,

$$P(a) \times P(b) = k$$

where $P(a)$ is the risk for unauthorized use, $P(b)$ the risk that authorized use will not be carried out and k a constant (at least in the short run). Technical and organizational improvements may reduce k over time, so that the 'price' one has to pay on one dimension for a level of security on the other dimension may diminish - but it appears excluded that they can reduce k to zero, so the dilemma will always be there.

This dilemma is related to another one. Postures of nuclear deterrence suffer from having to satisfy at least two different criteria: on the one hand, they should be seen as being capable of deterring; on the other hand, they should be possible to legitimize politically. The most deterrent message would - according to traditional deterrence logic - be the following: 'If seriously threatened in a conventional war, we may get into first use of nuclear weapons, and this may happen even against the will of the decision-makers in the state owning the nuclear weapons or the state from or in which they are used. A local commander with his nuclear weapons PAL-cleared may come into an unforeseen use-them-or-lose-them situation; there may be no time to consult the other state as we ought to do; and so on.' The message that is most likely, or even necessary, in order to achieve domestic political legitimization, on the other hand, reads: 'There is absolutely no risk for unauthorized or inadvertent use of nuclear weapons. The President is the only person that can authorize it, and he is treaty-bound first to consult the national government of the state (from) where they are to be used'.

Obviously, these two messages are difficult to combine: the more deterrence you are seen to achieve (according to the theory), the smaller is the possibility for political legitimization, and *vice versa*; for the better the second message describes reality, the greater is the likelihood for self-deterrence. For example, it would be difficult for a Danish government to make credible that it would authorize the use of nuclear weapons on Danish soil; and if it managed to make it credible, it would in all likelihood have to resign, succeeded by a new government that does not authorize such use.

4.2 In the long run...

Reaching the top of the ladder of abstraction, let us consider an elementary statistical truth: as long as the failure probability of a system is non-zero, the cumulative probability gets higher, the longer time period we consider; and if the probability is constant, the cumulative probability is bound to increase asymptotically towards exactly 100 percent. This truth has repeatedly been referred to in the debate on accidental nuclear war, so we should have a look at what is says - and does not say.

First, it is a statistical truth, i.e. a tautology, and not a natural law: it *adds* nothing empirical to what it tells us about the consequences of empirical statements. To start with, it does not tell *when*: if the annual probability of an event is, say, one percent, then the probability that it will occur within the next ten, fifty or one hundred years is, respectively, 9.6 percent, 39.5 percent and 63.4 percent, and there is one chance in ten million that it will *not* have occurred within the next 1,600 years. It is therefore more likely than not that the event *will* occur within the coming century, and more likely than not that it will not happen within the next ten years. This does *not* exclude that the coming century is accident-free, nor that the accident happens tomorrow.

Second, the increase towards 100 percent presupposes statistical independence: that what happens in one year does not affect what happens in following years. This assumption appears to be largely valid, and the prediction is actually strengthened by the exception already referred to: that non-occurrence may lead to relaxation of security and therefore to an increasing risk.

Third, it is essential for such an asymptotic cumulation that the annual risk is *constant*; if it is decreasing, e.g., due to technical improvements in security, then the risk need not cumulate to 100 percent (Avenhaus et al., 1989). This argument obviously *has* some empirical backing: such efforts have indeed been - and continue to be - made at great cost, and we must assume that they have some effect. On the other hand, the mathematics of it indicates that the normal effect of such improvements is to buy some time, in the sense that we have to consider a somewhat longer time period than in the simple case to reach the same level of probability that the event will have occurred. In order for technical improvements to be able to counteract cumulation to an eventual 100 percent, however, they have to create a continuous *exponential* decrease of risks: they have to be reduced at least as quickly as a process of radioactive decay - all the time. It appears extremely unlikely that such a reduction can be achieved throughout an indefinite future, and the authors of this third reservation do not even attempt to make that credible. In addition we have to consider what risks are being *added*. Let us devote the next section to some of them.

5. In the short run

As already stated, it is probably meaningless to try to present a single indicator of whether the accumulated risk of accidental nuclear war is going up or down: different trends point in different directions. Let us therefore review the more important ones: *who* have *how much* of what kinds, *what* are they doing with them, and *how has the context changed*?

5.1 Horizontal proliferation

Since the USA came first in 1945 and the USSR second in 1949, the number of Nuclear Powers has continued to increase. By the mid-1960s, Great Britain, France and China made five 'official' members of the nuclear club, and it has not increased since then. However, some 'unofficial' members have joined. They all officially deny that they have nuclear weapons, so their membership may be a matter of speculation. There appears to be general consensus that Israel has a two- or three-digit number of nuclear warheads; India's detonation in 1974 of what was described as a peaceful nuclear device naturally put it on the list of suspected possessors with fissile materials to build dozens (Japuncic et al. 1993). While South Africa was on the list of suspects, its own government was first to confirm that it had in fact built six bombs and was working on a seventh when ending the project in 1990, later destroying the bombs and joining the NPT in 1991 (*International Herald Tribune*, 14 May 1993, p. 6). Pakistan is another 'unofficial', possibly having a few bombs already (Japuncic et al. 1993). A number of other states are believed to be able to get nuclear weapons; Bracken & Leavitt (Ch. 12) list the near-nuclear Third World countries.

Whether this record provides grounds for optimism or pessimism is a matter of what is the basis of comparison. If we look at nuclear weapons only, a comparison with *SIPRI Yearbook* (1972) is instructive. It indicated 15 countries as 'near-nuclear', but had already narrowed the field considerably by excluding those (e.g. Sweden and Canada) that had both signed and ratified the Non-proliferation Treaty (NPT); at that time, it was sometimes guessed that 30-40 countries might be able to get nuclear weapons by the year 2000. Eight industrial countries appear in the SIPRI list only (all have ratified the NPT since then). Seven appear in both lists: the 'unofficials' plus Argentina, Brazil and Egypt. Among those in the list by Bracken & Leavitt that do not appear in SIPRI's list, Iran, Iraq, Libya, Syria and Taiwan had been excluded by SIPRI on the basis of having signed the NPT. South Korea signed the NPT in 1975, but reportedly carried its nuclear weapons project on until 1979, when it was cancelled a couple of years before expected completion (*Jane's Defense Weekly 1993, no. 9. p. 6)*; North Korea joined in in 1985 and Saudi Arabia in 1988 (Goldblat, 1990). All of these states are marked by Bracken & Leavitt at least as 'possible beyond the year 2000'.

This, in fact, looks like a rather impressive record for the NPT: the number of states that are now seen as possible possessors of nuclear weapons by the year 2000 is far smaller than it was twenty years ago, and the number of NPT states reached 155 in November 1992 by Myanmar acceding. In the last couple of years, China and France have joined as the last 'officials'; this will further limit the access to technology of near-nuclear nations.

In addition, the list of signatories that permit IAEA inspection gets longer. Even North Korea announced in 1991 that it would do so, but made that conditional on the withdrawal of US nuclear weapons from Korea (Sanders 1991). The Bush Initiative later that year would seem to satisfy that condition; at least, North Korea joined, but only to collide with the IAEA in 1993 (see below).

There is the other side of the coin, however. This was in particular illustrated by the issue of possible Iraqi nuclear arms in 1990-91. One of the foremost specialists on nuclear proliferation, Leonard Spector (1988: p. 210), had expressed the opinion that the nuclear program of Iraq had been brought to a virtual impasse and that this situation would hardly change within a near future, and even two years later (Spector & Smith, 1990: p. 198) judged that 'it is highly unlikely that Iraq will be able to acquire them before the mid- to late 1990s.'

It soon turned out that Iraq had been able to do much more than assumed. Already before the UN inspection team had reported, there were several indications that previous estimates have to be revised.

Thus Albright & Hibbs (1991b: p. 15), revising their earlier assessment (Albright & Hibbs, 1991a), wrote that '(w)e remain convinced that Iraq would have needed about a year to build a crude explosive device, but we now believe that Iraq might have developed a usable nuclear arsenal in as little as two or three years.' In addition, the spokesman for IAEA, Mr. David Kyd, stated that there is now tangible evidence that Iraq - in spite of having steadfastly denied this - was indeed studying detonators for nuclear warheads. (*International Herald Tribune*, 1 October 1991, p. 1 and 4). Later reports confirmed massive Iraqi violations of the NPT (Ekéus 1992, Müller 1992), and even when the UN inspectors had eliminated all of Iraq's known nuclear weapons facilities in June 1993, it retained its scientists and know-how, and a Clinton official stated that Iraq could rebuild a nuclear bomb capacity unless monitored (*International Herald Tribune*, 30 June 1993, p. 4).

This brings us to another important lesson, which concerns the IAEA safeguard system. There has been much debate about the ef- ficiency of IAEA inspections; but Iraq constituted the first case where concrete evidence could be compared with IAEA reports. As late as in November 1990, the IAEA inspection in Iraq did not reveal evidence of plans to produce nuclear weapons. This reflects less on how the inspection was carried out than on what was inspected: as the safeguard agreement - or the prevalent interpretation of it - prescribed, it studied officially notified installations and activities only. There were therefore good reasons to review how the IAEA safeguard system could be revised to form a better supplement to the NPT, and this matter has been discussed at several Board meetings of the IAEA (Müller 1992). At its June 1991 session and later, it Director General Hans Blix stated three conditions for operations like those of Iraq to be discovered: (a) unlimited access to all 'suspect' facilities within a country; (b) a supply of intelligence on such facilities by member states capable of collecting relevant data (e.g., by observation satellites); (c) full backing by the UN security council. The discussion on these conditions, in particular (b), seemed to reopen the North-South divide and the difficulties that can be foreseen are related to the general problems with the NPT.

For while the NPT is often seen as a dam against nuclear proliferation, fears have repeatedly been voiced as to when it might burst. The quinquennial Review Conferences have indeed revealed considerable differences between the 'Haves'and the 'Have-Nots' (most, but not all of which are also in the South). The Haves tend to argue that it is in the self-interest of the Have-Nots not to have - and have found it hard to sell this argument as long as they simultaneously argue that it is in their own interest to have. The next Review Conference in 1995 will be the first where the Haves can counter the traditional criticism from the Have-Nots by some negotiated or unilateral reductions of the nuclear arsenals of the USA and Russia. At the same time, the issue above is likely to become controversial. Apart from Iraq, the new and strengthened IAEA regime was tested for the first time against North Korea in 1993. When IAEA insisted on access to non-notified installations in North Korea, which is suspected of a nuclear weapons project (Chauvistré 1993) the countermove of North Korea was to give notice, on 12 March 1993, that it would leave the NPT on 12 June 1993. The Security Council limited itself to a resolution on 11 May 1993 calling upon North Korea to comply with the IAEA safeguards agreement. It was eventually persuaded to remain in the NPT, but the inspection issue remained, also becoming a matter of talks between North Korea and the USA, in connection with which the US Secretary of State, Mr. Warren M. Christopher stated that 'any effort to build a nuclear bomb would not be tolerated by the USA' and President Clinton that it was not something the USA could afford to let happen (*International Herald Tribune*, 5 July 1993).

As the present book goes to the printer, the final results of these developments are not known. They point, however, at a general dilemma within the NPT and IAEA regimes. On the one hand, the broadening of the IAEA regime and the willingness of the USA and possibly the Security Council to exert pressure to prevent NPT members from leaving and to back the broadened IAEA regime up may make the regime stricter and reduce the risks of violations. On the other hand, the same pressure might persuade a number of near-nuclear non-members of the NPT that it has come to include more obligations than before and in addition has become very difficult to get out of, once joined, notwithstanding the provisions for this in the treaty. This may have provided them with a new and strong argument against joining the NPT.

This is not the place to review the differences between Haves and Have-Nots, many of which will depend heavily on political sympathies. However, Bracken & Leavitt contribute one essential non-political argument to that debate. They point out that a number of the institutional and relational factors that have contributed to reducing the risks within and between the two superpowers are weak or absent in several near-nuclear states, and would be extremely costly and time-consuming to create. In addition, the warning times between new nuclear neighbors would be very short. The emergence of new nuclear states would therefore have at least a short- to medium-term effect of strongly increasing the risk of inadvertent nuclear war, and would have a long-term effect of increasing it. There is also a paradox involved: *if* one of these states went nuclear, it would be in the interest of Nuclear Powers to assist it with C^3I technology, at least for negative control, to reduce the risks for an accidental nuclear war; but at the same time, it is decidedly *not* in their interest to tempt any state to go nuclear by making such promises.

There is another set of issues to consider under the headline of horizontal proliferation: the fate of nuclear weapons in the fifteen or more republics resulting from the dissolution of the former USSR. Initially there were nuclear weapons in at least ten of them, and strategic nuclear weapons in four: Russia, Ukraine, Belarus and Kazakhstan. Much of the fears turned out to be groundless, however. By April 1992 all tactical nuclear weapons had been withdrawn to Russia, and the three later states had signed a START I protocol with the USA where they agreed to adhere to the NPT as non-nuclear weapons states 'in the shortest possible time', keep nuclear weapons under 'a single unified authority' and implement the limits and restrictions of START (Blair 1993: p. 14).

All is not well, however. While Belarus has ratified the START, adhered to the NPT and agreed to ship all of its 81 nuclear-tipped SS-25 missiles to Russia by the end of 1994 for dismantling, Kazakhstan has only ratified the START, and Ukraine has done neither (*International Herald Tribune*, 16 April 1993). Ukraine furthermore legislated in June 1993 that all nuclear weapons on Ukrainian soil were Ukrainian property, and its parliament is obviously split on whether to ratify START or not. In addition, the supreme command of CIS was dissolved in June 1993, leaving the control of these nuclear weapons an open issue at best and a bone of contention with Russia at worst.

Judged by the debate and demands, three motives underlie the hesitation of Ukraine. Nuclear weapons serve as a status symbol; Ukrainian politicians have drawn parallels between Ukraine and France. They serve as deterrence; Ukraine is holding out for strong security guarantees from the West before relinquishing them. And they serve as bargaining chips; Ukraine is asking for many times more economic support than the West has offered so far. It is obvious that it will take new rounds of negotiations between Ukraine, Russia and the USA before the START can come into effect, and that this will involve thorny issues.

5.2 Vertical proliferation

At the NPT Review Conference in 1995, it will be less easy than before for the Have-Nots to argue that the Haves have neglected the commitment to serious negotiations on nuclear disarmament expressed in Article VI of the treaty. The destruction of the whole INF category of missiles has been completed in the USA and Russia by the deadline, 1 June 1991 (although it is permissible for them to redeploy the warheads on other carriers). The START negotiations resulted in the summer 1991 in an agreement on considerable cuts (on average about one third) in strategic nuclear weapons, with a number of sub-ceilings and an unprecedented verification regime (Cowen Karp 1992). After the last Soviet short-distance nuclear weapons outside the former Soviet Union had been withdrawn (from Germany) in about August 1991 (Blair 1993: p. 10) - and after the failed coup in Moscow in August 1991 - a series of initiatives by Bush, Gorbachev and Yeltsin in 1991-2 provided an epoch-making set of unilateral measures and proposals for agreement (Fieldhouse 1992). The Bush Initiative on 27 September 1991 provided for all American land-based short range nuclear missiles and warheads in Europe and South Korea to be withdrawn and cancelled the plans for a new short range missile. In addition, all sea-based tactical nuclear weapons - including cruise missiles - were to be removed from ships and attack submarines, most of them to be destroyed; the alert levels for strategic bombers and missiles were reduced, the warheads of the bombers would be stored and the strategic weapons that the START treaty has marked for destruction to be removed immediately from their existing positions. These measures were not conditioned on any Soviet action, although President Bush asked the Soviets to match these actions by unilateral cuts of their own. So President Gorbachev did, nearly item for item, in his announcement on 5 October 1991; he went further to announce that the Soviet Union would reduce its strategic forces to 5,000 START Treaty-accountable warheads (1,000 below the treaty ceiling), proposed the destruction rather than storing of the withdrawn tactical nuclear weapons, and abolished a number of nuclear weapons programs. Further initiatives by President Bush on 28 January 1992 and by President Yeltsin on 29 January 1992 contained another set of unilateral moves and proposals for agreement defined a halt to production of new nuclear weapons and called for negotiations about even deeper reductions in terms of various START ceilings. Great Britain and France have also announced some measures in line with all these initiatives.

From the point of view of accidental nuclear war, much has therefore been moving in the right direction, at least in the two major nuclear powers. In the USA, there have also been massive programs to increase security in the 1980s, and the Panel on Nuclear Weapons Safety (1990), in addition to suggesting more measures, noted that no external information had to be provided to submarines in order physically to enable a launch of ballistic missiles, concluding the report with the sentence: 'It is also important to evaluate the suitability of continuing this procedure into the future'. Congress then mandated that the Defense Department submit a report evaluating the proposal that PALs be installed on all nuclear forces at sea (Blair 1993: p. 283).

The picture of the former Soviet Union is more complex, the situation being continuously fluid. The traditional desire for very centralized control over nuclear weapons seems to have kept much of the potential effects of the political fluidity in check, however. One of the challenges was the deconstruction of the Soviet Union; it has now boiled down to the issues described above: who - if anybody else than Russia - is to retain nuclear weapons and what will be the division of constitutional control of them between Russia and those republics who retain them, or have not yet gotten rid of them. There seems to be agreement on a 'dual control' system, with Moscow in positive control and the governments of these republics in negative control. How that is to be worked out in detail is not yet clear, and the devil may be in the detail: at least Ukraine has called for that negative control meaning not only consent to launch from the Ukrainian President, but also physical means for him to block any launch. He now seems to be able to block launch orders for nuclear weapons in Ukraine (Blair 1993: p. 75).

The second major challenge was illustrated by the failed attempt at a coup d'état in August 1991, which raised many speculations as to who had release authority. While there has been domestic fighting in some nuclear weapons states previously - the cultural revolution in China and the coup attempt in France in 1961 - this was the first time that the central command of nuclear weapons was affected. The coup leaders were reported to have seized President Gorbachev's codes for releasing nuclear weapons, but it was pointed out already by Rowen & Hoffman (1991) that this did not mean that they were not under control or that they could easily have been launched amid the chaos surrounding the coup. In fact, Blair (1993: p. 83) states that the three CINCs of the strategic forces had agreed not to obey any orders from the coup plotters and had arranged the system in such a way that it would be impossible for them to give any direct orders to lower commanders. A future collapse of responsible authority on highest level cannot be dismissed, however; but this threat is of a political nature, rather than a more narrowly organizational one.

5.3 The context
It is almost a tautology that the risk of 'intentional' nuclear war is related to international tension, especially if we operationalize 'tension' in terms of expectations of war. How the risk of accidental nuclear war relates to it is more of an empirical matter (Petersen & Smoker, Ch. 11). Opinions differ on the exact relationship (linear, threshold effect, etc.), but there is general agreement that when tension decreases, risks for accidental nuclear war also decrease, perhaps even more, or much more, rapidly. From this point of view, there have been great improvements in the last few years. There have also been other détente effects in the same direction, such as the indications from NATO that it may change its doctrine to make nuclear weapons an instrument of last resort, which is largely what the advocates of No-early-use have been asking for.

To the extent that history teaches us anything, one main lesson appears to be that international tension is variable. It has gone up and down before, and is likely to continue to do so. The recent European transformation *may* mean that next up-swing is less steep - and it may not. If the USA failed to deter Iraq from attacking Kuwait, Iraq in turn failed to deter the USA from attacking Iraq. In some parts of the Third World, like India, many seem to have drawn the dangerous conclusion that nuclear weapons are necessary for deterrence (Navlakha, 1991).

Apart from providing a temporary reduction of the risk for accidental nuclear war, the present phase of detente also offers possibilities for future reductions. Its main contribution here is twofold. It consists in making some unilateral measures possible and, if reciprocated, eventually cemented in treaty form. It also creates a window of opportunity for such solutions that cannot be achieved unilaterally, because they derive from the structure of the strategic situation, rather than from what individual states are or do. If such structures can be changed now - or if they can at least be surrounded by durable regimes - we may be able to create a *ratchet* effect, preventing next downturn in relations from being as deep and ominous as it otherwise would. The issue is not only, perhaps not even primarily, one of reductions, even if they may help much in addressing the central issue of changing the structures of the nuclear systems - deployment, countermeasures, command and control - in such a way that a possible return of tensions do not squeeze the Nuclear Powers into mutually reinforcing postures of 'launch on warning' again. Avoiding such a return involves several types of measures, including revisions of overall declaratory and *de facto* nuclear doctrines; agreements to keep SSBNs far away from each other's coasts; agreements concerning the use of stealth technology, perhaps limiting it to conventional arms only; agreements on a joint early warning centre, and so forth.

There is, unfortunately, another side to this: while creating this window, detente - and the ensuing reduction of risks for accidental nuclear war - may also make it appear less urgent to use it. This can lead to a dangerous myopia; for negotiations take time, often long time, and if occasions are not seized, it may quickly become too late. From this point of view, the measures deriving from the Bush, Gorbachev and Yeltsin initiatives have been major steps forward. Yet even after their being carried out - and that will take several years - there will still be many thousands of nuclear weapons distributed over several countries, and future increases in global or even regional tensions might bring us back to a new period of higher risks of inadvertent nuclear war. The time to save for the seven lean years is the seven fat years. And that brings us to the agenda for how to use the time.

5.4 Where do we go from here?
A major aim of this book has been to review the state of the art of research relevant to accidental nuclear war, thus updating a number of earlier volumes like Hellman (1985a) and Paul et al. (1990). We

have also wished to go more than traditionally beyond that in terms of studying proposals as to what could be done by whom in this respect. Part V is therefore devoted to contributions (Intriligator & Brito, Kislov, Belous, Ahlstrand and Kanninen) that focus on potential action on various levels and by various actors. Among the proposed actors, we find states (nuclear and non-nuclear), pairs and groups of states (proposed negotiations and treaties) and the international community as represented by various organizations within or outside the United Nations system.

In addition, we have reprinted as Appendix B the important declaration emerging from an international symposium arranged in Stockholm in November 1990, by the Swedish Initiative for the Prevention of Accidental War. At this symposium, which was supported by all political parties in Sweden, there were a number of outstanding international experts present (many of whom are among the authors in this book), and the proposals emerging from it are therefore to be seen as a valuable supplement to those put forward in Part V. Some of the measures proposed are already being carried out, and others have been added elsewhere, such as in Wedar et al. (1992) and Hellman (1992), as well as Blair's (1993, Ch. 8) rules for 'responsible nuclear custodianship'. Taken together, all these measures should go a long way to reduce the risks of accidental nuclear war, even if it may be impossible to disinvent nuclear weapons.

Chapter 2

Accidental Nuclear War in the Context of Global Problems

Karl K. Rebane

Global problems are man-created problems that have a tendency to grow into global threats and later catastrophes, provided that present trends in the development of mankind continue. They are not results of man's stupidity, rather the opposite: in his struggle for life man has been *clever* in expanding his exploitation of natural resources, doing it faster than his rivals and - for the sake of being faster and stronger today - paying little attention to the future consequences. Such behavior has become a basic part of man's nature, for which reason it is extremely difficult to really innovate patterns of thinking and action. According to the Second Law of Thermodynamics, the winners are those species and communities that by the final count have been most active in producing entropy and causing pollution of the environment (Rebane, 1990).

Global problems are both interconnected and interdependent. For instance, the exhaustion of global resources (oil, coal, pure water and air, etc.) will lead to a despair, which will, in its turn, induce aggressive thinking. The probability of wars, including intentional and accidental nuclear wars, will increase. The greenhouse effect of global warming might therefore soon become a contributory cause of great social disturbances and a mighty wave of aggressivity.

Conversely, if the probability of war decreases, it becomes possible to reduce the military consumption of - natural and other - resources, as well as a part of the environmental pollution caused by the military industry. The resources freed from the arms race can be used for combating the greenhouse effect and other environmental disasters.

Such a conversion from military to environmental use can have many forms: reorienting research and technology, establishing rapid action forces for environmental disasters, and even the substitution of environmental for military service. It will contribute to decreasing the likelihood of war by improving the environmental situation on a global scale providing a possibility to slow down the man-created production of entropy (Rebane, 1978).

Another new global problem consists in the safeguarding of hundreds of nuclear power plants. The risks of damage and of large leaks of radioactive material increase considerably when social revolts occur, when changes in climate or food shortages affect the minds of people working at the plants. Technical accidents and human errors become considerably more likely when transportation systems and the supply of energy, water and materials are adversely affected by economic difficulties.

By damaging nuclear power plants, even a conventional - civil or international - war may engender catastrophic radioactive pollution and devastate nature globally. This is another of the instabilities that could contribute to increasing the risk of accidental nuclear war.

Yet mankind has to live with nuclear power plants: at least for the next few decades, there is no other option, if we want to keep the concentrated energy production on the level necessary for modern civilization.

To keep the huge amounts of radioactive materials under control, elaborate and extremely reliable systems have to be designed, built and maintained in excellent operational order. Extensive and open international cooperation here will help in meeting these high technological and organizational requirements - and contribute to personal contacts, mutual understanding, and a better political climate.

Accidental nuclear war is thus quite similar to nuclear power disasters: today, and most probably for some time to come, mankind has to live with these risks. Too many people in power keep thinking that the threat of nuclear retaliation and Mutual Assured Destruction is the only factor that averts full-scale wars between nuclear power states. It is, of course, really dangerous to have piles of nuclear warheads and complicated systems of control, targeting, transportation, etc., which are reliable, but far from absolutely so; but according to these considerations, there is no other way to preserve peace on the global scale today. As long as they predominate - and today they do - it is of primary importance to develop the control systems, so as to keep the probability of accidental nuclear war as low as possible. To reduce this threat, we need an international cooperation and control that is as wide and as open as possible. They will contribute even more than cooperation on nuclear plant safety to contacts, mutual understanding and a better political climate.

During political thaws between great powers, an effect of the decreased risk of an intentional nuclear war is that the *relative* probability of an accidental one increases (Intriligator & Brito, 1988), for which reason the risk of an accidental nuclear war requires even more attention than before. The most important problem is, however, whether its *absolute* probability will increase, too. If we could rest assured that the opposite is true, so that the absolute probability decreases considerably with political thaws, we would have a reason to stop worrying and to turn at least the main part of our activities away from the problems of accidental nuclear war.

Different inputs to the absolute probability may obviously change in different directions: some contributing factors decrease, others may increase, and a considerable increase in merely one of of the latter may result in considerable increase of the composite absolute probability of an accidental nuclear war. *One* of the potentially dangerous factors is obvious: giving less attention to technological and human aspects of nuclear weapons will tend to increase that probability.

Nuclear submarines constitute a delicate point. Today, decision-making and launching of SLBMs are delegated to their commanding staff, remaining for long periods out of governmental or other central control, due to lack of proper communication with submerged submarines. There are dozens of nuclear submarines deployed at sea at any time. They carry hundreds of missiles with several thousands of warheads. A Trident II missile has performance capabilities (accuracy and nuclear yield) equivalent to those of an ICBM (Perry, 1989).

The risk of accidental nuclear war would be considerably diminished by a reliable channel of communication with submarines deep under the surface. If it could be a high-capacity channel, the crew might receive a flow of fresh information, feel themselves less isolated from mankind and thereby experience less of the resulting stress. It would assist in avoiding an accidental launching caused by mental instability. We would get a crucial effect from 'strategic locks', installed in the missiles on submarines and controlled from the centre (preferably by the government or some other high-level council). Decision-making would then be lifted off the commanding staff of submarines.

Given modern technical means, especially progress in optical laser communications, it must be quite possible to create the necessary link of communication. It should be possible to provide an 'optical lock,' using medium power lasers (1-10 Joule per pulse), improved filters for discerning signals from noise, and an optical cable as antenna to connect the information processing station in the submarine with the ocean surface which is illuminated by means of an orbiting laser (Zuev & Rebane, 1990).

In spite of the possibility that such links - like any technological innovation - may also be used for purely military purposes, we should search for international cooperation in solving the technological (and political) problems of establishing them.

Deterrence by nuclear retaliation is the central issue for holding balance and providing peace between nuclear power states in our contemporary world. The issue at stake has been how many and what kind of missiles can guarantee a total destruction of the enemy in a second strike. ('Unacceptable damage' actually comes to the same thing: once the exchange of nuclear strikes has started, it appears technically very difficult to stop before total destruction.) At the same time, the technology for the second strike should be limited to precisely that, and should not be possible to be used also for a first strike.

As a physicist, there seems to me to be only one clear-cut answer if we take both these conditions seriously: that a nuclear state has one single nuclear charge, really large and powerful in its destructive capacity, and that it has it *at home*.

That warhead might be designed to cause a total destruction of our civilization, whether by the explosion itself or its radioactive fallout. By fulfilling the first aim - the horror of the guaranteed destruction of the enemy (and everybody else) - it would also be retaliatory, thus providing a perfect version of Mutual Assured Destruction (MAD).

It is very difficult, in fact impossible, to find countermeasures preventing the use of that kind of suicidal counterstrike. The domestic device ('under the presidential desk') may be designed in such a way that any attack against it triggers its full-scale explosion. The second condition, first strike inability, is also completely fulfilled. The probability of an accidental nuclear war would furthermore be much smaller: because of the direct and simple 'launch' control by highest-level authorities, the very complicated systems of delivery to other continents become superfluous.

There is, of course, one serious disadvantage. When activated, this domestic nuclear device means certain and immediate death for the person who pushes the button, his home, relatives and countrymen. But would the actual situation in a country after this be much worse than after a nuclear exchange? Does it make any difference whether the nuclear explosions and radioactivity in your country are imported or of your own making? Do we still not want to realize how very small is our common home Earth? *Selective* nuclear weapons, which may be aimed with high precision against certain targets, are always to a considerable extent first strike weapons.

The crucial difference would be the possibility of having any hope that there can still be a winner even in a full-scale nuclear war. If there can, then new effective ways to win a nuclear war and survive it have to be searched for - but so will the other side, and we will just get to a new stage of the arms race. The domestic nuclear device, by being a full guarantee of MAD, would eliminate any such hope, thereby making senseless any further development of nuclear arms or other weapons of mass destruction.

The idea of such a domestic nuclear MAD device may admittedly appear naive. On the other hand, if it is considered naive, does this not finally mean that policy makers are still harboring some hopes about winning a nuclear war or that they are prepared to live forever with nuclear weapons and the arms race?

PART II

The Systems and their Components

Chapter 3

Strategic Defense and Inadvertent Nuclear War

Herbert L. Abrams

The possibility of deep and meaningful cuts in the nuclear stockpiles of the great powers has sharply diminished the concern over the threat of a nuclear holocaust. There is a growing shift in emphasis from the military to the economic equation in international affairs, a belief that the military giants of these past decades may be relegated to lesser positions by the extraordinary forward productive thrusts of the East Asian and middle European powers.

Nevertheless, none of us can feel secure with thousands of nuclear weapons still pointing in our direction. Because rational leaders of the great powers would not intentionally initiate a destructive massive exchange, nuclear war, if it comes, is more likely to arise from misunderstanding, miscalculation, or accident.

In a period of profound change, the explosive forces in the East, and the persistence of the threat of nuclear weapons compel us to look critically at the interaction of strategic defense with accidental nuclear war. While the funding of the 'Strategic Defense Initiative' (SDI) has expanded less rapidly than its proponents had hoped, over $20 billion dollars have been invested in it since 1983. Recent cuts in the SDI budget should not obviate the fact that billions continue to be appropriated in support of the program.

This analysis will concentrate on the full fledged effort that President Reagan called for in his 'Star Wars' speech of March 23, 1983, nothing less than the 'layered' defense embodied in the initiative. Is it reasonable to focus on the full system? The director of the strategic defense program in the United States, General George Monahan, was explicit on this matter in March, 1990: 'Our policy,' he said, 'calls for the layered defense...that's all remained the same. The strategic capability of the Soviet Union has not changed. They've modernized their ballistic missile force and they are continuing to do so' (Monahan, 1990). While current Defense Department goals are more modest, there remain strong and vocal supporters of a massive strategic defense effort.

*   *   *   *

The history of nuclear weapons can be summed up in six words: decreasing delivery time and increasing accuracy. The two considerations of time and space have played a central role in creating an unacceptable risk in the nuclear stockpiles of the great powers.

Space. On October 4, 1957, the Soviet Union launched Sputnik 1, to the surprise of the US space program and of Americans in general. What followed was not so much a 'race to space' as an arms race in space. The United States accelerated its program, launching 30 satellites between Sputnik 1 and the first moon probe - the Soviet Luna 1 - in September 1959. The launches included the first US military satellite for photographic reconnaissance in February 1959. Of the 30 launches, 19 failed. The Soviets completed 5 launches during this time, all successful (Jasani and Lee, 1984: p. 8). In late 1959 the United States began tests on anti-satellite (ASAT) weapons, but continued to experience 10 to 15 launch failures per year until 1962. By then, the American space program had 'caught up' to the Soviets and both countries regarded space as an important military asset. Soviet ASAT research began in 1963 (Jasani, 1984: pp. 11-14).

Doctrine. In the 1950s and 1960s neither the United States nor the Soviet Union had ballistic missiles of sufficient accuracy to pose a credible threat to the hardened nuclear forces of the adversary. All either side could do was to hurl nuclear bombs into the other's country. The strategic doctrines of the period - massive retaliation and assured destruction - reflected these technological capabilities (Shapley, 1984).

Space technology made both sides' ICBMs more accurate in the 1970s. Dramatic improvements in inertial instrumentation, re-entry technology, and our understanding of the earth's gravitational fields made missile silos and other military assets vulnerable to offensive missile strikes, challenging the retaliatory capacity (Kerr, 1984).

Technological advances contributed to stability, however, because of superior global communications, and reconnaissance. Early warning satellites reduced uncertainty about a Soviet first strike and afforded the National Command Authority more time and information upon which to base a response. They also made launch-on-warning (LOW) more credible: ICBMs could be launched before the incoming missiles could destroy them. Stability was augmented through verification and early warning, while war-fighting capabilities were enhanced (provided the satellites survived and worked). Since neither side had effective ASAT weapons, space became a 'sanctuary' for these systems that were simultaneously stabilizing (better information) and destabilizing (possible Launch on Warning; augmented war fighting capacity) (Shapley, 1984: pp. 59-61).

In the 1970s the United States developed a counterforce doctrine that relied on highly accurate ICBMs to destroy Soviet nuclear and general military forces. Counterforce doctrine supplemented assured destruction's singular response, providing options for limited retaliation at lower levels of escalation. As such, counterforce was thought to provide *extended* deterrence. The survival of global military command and control (C^3I) was essential in order to carry out a limited nuclear war. Since 80 percent of US military communications are carried out via satellite, space became an asset vital to counterforce doctrine. Military satellites also became a logical target if one side wanted to destroy the other's war-fighting capabilities or paralyze its warning systems.

Warning systems. The sophistication of doctrine and forces has not been matched with equivalent leaps forward in C^3I (Blair, 1985: p. 211). Even after planned improvements, the C^3I system might be incapable of supporting nuclear war fighting strategies. Furthermore, it remains vulnerable to a 'decapitation' attack. This dual vulnerability has led many to consider 'launch on warning' and ballistic missile defense as viable responses to first-strike weapons (Garwin, 1979; Easterbrook, 1983; Gray, 1977; Waller, et al, 1986). Such responses are totally dependent on a warning system that has not kept pace with improvements in weapons systems.

The missile warning system operates at three levels: data collection; assessment; and decision-making. Satellites with infra-red sensors for launch detection and ground-based radars collect the data. Computer centers and communications-links record, correlate and relay the data. Finally, personnel at four command posts interpret, analyse and act upon the warning information.

When the sensors indicate a potential threat or convey ambiguous information, a *Missile Display Conference* is called among all four commands. The frequency of such conferences reflects the great sensitivity of the satellites that stimulate the warning process (US Congress, 1980).[1]

Conferences called to evaluate threats are a more serious category of response. They act as a double check on the more threatening or ambiguous attack warnings.

If the Commander-in-Chief of NORAD decides there may be a real threat, he convenes a *Threat Assessment Conference*. More senior personnel, including the Chairman of the Joint Chiefs of Staff, appraise the warning. When a threat reaches such serious proportions, fighter aircraft have been launched, land-based missiles brought to a higher state of readiness, and Strategic Air Command (SAC) bomber crews have boarded and started their engines.

The Threat Assessment Conference is the last step before the *Missile Attack Conference*. At this highest level, which has not been required thus far, the President and other senior personnel confer on the actions to be taken, and it is sometimes assumed that a decision can be made within minutes (US Congress, 1980; Wallace et al, 1986).

False warnings. All told, there have been thousands of routine Missile Display Conferences and hundreds of Possible Threat Conferences. From 1977 to 1984, 20,784 false indications of missile attacks on the United States were generated by our early warning systems. Over 5 percent were serious enough for bomber and intermediate missile crews to be placed on alert. In 1978, 1979 and 1980, there were a number of warnings that required Threat Assessment Conferences.[2]

Two events in 1978 involved the malfunctioning of SLBM warning radars off the West Coast, which triggered a launch and impact report. The sensors have since been replaced with Pave Paws radar (NORAD, 1983).

On October 3, 1979, an SLBM radar picked up a low-orbit rocket body that was close to decay and generated a false launch and impact report (US Congress, 1980).

On November 9, 1979, NORAD's operational missile warning system indicated a mass attack on North America. During the next six

---

[1] NORAD 1985. 'Letter to David Morrison', *Center For Defense Information*, February 19.

[2] NORAD 1985. 'Letter to David Morrison', *Center For Defense Information*, February 19.

minutes, while the attack warning was being evaluated, ten jet interceptors scrambled aloft, and the US went on low-level nuclear alert. The emergency was caused by a 'war game' tape simulating missile attack data that was fed into a NORAD computer in the course of system testing. Through human error, the computer remained connected to the warning system (US Congress, 1981: pp. 116-117; US General Accounting Office, 1981; Sulzberger, 1979).

On March 15, 1980, as a part of Soviet training exercises, four SLBMs were launched from the Kuril Islands, a Soviet possession. The trajectory of one missile appeared to project an impact point in the United States. If this had been confirmed, a Missile Attack Conference would have been initiated (US General Accounting Office, 1981: p. 3).

At 2:26 a.m. on June 3, 1980, the display system at the SAC Command post disclosed that two Soviet SLBMs had apparently been launched towards the United States. Immediately thereafter, additional launched missiles were visible on the display system. Alert crews were directed to their aircraft to start the engines in preparation for take-off. At the outset, a Threat Assessment Conference was initiated. The airborne command post of the Pacific Command in Hawaii took off, prepared to send instructions to US warships. The President's emergency aircraft was also readied for take-off.

Three minutes and 12 seconds after the first attack warnings, the alert was called off and SAC aircraft crews returned to their barracks.

The cause of the false warning remained unclear. Over the next several days it was finally traced to a malfunctioning integrated circuit. This 46¢ computer chip was part of a communications multiplexer, which forms the message constantly transmitted from NORAD to the other commands (US Congress, 1980; Bunn & Tsipis, 1983).

These false alarms prompted several government investigations into NORAD's missile attack warning system and the command and control system in general. A 1982 report by the Committee on Government Operations stated:

> The NORAD facility had been mismanaged over the last decade by the Air Force, the Joint Chiefs of Staff, and the Department of Defense, resulting in obsolete computer systems (US Congress, 1982: p. 2).

One danger of false warnings is that the response by *one* side might provoke the *other* side. If nuclear forces are placed on alert in crisis as a result of erroneous attack warnings, an adversary, witnessing these apparently offensive maneuvers, might feel compelled to heighten their alert status as well. The 'ratcheting' effect might move both parties to ever higher levels. This sequence is possible because the major nuclear forces have become tightly coupled and interactive, behaving like a single system. Small perturbations in the system may well have major repercussions.

Multiple errors in the warning system pose a special risk to nuclear stability. The history of major technological accidents shows that, in each case, a combination of errors or malfunctions led to the catastrophe (Bracken, 1983).

The problem is intensified by short missile flight times with correspondingly limited response time (Frei & Catrina, 1983: p. 109-137).

Timelines. Russian ICBMs take 25 to 30 minutes to reach the ICBM fields in the central United States (see Table 1). Russian SLBMs take 8 to 15 minutes to Iowa, but only 5 to 10 minutes to coastal targets, like Washington, DC. Thus, vital command and control assets could be destroyed early in an attack.

Table 1
Current Timelines -- Attack

Soviet ICBMs:	25 - 30	Minutes (US ICBM Fields)
Soviet SLBMs:	8 - 15	Minutes (US ICBM Fields)
	5 - 10	Minutes (Washington, D.C.)
	1 - 7	Minutes (EMP Blast)[a]

[a] A Russian SLBM launched 1000 miles off the Atlantic Coast could produce an electromagnetic pulse over the Eastern Seaboard in 1-2 minutes. A detonation over the Midwest to blanket the nation's communications system would probably take 5-7 minutes.

The Russian would face similar timelines from US ICBMs and SLBMs (see Table 2). Submarine-launched cruise missiles might place additional pressures on a Soviet response. In a coordinated launch of hundreds of ICBMs and SLBMs, the first processed signals from infra-red satellites and peripheral radar would arrive about 2 minutes later. Within 12 to 15 minutes after launch, the Ballistic Missile Early Warning System (BMEWS) radars would provide independent confirmation of ICBM attack. Decision time would be very short.

Command authorities might have to make unprecedented choices in 3 to 20 minutes. One SLBM could destroy Washington, DC within 5 minutes of launching (US Office of Technology Assessment, 1981: S-7439; Steinbruner, 1984: p. 43; Ball, 1981: p. 36).

Table 2
Current Timelines -- Attack

US ICBMs:	25 - 30	Minutes (Soviet ICBM Fields)
US SLBMs:	8 - 15	Minutes (Soviet ICBM Fields)
	5 - 10	Minutes (Moscow)
	7	Minutes (EMP Blast)
Cruise Missile:	Hours	Undetectable

The potential tightness of the decision framework is formidable. As Wallace and his colleagues have emphasized, a minimum period of four to eight minutes from missile launch through the Missile Attack Conference is required before a decision can be made (see Table 3) (Wallace et al., 1986). A full assessment might move beyond 'decision' time; weapons would have reached their targets.

1. The effect of Anti-Satellite Weapons (ASAT)

In the era of intercontinental ballistic missiles, time has decreased; and space - which once served as a sanctuary and buffered some of the problems of time - has become a new battleground. In this light, launch on warning, ASAT, and the Strategic Defense Initiative (SDI) can be seen as an attempt to regain time and space. Instead, they may in fact take decisions out of the hands of the National Command Authority and place them in sensing devices and a command and control system that are fallible and made more so by urgent time pressures.

US and Russian ASAT systems developed thus far, but not deployed, can only attack satellites at relatively low altitudes - especially the Russian weapons (Jasani, 1984). Though comparable, the US ASATs pose a greater potential for instability. While one-third of US satellites are in a low or medium orbit, eight out of nine Soviet satellites are either in low, medium or an elliptical orbit in which they pass as low as 400 kilometers above earth. Furthermore, the US military early warning satellites are in high, geosynchronous orbit. Only photo reconnaissance and some naviga-

tion satellites are in low-orbit. The Soviets have responded to the
threat with plans to place vital early warning, navigation and
communication satellites into high-orbit.

ASAT and satellite technologies may converge in such a way as
to destabilize space. Technological improvements that support
command and control make satellites more valuable targets, while
ASAT technology provides the potential for a high precision, high
confidence weapon that is hard to detect. These technologies move
side by side with SDI. In fact, SDI research will produce an ASAT
potential long before it reaches an anti-missile capability. Both kinetic
energy and laser technologies are currently under exploration and
development (Norman, 1990).

2. The Strategic Defense Initiative

SDI, in its final deployment, would depend on layered defenses that
would successively 'thin out' incoming warheads. The first layer would
intercept boosters and post-boost vehicles before reentry vehicles
(RV) and decoys dispersed (see Figure 1). Boost phase currently lasts
three to five minutes (US Office of Technology Assessment, 1986).

Figure 1

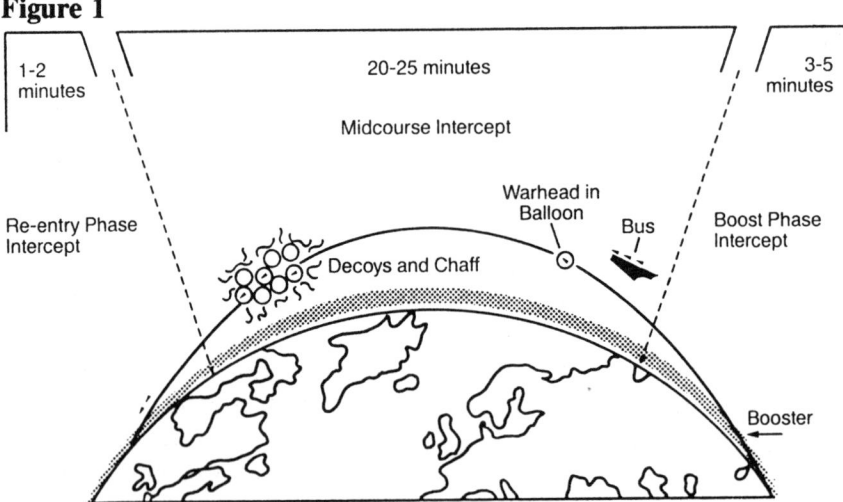

'Layers' of defense start over Soviet Union, where missiles rise from silos. The 'bus'
atop a missile dispenses warheads. Altogether, it takes warheads about 30 minutes to
reach targets.

Source: Union of Concerned Scientists, 1984. Reproduced by permission.

The second layer would correspond with the mid-course phase, which lasts about 20 minutes for ICBMs, but can be much shorter for SLBMs. The third layer would correspond to the terminal phase, which lasts less than two minutes as the RVs re-enter the atmosphere and explode.

If SDI is feasible, will it be a dependable system? There are five possible sources of unreliability: weapons, computer hardware, sensors, software, and human error.

Weapons degrade and break down. Computer hardware wears out and is sensitive to even small amounts of natural radiation that can destroy the information it contains. Preventive measures may help, but cannot eliminate hardware errors (Travis & Stock, 1983).

SDI sensors will be extremely 'computation-intensive', and subject to both hardware and software errors. Sensors and computers cannot always discriminate; objects in space may be mistakenly identified as incoming warheads.

Software will tell the computers what to do, i.e. how to integrate the sensors and weapons into an effective defense system. This will require 10-50 million lines of code. This software requirement is 5 to 25 times more complex than the largest single military software system, the one used in the Safeguard ABM system.

By comparison, the space shuttle has about 500,000 lines of code in its operating software (Wilentz, 1980). During a simulated flight, space shuttle astronauts decided to abort the flight, changed their minds, and then tried to abort again. The program in their on-board computer went into an 'infinite loop,' rendering itself useless. Programmers had not foreseen that the astronauts would try to abort the same shuttle flight *twice*. Two Mariner space flights were lost because one program had a period where there should have been a comma, and the other was missing the word 'not' (Travis and Stock, 1983).

Only full-scale testing or operation can reveal most software errors. With SDI the only full-scale test would be a nuclear war. Since such a test is unacceptable, the only alternative is simulation in real time. In essence, another large computer system with complex software would be needed to find the errors in the large SDI computer system with its complex software. The software would be subject to the same kinds of errors that have previously caused problems with the space shuttle and the warning system (Nelson & Redell, 1986; Borning, 1985).

Deficient communications security is still another hazard. Deceptive messages can be entered into a nation's communications system. Israel sent false intelligence messages to both Egypt and Jordan during the October 1967 war. Navigational systems and command satellites can also be tampered with.

The vulnerability of these complex computer systems was vividly demonstrated in November 1988, when a nationwide US computer network used by military installations and research centers was disabled by a graduate student's insertion of his own program, and more recently by the massive disruption of the American Telephone and Telegraph Company's long distance switching system on January 15, 1990. In the AT & T problem, a single computer program designed to improve the system malfunctioned and produced a chain reaction (Markoff, 1990; Sims, 1990).

How will the defensive system respond? The government Fletcher Report on SDI concluded: 'Some degree of automation in the decision to commit weapons is inevitable' (Fletcher, 1984).

Time available. With current missiles, boost phase lasts 150-300 seconds for ICBMs and 150-200 seconds for SLBMs. With completion of the boost phase in 150 seconds, decision time of 120 seconds allows at best two minutes to process false alarms before defensive weapons are fired.

Current time needed. Existing procedures to clear serious false alarms require time that may exceed even present boost phase duration (see Table 3). But 'fast burn' technology can reduce a missile's boost phase to 50 seconds. Decision time would likewise be reduced to tens of seconds.

Table 3
Time Needed to Clear Serious False Alarms

STEPS TAKEN	TIME USED
1. Alarm processed and labelled potential threat or non-threat	30 seconds
2. Missile Display Conference	2 minutes
3. Threat Assessment Conference	30 seconds - 2 minutes
4. Missile Attack Conference	1-2 minutes

Time Span: 30 seconds up to 6 minutes, 30 seconds
Source: (Wallace, Crissy et al., 1986)

As the SDI decision time decreases from two minutes to tens of seconds, the number of false alarms that exceed decision time may increase dramatically (see Table 4) (Wallace et al., 1986). Sooner or later, a false warning misperceived as a true warning could trigger the system during a crisis. Then the defensive machinery would come into play and might attack all objects within its field of view. Among those objects, the satellites of an adversary might suddenly be destroyed, with loss of the sensing surveillance devices that have provided assurance of good intentions. It is at that point that a country might launch its first salvo in a time of crisis, certain that its windows on the world had been deliberately destroyed. As the missiles thrust beyond the boost phase, and the re-entry vehicles move into independent flight, thousands of decoys will accompany them. The SDI umbrella, its holes incapable of handling the assault, will itself be useless as the space management command is destroyed.

Table 4
Number of False Alerts that Exceed Decision Time

ALERT TYPE	LENGTH	NUMBER	PERIOD
Routine	30 sec.	5-10	Daily
Potential Threat	Less than 2 min.	1	Every Two Days
Serious Threat	More than 2 min.	1	Every Two Months

Source: (Wallace, Crissy et al., 1986)

Countermeasures. Strategic defense may also contribute to the likelihood of inadvertent nuclear war by creating a false sense of security in an untested system. Decision-makers may be emboldened to embark on more provocative measures than otherwise, even though numerous countermeasures will be available to the adversary. Most of them will be based on inexpensive off-the-shelf technology - designed to enhance the opponent's ICBM effectiveness, protect its RVs or warheads, and otherwise neutralize the system. Electronic-countermeasures (ECMs) can be as simple as strips of aluminum or chaff to 'foil' enemy radar (Travis et al., 1983).

Warheads can often be 'salvage fused' so as to explode upon impact with non-nuclear interceptors (including shrapnel) and thermal lasers rather than being disarmed by them (Garwin, 1985). In such an explosion, intense electromagnetic radiation at all frequencies and the explosion's fireball may 'blind' sensing devices, while background signals from the explosion could disrupt distant sensors.

Exoatmospheric explosions create large electromagnetic pulses (EMP) that might damage defense battle management and C^3I and disable or destroy large power grids (US Office of Technology Assessment, 1986: p. 171). The higher the explosion, the larger the ground surface area affected by EMP. A one megaton explosion at 500 kilometers above the central United States will cover the entire country and parts of Canada and Mexico. Uncertainty and ambiguity are the ferments from which miscalculations are brewed in time of crisis, and no one will be certain of the effectiveness of countermeasures.

The most likely countermeasures are hundreds or thousands of missiles and warheads that could easily be built for the hundreds of billions that a full fledged space-based defense will cost.

3. The offensive potential

The borderline between defense and offense is tenuous. The inherent offensive capabilities of SDI will contribute to crisis instability.

1. Strategic defense will be perceived by an adversary as important support for a first strike (US Office of Technology Assessment, 1986: p. 93; Marsh, 1985; Drell et al., 1984).
2. The system will have enormous ASAT capabilities that could be used against an opponent's space-based defenses, early warning and communications.
3. If defense weapons are able to penetrate the atmosphere - like visible lasers - they might be able to attack cruise missiles, bombers and airborne command posts, provided they could locate these targets.
4. Weapons that penetrate the atmosphere might also be able to attack ground targets (US Office of Technology Assessment, 1986).
5. There will be important technological spinoffs for conventional warfare. Exotic instruments such as anti-tank lasers might result in a new class of weapons that would be threatening in a crisis (Glaser, 1985).

4. Crisis stability

While ASAT and SDI technologies overlap, ASAT weapons require lower power levels. The development and deployment of directed-energy ASAT weapons would therefore be a transition in the development of boost-phase or mid-course intercepts that would require higher power levels. Thus, the ability to destroy the space-based components of a missile defense system would precede the system.

ASAT advances on one side would undoubtedly create suspicions on the other that an SDI breakout was close at hand. Malfunctions of vulnerable satellites could exacerbate an ongoing crisis, increasing the likelihood of accidental nuclear war (Garwin & Pike, 1984).

In crises, the time for decision-making is compressed, the data frequently ambiguous, the choices few, and the pathway chosen important for an appropriate outcome (Ury & Smoke, 1984). All of these elements increase stress, which degrades decision-making (George, 1986).

Strategic defense will render the dynamic of crises particularly unstable:

1. Time is severely reduced.
2. Uncertainty is high because unknown defensive capabilities must now be taken into account.
3. Choices are few: 'Use them or possibly lose them.'
4. The stakes are high: Experience a first strike, or initiate one.

These factors combine to augment the urgency of action and impair the capacity for deliberation and negotiation.

With the relaxation of tensions between East and West of the recent period, the deep suspicions of the adversary's intensions are abating. But they still lie just beneath the surface. A deployed US missile defense might profoundly affect crisis stability if a confrontation gets out of hand - perhaps leaving the Soviets with the perception that they have one viable option: preemption. The more capable a missile defense becomes for one side, the more likely 'use or lose' becomes the only option. The other side may perceive that defense will encourage a first strike by assuring the first side of its ability to handle the 'ragged' response of a partially destroyed Soviet strategic arm. Given that perception, they will feel they have no option but to strike first so as to cripple the defense by destroying its command, control and battle management stations.

In summary, SDI increases the likelihood of unintentional nuclear war in several ways:

1. The danger of false warnings.
2. The time available versus the time needed for decision-making.

3. Increased crisis instability with an incentive to strike first.
4. Arms race instability with the perception that offensive and defensive weapons must be increased.
5. The offensive potential in defensive weapons.
6. The weaponization of space.
7. ASATs versus Strategic Defense, with the potential loss of sensor and intelligence data.

*   *   *   *

SDI represented a super-highway to instability in crisis. If the design to protect against annihilatory weapons promotes the likelihood of their use in time of crisis, it cannot be justified by an appeal to national self-interest or national security.

Of the many policy recommendations that flow from the foregoing considerations, a few deserve special emphasis:

1) SDI is a poor investment and should be scrapped. It is useless against cruise missiles, stealth technology, depressed trajectory SLBMs, nuclear terrorism (smuggling weapons into the country), or any truly determined adversary. A maximum of $200 million per year might be devoted to research and development.

2) The ABM Treaty must be reaffirmed in its strict interpretation as a mutually beneficial safeguard, and should be extended to include all nuclear nations.

3) A multilateral anti-satellite weapon treaty is essential.

4) A treaty banning all weapons in space is essential - any weapons designed to interfere with spacecraft or to inflict damage on earth, in the atmosphere, or on objects placed in space.

5) Investments in command and control - in computer systems, sensing devices, and in their protection - increase stability.

6) Information exchanges on Permissive Action Links, Personnel Reliability Programs, and all measures that cut the likelihood of unauthorized launch, strengthen common security. Command

destruct capability on strategic missiles would be a major forward step, as would Permissive Action Links on all naval vessels.

7) A comprehensive test ban might signify to all countries that the era of unbridled vertical proliferation by the two superpowers is coming to an end, and that they are prepared to respect their obligations under the Non-proliferation Treaty. Only then can a credible case be made for dissuading nuclear-capable nations from moving relentlessly forward on their own nuclear weapons programs.

*   *   *   *

Such measures would fit naturally into the developing arms control regimen on nuclear weapons, conventional forces, and confidence - and security - building measures.

While the risk of accidental nuclear war will persist as long as tens of thousands of weapons of mass destruction remain in the United States, Russia, the Ukraine, Belarus, Kazakhstan, England, France, China, Germany, South Korea, Greece, Turkey, Israel, India, Pakistan and other nations, that risk can be minimized by a rational agenda of prevention coupled with progressive deep cuts in the arsenals. By the same token, all measures that contribute to instability - such as the Strategic Defense Initiative - render more dense the 'fog of war' and the likelihood of misperception in crisis leading to irrevocable actions.

Chapter 4

Accidental Nuclear War Considered from the Area of Reliability of Large Technological Systems

Bent Natvig

1. Introduction

On 15 September 1987 an agreement was signed in Washington, DC by the US and Soviet Secretaries of State George Shultz and Eduard Shevardnadze establishing 'nuclear risk reduction centers'. These centers, to be located in Washington, DC and Moscow, will exchange information on matters that might be misinterpreted, such as an accidental missile launch or a commercial nuclear accident like the Chernobyl reactor fire. The centers will act as 'high-tech supplements' to the Washington-Moscow hot line. Four years of work led to this agreement, with US Senators Sam Nunn and John Warner as key promoters. The original plan was to have a mixed US-Soviet staff at both centers. Now there is to be only US staff in Washington and only Russian staff in Moscow - which is obviously a great drawback.

In this paper, which is an expanded version of earlier papers (Natvig, 1988 & 1989), we will look at this agreement in a broader perspective. In particular, we will view the problem of accidental nuclear war as a problem within the area of reliability of large technological systems. In Gregory & Edwards (1989), a list was provided of more than 230 nuclear weapons accidents involving the USA, the USSR and the UK between 1950 and 1988. Only nine of these accidents are categorized as 'any accidental or unauthorized incident involving a possible detonation of a nuclear weapon, which could create the risk of a nuclear war.' These few accidents should not be mixed up with the rest, however, since the consequences represent quite another dimension. After an accidental nuclear war there will not be many left to learn the lesson: whereas, for instance, the Chernobyl accident led to improvements in nuclear reactor safety all over the world, or so we may hope even in the Commonwealth of Independent States (CIS).

The best current information on the problem of accidental nuclear war seems to be the *International Accidental Nuclear War Prevention Newsletter* (see Babst). In addition, several conferences have been held on this issue. 'Nuclear War by Mistake - Inevitable or Preventable' was held in Stockholm, Sweden, 15-16 February 1985 (see Hellman, 1985). Here the late Swedish Prime Minister, Olof Palme, concluded his excellent introductory address by saying: 'Your conference is therefore addressing the most vital issue we have to face in the world today'. This conference was followed up by 'The Risk of Accidental Nuclear War' held in Vancouver, Canada, 26-30 May 1986 (see Demchuk, 1987). Furthermore, accidental nuclear war was the topic of both the fourteenth Pugwash Workshop on Nuclear Forces held in Geneva, 13-14 December 1986 and the eighteenth, held in Pugwash, Canada, 18-20 July 1989 (see Paul et al., 1990). Finally, the conference 'Implications of the Dissolution of the Soviet Union for Accidental/Inadvertent Use of Weapons of Mass Destruction' held in Pärnu, Estonia, 23-25 April 1992, presented new frightening perspectives.

We will conclude this section by reproducing the press release from the Vancouver conference.

INTERNATIONAL CONFERENCE WARNS OF NUCLEAR WAR RISK
The Conference on the Risk of Accidental Nuclear War held at the University of British Columbia, Vancouver, on May 26-30, concludes that the danger of accidental nuclear war is substantial and increasing for the following reasons among others:

1) Deteriorating global political relations coupled with a lack of real progress in disarmament and arms control, and the high frequency of international crises;
2) Escalation of the arms race leading to the development and deployment of destabilizing weapons systems and technologies;
3) Increasingly complex and unmanageable command and control systems with reduced warning times demanding decisions and actions on a time scale exceeding human capabilities;
4) Increasing reliance on automated decision-making systems leading to a greater likelihood of catastrophic error.

Measures must be taken to halt this continuing drift towards unparalleled catastrophe. The forthcoming Conference report will include detailed proposals for reducing the risk, but cautions that purely technological measures will not eliminate the risk.

Concerning 1) and 2), it is worth noting that at least 1), fortunately enough, seems less valid today than in 1986: 3) and 4), however, are as valid as ever.

2. Reliability

At the 18th European Meeting of Statisticians in Berlin, GDR, on 22-26 August 1988, the author of this article organized a session on 'Reliability of large technological systems'. This topic is obviously a hot one, due to e.g. the Chernobyl catastrophe on 26 April 1986. Some have claimed that this accident was totally unexpected; but this is to ignore the fact that even before the Three Mile Island accident on 28 March 1979, the American Reactor Safety Study (1975) had been strongly criticized (Lewis et al., 1978; Natvig, 1979). Laaksonen (1986), of the Finnish Center for Radiation and Nuclear Safety, has expressed the following opinion on the Chernobyl accident:

> The Chernobyl accident provided a discouraging example of a phenomenon which would be extremely difficult, if not impossible, to foresee and take into account in a probabilistic risk analysis. Also the events which are usually considered in the safety analyses have almost been standardized 15 years ago.
>
> The accident took place when the operators were decreasing the reactor power, prior to taking the plant out of service for scheduled maintenance. A special test of electrical systems was to be made at the stage the reactor had reached the power of 700 - 1 000 MW (20-30% of nominal power). At the beginning of the test the reactor was to be scrammed automatically and thus no interaction was expected between the reactor and the other plant systems.
>
> In the course of test preparation a coincidence of unfavorable operational steps brought the reactor to a state where it could reach prompt criticality in a few seconds. The dangerous core characters were evoked by the operators who were lacking sufficient knowledge in reactor physics. During the 12 hours preceding the explosion the operators committed deliberately at

least six severe violations of operating rules. Four of these were
such that without any of them the accident would have avoided:

1. Continued reactor operation without the necessary differential
reactivity worth in the control rods (operation below the permissible value was indicated clearly on a computer printout).
2. Continued reactor operation below the minimum allowable
power level.
3. Blocking of the reactor scram signals associated with steam
drum level and reactor coolant pressure.
4. Blocking of the reactor scram signals associated with trip of
both turbogenerator units.

The operator behavior was of course unforgivable but I think
it can be understood from the following viewpoints:
· a common attitude on operational rules in the Russian plants
  has been obviously quite relaxed: the rules have been taken as
  guidelines and not as strict orders
· the safety record of RBMK-reactors was good and no precur-
  sory events of this type had ever occurred
· Chernobyl unit 4 had an excellent reputation among the
  RBMK plants and the operators were evidently too self-
  confident
· the operators were not able to raise the reactor power above
  200 MW with the normal control systems (the power level
  followed changes in the coolant void content but the operators
  did not realize the situation clearly enough).

*What the Chernobyl accident really did was to call into question the
existing risk and safety analyses of large technological systems.*
    This was further underlined by the *Piper Alpha* oil-rig accident in
the North Sea on 6 July 1988, where 167 people were killed, and will
now be discussed more closely.
    In applying reliability theory to such systems, the following
problems arise:
· Lack of relevant data;
· Lack of knowledge on the reliability of the human components;
· Lack of knowledge on the quality of computer software;
· Lack of knowledge on dependencies between the components.

This makes it almost impossible to assess the probability of failure of a large technological system. Hence, the use of risk analysis to back political decisions on controversial safety issues is dubious, to say the least. If, however, a political decision has already been made, risk analysis and reliability theory can contribute essentially to *improving* the safety of a system. This is just the case for Norwegian offshore activities and for the Swedish nuclear power industry. It should, however, be noted that the latter is in deep trouble after the incident in the Barsebäck reactor on 28 July 1992. The site is very close to Copenhagen and the Danish environmental movement OOA has on the basis of a report from the present author claimed the plant to be closed down for a second time in a year.

We then need measures of the relative importance of each component for system reliability. Barlow & Proschan (1975) suggested that the most important component is that having the highest probability of finally causing system failure by its own failure. The present author has since developed a theory supporting another measure (Natvig, 1985a). The component whose failure contributes most to reducing the expected remaining lifetime of the system is the most important one.

The Chernobyl accident provided new data on nuclear power plants. What type of theory do we have to benefit from such data in future risk analyses in the nuclear industry? The characteristic feature of this type of theory is that one benefits both from data for the system's components and for the system itself. Furthermore, due to lack of sufficient data one is completely dependent on benefiting from the experience and judgement of engineers concerning the technological components and on those of psychologists and sociologists for the human components. This leads to a methodology of statistical inference that can deal naturally with subjectivistic probabilities. Such a methodology is called Bayesian after the English reverend and probabilist Thomas Bayes, who died in 1761. A textbook in this area is Berger (1985). One starts out by using expert opinion and experience as to the reliability of the components. This information is then updated by using data on the component level from experiments and accidents. Based on the information on the component level, the corresponding uncertainty in system reliability is derived. This uncertainty is modified by using expert opinion and experience on the system level. Finally, this uncertainty is updated by using data on the system level from experiments and accidents.

Hence, it is only in the final step that data from the Chernobyl accident can be used. Theory in this area is under development at the University of Oslo (Natvig & Eide, 1987).

In the magazine *Nature* (1986), there was an article on a situation coming close to a catastrophe, which occured in the night of 14 April 1984 in a French pressurized water reactor (PWR) at Le Bugey on the Rhône river, not far from Geneva.

> The event began with the failure of the rectifier supplying electricity to one of the two separate 48 V direct-current control circuits of the 900 MW reactor which was on full power at the time. Instantly, a battery pack switched in to maintain the 48 V supply and a warning light began to flash at the operators in the control room. Unfortunately, the operators ignored the light (if they had not, they could simply have switched in an auxiliary rectifier).
>
> What then happened was something which had been completely ignored in the engineering risk analysis for the PWR. The emergency battery now operating the control system began to run down. Instead of falling precipitously to zero, as assumed in the "all or nothing" risk analysis, the voltage in the control circuit steadily slipped down from its nominal 48 V to 30 V over a period of three hours. In response a number of circuit breakers began to trip out in an unpredictable fashion until finally the system, with the reactor still at full power, disconnected itself from the grid.
>
> The reactor was now at full power with no external energy being drawn from the system to cool it. An automatic "scram" system then correctly threw in the control rods, which absorbed neutrons and shut off the nuclear reaction. However a reactor in this condition is still producing a great deal of heat - 300 MW in this case. An emergency system is then supposed to switch in a diesel generator to provide emergency core cooling (otherwise the primary coolant would boil and vent within a few hours). But the first generator failed to switch on because of the loss of the first control circuit. Luckily the only back-up generator in the system then did switch in, averting a serious accident.

The article in *Nature* furthermore stated:

But the Le Bugey incident shows that a whole new class of possible events had been ignored - those where electrical systems fail gradually. It shows that risk analysis must not only take into account a yes or no, working or not working, for each item in the reactor, but the possibility of working with a slightly degraded system.

In 1978 Barlow & Proschan initiated the development of a theory of reliability where both the components and the system are described in a more refined way than just as functioning or failing. During the 1980s, the University of Oslo has been central in the development of this theory (Natvig, 1985b). It has also been indicated how this theory can be applied to offshore electrical power supply systems and pipeline networks. Furthermore, efficient algorithms and computer software based on this theory have been developed.

Avoiding accidental nuclear war has a lot in common with avoiding nuclear power plant catastrophes. Hence, the reliability aspects commented on above are indeed relevant also when discussing accidental nuclear war. This fact seems to have been overlooked in earlier assessments.

3. The 'Launch on Warning' strategy

In considering risk analyses of launching systems and early warning systems for nuclear weapons, an additional problem arises, at least for a civilian analyst: Lack of knowledge of the system.

Thanks to the information sources mentioned in Section 1, we are, however, not completely ignorant. One of the key contributions of the Vancouver conference was given by Bruce Blair, author of a book on strategic command and control (Blair, 1985). We quote from his presentation:

> Both have low confidence in their ability to absorb an attack before retaliating. And hence both sides have a de facto strategy of *launch on warning*. This is considered their principal strategic option, and at least the United States is operationally geared for this option. Therein lies a real danger of accidental war.

To illustrate this strategy, let us consider the following scenario from Wallace et al. (1986). A US early warning satellite gives a signal of an ICBM attack observed 1½ minutes after a possible launch in the

Soviet Union. It takes 2½ minutes to evaluate the signal from the satellite, and one fears that it is correct. A *Missile Display Conference* (MDC) is called after 30 seconds. This gathers further information and evaluates it. After 2 minutes of the conference, the situation is regarded as very serious and a *Threat Assessment Conference* (TAC) is called. Here, senior military personnel are immediately gathered to evaluate the threat. Now, 6½ minutes have passed since the possible launch. After 2 more minutes, a land-based radar gives a signal of an ICBM attack. The situation has become critical, and a *Missile Attack Conference* (MAC) is immediately called. In principle, a MAC includes all the senior personnel and the US president (if or when he is available). Preparations for launching one's own missiles are started. Two minutes later, one gets a message fearing the radar signal to be correct. There has been no message indicating that the satellite signal is false. Now 10½ minutes have passed since the possible launch. The time from issuing a launch order to a successful launch of the retaliatory missiles can be 6 minutes. These must be launched before the possible Soviet missiles reach their targets after 25 minutes. Thus the *Use Them or Lose Them Point* comes 19 minutes after the possible launch. Hence the US President has 8½ minutes to consider the situation and gather any further information. If he is really following the 'Launch on Warning' strategy he will then have to push the button. The peril of such a strategy was illustrated by the shooting down of an Airbus 300 from Iran Air over the Persian Gulf on 6 July 1988, killing 290 people. The lesson learnt is that governments should deploy the nuclear forces they have - as long as they have them - in such a way that the analogous decision situation does not arise.

Due to the US Freedom of Information Act, we know that the number of MDCs increased from 43 to 255 in the period from 1977 through 1983 (Wallace et al., 1986). None of these were just 'routine'. In 1978, 1979 and 1980 there were 2 TACs each year. Four of these were listed in Gregory & Edwards (1989). There is no information of any MAC. These figures thus indicate that the number of false alarms is alarmingly high.

A key point of the INF Treaty was to remove destabilizing weapons systems from Europe. Consider, for instance, a hypothetical situation in the past where a Soviet early warning satellite gives a signal of a US Pershing II attack being observed 2 minutes after a possible launch in Western Europe. If the missiles reach their targets after 8 minutes, and if one is optimistic and believes that it takes 4 minutes from issuing a launch order to the successful launch, then there are just 2 minutes left to evaluate the signal and reach a decision. The situation above still seems realistic today, if we consider a US SLBM attack on the CIS from the Barents' Sea or a corresponding CIS attack from the Atlantic.

Another contribution in this area was given at the Vancouver conference by Linn Sennott (1986). She presented two probability models related to aspects of the behavior of false alarms in the early warning systems. A potentially dangerous situation may arise when two false alarms are in the system at the same time. To model an overlap, one assumes that false alarms from all sources arrive to some central processing center according to a so-called Poisson process (Barlow & Proschan, 1981), with the rate λ. This rate could typically be 200 false alarms per year. The resolution time for each alarm is, for simplicity, assumed to be exactly r minutes. In our example r equals 3.5 minutes. One is interested in the distribution of the following random variable:

Z = the time until the arrival of the first alarm that finds another alarm still being resolved.

The theoretical average of Z, its expected value EZ, can be found by elementary probability calculus, and is approximately given by

$$EZ \approx \frac{1}{\lambda^2 r}$$

The inclusion that a doubling of the false alarm rate reduces the expected time until a false alarm overlap by a factor of four is a non-intuitive insight provided by this model. This shows the importance of making the early warning system extremely reliable. Having 200 false alarms per year and a resolution time for each alarm of 3.5 minutes, the expected time until a false alarm overlap is 3.8 years.

The second model is an attempt to quantify the gain in safety resulting from the required 'dual phenomenology', that is, the requirement that an indication of attack picked up by satellite sensors be independently verified by radars. In this model, one assumes there are two independent false alarm Poisson processes, with rates λ_1 and λ_2 respectively. The alarms from the first stream are resolved as they arrive and the resolution time is again assumed to be exactly r minutes. Now one is interested in the distribution of the following random variable:

> W = the time until the arrival of the first alarm from stream 2 that finds an unresolved alarm from stream 1 in the system.

The expected value, EW, is approximately given by:

$$EW \approx \frac{1}{\lambda_1 \lambda_2 r}$$

Again, a doubling of the false alarm rates reduces the expected time to a 'critical' alarm by a factor of four. With 200 false alarms per year from the two streams together and a resolution time of 3.5 minutes for alarms from the first stream, the expected time until a 'critical' alarm is again 3.8 years. Sennott leaves it to the user of these models to specify what constitutes a false alarm and to estimate their rates.

It has been questioned whether the United States does in fact have such a 'Launch on Warning' strategy. Let us quote Dr. William J. Perry, Deputy Under-Secretary of Defense for Research and Engineering: 'While launch on warning will remain an option it would not be prudent to rely solely on this option for ICBM force survivability' (Perry, 1980). This statement makes it clear that the USA at least does not deny having a 'Launch on Warning' option.

It goes almost without saying that in a critical situation opinions at different levels might differ as to the proper response, including whether to launch retaliatory forces. In the USA there might be disagreement between the President, the Vice President, the North American Aerospace Defense Command (NORAD), the Strategic Air Command (SAC), and so on. A similar disagreement is likely to occur in the USSR. Let us hope that the attitude that a nuclear war cannot be won will influence the decisions made by politicians and the military in a future crisis. All in all, there are several uncertainties as to the consequences of a 'Launch on Warning' strategy in a crisis situation. There is also some hope. Yet uncertainties and some hope are simply not good enough!

4. 'Permissive Action Links' and the human factor

Another key point in the discussions at the Vancouver conference centered on the so called 'Permissive Action Links' (PALs), which are electronic locks to prevent undesired local use of nuclear weapons. In a situation of an international crisis, the codes to unlock these circuits (and thereby activate the weapons) are transmitted from the central national authorities. This will increase the probability of a chain reaction leading to a nuclear war. In addition, what is frightening is the fact that the PALs are mainly designed not to prevent an unintentional nuclear war, but to prevent the enemy from using these nuclear weapons. It has thus been stated that there are no PALs on US submarines. Hence, even in the absence of an international crisis a sufficient number of the crew of a submarine might agree on launching one or more missiles on their own, having, for instance an erroneous perception of an acute threat. From a technical point of view it would probably suffice that two of the senior officers break the safety measures and are helped by a few of the crew members to launch the missiles.

One may object that such a situation is very unlikely. It must however, be recalled that submarines may be on a mission for 60-70 days, and that drug abuse among US military personnel is alarmingly high. This has been documented in Dumas (1980). Against this background, it is astonishing that there are no PALs on US submarines, even though PALs may help the enemy to discover them. One reason, according to Blair, is that the US Navy does not want any intervention from civilian authorities in matters considered to be their own concerns. *This really shows that a total risk analysis of command and control systems can never have been carried out in the USA.* The fact that there have been no such 'unauthorized launches' since 1945 is not a sufficient reason for not worrying about this problem. Before the Chernobyl accident (and even after it!), most 'experts' felt that the problem of nuclear power plant safety was under complete control.

5. Conclusions and proposals

I am convinced that it is impossible to give accurate estimates of the probability of an accidental nuclear war - which means that earlier attempts in this direction make no sense at all. I am, however, equally convinced that it is unacceptably high, given the consequences of the

event. Hence, judging from the information at hand, we may
reasonably fear such a war before the year 2000 - if nothing is done!

Still, reliability theory and risk analysis can be applied to improve
the reliability of a system, even if this reliability is unknown. The
nuclear risk reduction centers can be dramatically improved. Systems
can therefore be redesigned; technical components can be improved
and more redundancy introduced; procedures for the human beings
in the systems can be improved to ensure real, independent control.
Software failures however, are extremely hard to deal with, and here
it does not help to have program backup. Unfortunately, there is no
reason to believe that the quality of research workers and safety
analyses is any better in the military sector than in the civilian
nuclear power industry, where it is poor enough. In addition, there is
reason to believe that it is poorer in the CIS than in the USA.

To focus on these problems, an International Academic
Committee on Accidental Nuclear War has been established,
including among its members the Soviet academicians Yuri Kagan
and Boris Raushenbach. One aim of this Committee is to hold a
major international conference dealing with Accidental Nuclear War,
where politicians and scientists can meet. At the 38th Pugwash
Conference in 1988, I proposed that such a conference should be held
in Moscow in 1989. The mentioned Pärnu Conference in 1992 came
as an answer to this proposal. I also stressed the need for having
complete figures on false alarms also from the Soviet side. This will
show the world the need for proper action.

There is, however, no purely technological solution to the problem
of accidental nuclear war. Only deep reductions in nuclear weapons
arsenals can lead to a dramatically reduced, albeit still unknown,
probability of such a war. This follows from a probabilistic fact about
situations where many events (here: accidental launches of individual
weapons) each have a low probability: the probability of *at least one*
event occurring is approximately the sum of all the probabilities for
individual events. (This is true even if the events are dependent.) We
should indeed get rid of the most destabilizing weapons first. We
should also be aware that the situation may change when the number
of nuclear weapons systems approaches zero; but the 'instability close
to zero' problem does not have to be solved tomorrow. Meanwhile,
this probabilistic fact indicates a political solution to the problem of
accidental nuclear war - and at the same time provides an excellent
motivation for nuclear disarmament. This is of utmost importance

now due to the complete lack of political stability inside the CIS and to the serious disagreement, also witnessed at the Pärnu conference - between Russia on the one side and Belarus, Kazakhstan, Ukraine on the other - on the future of nuclear weapons on the CIS territory.

Chapter 5

Computers and Accidental Nuclear Conflict

Boris V. Rauschenbach

If we talk about *nuclear* war, few people still share Clausewitz' belief that war is an extension of diplomacy by other means. Today, there is general consensus that a nuclear war can result in no winner, but quite possibly in the mutual annihilation of the belligerents, the end of the human race or even of life on Planet Earth. Such an outcome can hardly be the object of a diplomacy pursued by other means, for which reason intentional nuclear war must be seen as unthinkable - and we should focus on the risks of an accidental one.

Even if a 'normal' sequence of events leading to a nuclear war is ruled out, a nuclear conflict can be provoked by international terrorists or by some other group on the lunatic fringe, but would then in all likelihood remain a local one. While its consequences may well be horrific, it will not spell the end of the human race; for that, the major nuclear powers with their mind-boggling 'overkill' capacity would have to get involved. None of them seeming likely to risk precipitating a nuclear conflict endangering the earth, essentially only accident remains as a potential cause. One way of preventing it is to involve military experts and politicians in the final stage of the decision-making process, submitting to a further critical analysis the entire body of data that are seen as calling for the employment of nuclear weapons, also taking moral considerations into account. Yet we have no guarantee that this 'last chance' will always be used as it should. Its effectiveness decreases with the increasing computerization of the decision-making process. The participation of human operators in this process may well become meaningless, if the time available to them is reduced to fleeting seconds and even fractions of a second, like in some of the SDI scenarios. Should such versions of the SDI be deployed, starting a nuclear war will be up to the computers, rather than to human beings. In that case, the problem of fail safe functional reliability of sophisticated computer systems (and especially of their making erroneous decisions) becomes of vital importance in the literal sense of the term.

Erroneous decisions by computerized systems may be due to a variety of causes, above all malfunctions within the computers themselves as a result of component failure. This category of causes will always be of secondary importance, however, as malfunctions due to component failure can be remedied by available methods of stand-by duplication.

Errors slipping into computer software pose a far more serious challenge, and are now the subject of an extensive specialist literature. Their nature can be very diverse, including the inevitable mistakes made by computer programmers in developing highly sophisticated software packages; mistakes made in the process of matching different parts of the software developed by different programmers working in different locations; and mistakes arising from the impossibility of anticipating the consequences of complex logical side chains and sequences. Such mistakes can only be eliminated by repeated full-scale 'field' tests of the entire computerized system working in conjunction with the space weapons it is designed to control which would have called for the participation of a potential enemy with his own weapons deployed. The elimination of software errors can therefore even at the best of times only be partial.

Finally, even if we had fully functional and trouble-free computer systems, including the fire control systems, and even if they were programmed for defense only, there would be a danger of an accidental outbreak of hostilities in space. One of them may move into combat mode as a result of 'misreading' the behavior of the other side. This scenario of an accidental nuclear war has already been examined for those types of SDI weaponry that make the time available for decision-making infinitesimal.

In this case, the opposing systems do not have complete information about each other. In developing a program for repelling a potential attack, both therefore rely on their ideas about the potential enemy rather than on hard facts about him (the most important facts are usually subject to maximum secrecy). This disparity between actual facts and the data fed into the computer programs can cause 'errors of behavior,' erroneous interpretation of the intentions of the other side and, ultimately, erroneous responses. Such a response will mostly aggravate the situation and may even lead to hostilities, the logic of both systems being built on the ability 'to beat off' an inevitable attack. ('Inevitable' here refers to the natural attitude of the software developers, as the entire defensive system has been created with this sole object in mind.)

This scenario of a nuclear conflict involving the interaction of two independently developed computer systems permits us to discuss in general terms these dangerous types of interaction. Let us assume that three computers A, B, and C are integrated into a single system. Computers A and B represent the opposing space weapons systems. Their 'attack repelling' programs have been developed by different groups of software specialists working unbeknownst to each other in different countries. Computers A and B are only connected to computer C, which monitors the situation, but not to each other. If A issues a command to fire the rocket engine of an orbital weapons system, C will show a change in its orbit and this change will be observed by B. If the software of B interprets it as a signal to which it should respond, the appropriate commands will bring about a change in the picture of B on the display of C. Computer C will thus be the link connecting A and B into a single system, A + B. As the software for A and B was developed by specialists working in secrecy from each other, the behavior of the computer system A + B can be predicted by neither A, nor B. In the 'worst case' scenario, the system A + B may well start a nuclear war without any real justification, simply as a result of the mutual 'misunderstanding' between systems A and B.

Today, we can discuss these dangerous processes only in general terms; but there is an obvious need for a more detailed analysis of the mechanisms leading to disaster, or at least of some of their concrete characteristics. A complete solution to the entire problem still appears difficult; but already an analysis of simplified mathematical models of this type of conflict should be of considerable interest, given the incomplete and even distorted picture that A and B have of each other. As a first step in such a use of mathematical modelling we may offer the following analysis of a series of cases that are more elementary than that described above.

S. Bukharin at the Moscow Institute of Physical Engineering has studied a variety of hypothetical situations leading to a nuclear conflict. In a general pre-crisis political situation dominated by mutual antagonism, space weapons systems become particularly sensitive to events in outer space. Bukharin has examined a scenario where a sufficiently large number of objects are orbiting in outer space, including remains of space vehicles launched in the past which can be perceived by combat satellites as a potential threat. Each satellite is assumed always to have a sizeable 'sovereignty zone' around it, not to be invaded by anything. If sovereignty zone violations become frequent enough, they may be interpreted as an attack and thus provoke a conflict. In his (almost completed) work, Bukharin also takes into account such factors as strained relations between the opposing sides, the technical condition of space weapons systems, the data of earth observations from space and the frequency of 'sovereignty zone' violations. Significantly, in this scenario the conflict breaks out as a result of an erroneous interpretation of an observed event (the debris of a disintegrated space vehicle being mistaken for a space weapons system).

Getting back to the question of the interaction of opposing systems, we will find that proportional, flexible response is the simplest type of interaction. It means that if system B detects an increase in the combat readiness of system A, the former moves to a proportionately higher level of its own combat readiness. This type of interaction is known in control theory as positive feedback response. Today, this type of response underlies the arms race. The same mechanism was behind the outbreak of the First World War. In these cases, however, we had a slow unfolding of events. By contrast, computerized space weapons systems in a permanent combat mode, capable of virtually instantaneous target acquisition and destruction in a conflict situation, may precipitate such an avalanche of events that there is no possibility of human intervention in the development of the conflict.

In particular, the perception that system B has of an increasing combat readiness of system A may be the result of an erroneous interpretation of the observed processes. In this case an accidental outbreak of a conflict is very likely. The combination of the instability of positive feedback systems where parts A and B have incomplete information about each other with an atmosphere of mutual suspicion will almost always be sure to provoke hostilities.

The only radical solution to this problem calls for the parties to have full and reliable information about each other. In this case, barring a deliberate action to provoke a conflict, both sides will be receiving constant reassurances of mutual peaceful intentions, and positive feedback will not be able to display its dangerous characteristics. In a recent paper, A. S. Silbergleit and E. A. Tropp of

Leningrad attempted to reduce the dangers inherent in positive feedback. Given that potential enemies have agreed to declassify and coordinate some of the procedures of their response to the information coming into the weapons systems A and B, it becomes possible to introduce a measure of nonlinear dampening into the chain of automatic control and decision-making procedures, which will help in stabilizing the situation. Yet a more detailed analysis indicates that even so the danger is not entirely removed. Moreover, the behavior of the new system A+B turns out to be random and stochastic. Instead of the desired reliable stabilization we face the possibility of unpredictable 'outbursts' of runaway reactions with the result that the danger of an accidental nuclear conflict persists. In this case, creating a 'reasonable' system out of antagonistic subsystems is out of the question.

The only mathematically impeccable solution to this problem is offered by a joint development of the software for computer system A + B as an integrated unit. But this means total mutual transparency (openness) of systems A and B, and, in consequence, total mutual trust on the part of the sides they represent. Should that happen, systems A and B will no longer perceive each other as potential enemies and the entire problem becomes meaningless.

It would, perhaps, be more accurate and correct to say that the entire problem changes its content. If sides A and B with their enormous military potential come together to form a mutually open system A + B, the resulting united system may be capable of standing up to the challenge of the increasingly dangerous extremist and terrorist forces in today's world. And there is no need to fear that the world will get back to Square One, this time with system A + B confronted by a space weapons system deployed by the extremists. Only the great powers are capable of maintaining powerful space weapons systems supported by land, air and naval forces. The extremists are only capable of provoking local conflicts; and these can be successfully prevented.

PART III

How Humans May Err -
From Private to President

Chapter 6

Human Reliability, Instability, and the Control of Nuclear Weapons

Herbert L. Abrams

The problem of accidental or inadvertent nuclear war has been couched largely in terms of superpower confrontations during a crisis. Whether the focus is on the major powers, or on developing nations with ballistic missiles and possibly nuclear weapons capability, stability in those who handle weapons and careful safeguards on use are essential preventive measures.

The United States and the USSR have been careful to guard against unauthorized launch. All nuclear nations have been concerned with retaining ultimate control of nuclear weapons in civilian hands; with monitoring the reliability and stability of the forces that handle the weapons; and with preventing weapons from coming into the possession of outsiders.

In 1986, an analysis of the sources of human instability in those who handle nuclear weapons concluded that thousands of unstable individuals were involved in 'minding our missiles' (Abrams, 1986: pp. 491-528). The present paper serves as an update on the problem and deals in summary fashion with the availability of safeguards (Permissive Action Links, the two-man rule) that serve to mitigate the effects of unstable personnel. We will also examine some of the potential areas of increasing risk as the world changes.

1. Human reliability

1.1 A year in the life of Bangor
The Bangor Submarine Base in the state of Washington employs approximately 5,000 servicemen. Of these, 1,024 are certified under the Nuclear Weapons Personnel Reliability Program (PRP). They are responsible for the handling of 1,700 nuclear weapons: 1,500 of which are on board Trident submarines (Offley, 1990a & 1990b). Other weapons are kept at Bangor's Strategic Weapons Facility, the sole west coast site for assembling and loading Trident missiles for the Pacific fleet.

January 1989. At 9:30 p.m. on January 14, 1989, Lance Corporal Patrick Dale Jelly, an 18-year-old Marine, shot himself in the head with his M-16 rifle while stationed in a guard tower at the Bangor Strategic Weapons Facility. Jelly was PRP-certified and held a clearance which allowed him knowledge of 'asset location' (Offley, 1990c). [3]

His behavior had been unusual for several weeks.[4] He had talked about killing himself, punctured his arms with a needle and thread, and claimed to be the reincarnation of a soldier killed in Vietnam (Offley, 1990c). If this had been reported before his suicide, it would have led to his decertification from the PRP.

July 1989. On July 1, 34-year-old Tommy Harold Metcalf, a fire-control technician on the submarine *Alaska*, murdered an elderly couple by suffocation in their home after responding to an advertisement they had placed. Like all fire-control technicians, he was PRP-certified and was one of the crew members responsible for carrying out orders to fire the Trident's 24 nuclear missiles (Carter, 1989). Such personnel are classified by the Navy as 'critical', meaning that together with others they can cause the launch or use of a nuclear weapon. They also control or may use sealed authenticators, missile computer tapes, or other sensitive aspects of release procedures. A review of his records by the Navy was said to have found no problems with the screening process (Longo, 1990).

August 1989. Commander William Pawlyk was arrested in early August after stabbing a man and a woman to death. Pawlyk had served for five years aboard the nuclear submarine *James K. Polk*, and had commanded Submarine Group 9 at Bangor. At the time of the murders, he was head of a reserve unit in Portland, Oregon (Merrill, 1989).

---

[3] US Navy, 1989. 'Investigation to Inquire Into the Circumstances Connected With the Death of Lance Corporal Patrick Dale Jelly, USMC, on 14 January 1989', Lt. Thad A. Johnson, February 8, p. 1.

[4] Ibid., p. 5

January 1990. On January 15, Shyam David Drizpaul, a 23-year-old fire-control technician on the submarine *Michigan*, shot and killed one crew member in his living-quarters lounge, and then another one in bed.

The bodies of the victims were discovered when they and Drizpaul failed to report for duty later that morning. Meanwhile, Drizpaul had attempted to buy another 9mm pistol at a pawn shop. He grabbed the gun from the clerk, shot her to death, and critically wounded her brother. He then fled, checked into a motel near Vancouver, and killed himself with the same pistol (Barber, 1990; Offley, 1990d).[5]

Aftermath. All of these episodes were associated with a single submarine base. Similar breakdowns in behavior have occurred at other weapons facilities (Abrams, 1986). In this case, the events were sufficiently publicized to provoke concern in the state of Washington about the Navy's missile handlers. All had been PRP certified. Recent reviews disclosed no problems, behavior or attitudes that might have caused revocation of their PRP status.[6]

The Bangor base commander, Rear Admiral Raymond G. Jones, ordered a review of the PRP procedures and management (Offley, 1990a). Washington Congressman Norman Dicks called for a review of the Navy's PRP, saying 'Dramatic improvements (in the monitoring system) are necessary' (Offley, 1990c). A week later, Chief of Naval Operations Admiral Carlisle A. H. Trost told a House subcommittee that he had ordered a complete review of the Naval PRP because of the incidents (Offley, 1990b).

The experience at Bangor is a striking illustration of the difficulty of assuring stability in nuclear weapons personnel even when well developed systems of screening are employed.

1.2 Psychiatric problems

Psychiatric disorders are an important and difficult problem in the military (Abrams, 1986). A longitudinal study of 11,000 naval enlistees found that approximately 1 in 12 (8.7 percent of the total) was

---

[5] An attorney hired by Drizpaul's family disputed the official version, claiming Drizpaul was himself a murder victim (Offley, 1990d).

[6] Offley, Ed 1990. *Seattle Post-Intelligencer* reporter, communication with author, January.

discharged during his first enlistment because of psychiatric illness (Plag, Arthur & Goffmann, 1970). From 1980 through 1989, 95,000 individuals in the Army had psychiatric disorders. Over 6000 were schizophrenic, while an additional 7,000 had other psychotic disorders (see Table 1) (Department of the Army, 1985 & 1990). In the US Navy during the same period, there were 129,000 personnel with psychiatric problems (Department of the Navy, 1990).

Table 1
Distribution of psychiatric diagnoses in US Army (1980-1989).

DIAGNOSIS	TOTAL NUMBER
Alcoholic psychoses	1,033
Alcohol dependence	23,635
Drug psychoses	428
Drug dependence	1,602
Drug abuse	14,329
Schizophrenia	6,324
Other psychotic states	6,370
Neurotic disorders	4,919
Personality disorders	8,484
Mental disorders following organic brain damage	1,186
Other diagnoses	26,860
Total	96,134

Source: Department of the Army (1985, 1990)

The risk of mental illness is especially acute in nuclear armed submarines, on which crews remain for months at a time (Tansey, Wilson & Schaefer, 1979). In one study, 3.8 percent of nuclear submarine crew members required psychiatric consultation. Eight percent of those referred were psychotic (Satloff, 1967).

The available data suggest that, if anything, there has been an increased incidence of psychiatric disorders during the past five years (Department of the Army, 1990).

1.3 Drug and alcohol use in the US military
Drug use was not considered an important issue for nuclear weapons personnel until 1970 (Larus, 1970: p. 32). A 1980 survey revealed that

27 percent of the respondents had used drugs within the last 30 days (Burt, 1982). The 18-25 year old age group were most heavily involved.

A study in 1985 indicated a striking drop in the use of drugs, from the previously reported 27 percent to about 14 percent (see Table 2) (Bray et al., 1986). Furthermore, while prior studies showed comparable prevalence in the civilian population and the military population, current data indicate major differences (NIDA, 1988).

Table 2
Percentage of population using drugs, past 30 days, age 18-25 (1985).

	CIVILIAN	MILITARY
Marijuana	26.2	10.6
Cocaine	9.3	4.5
Psychoactive	8.3	4.9
Any Drug	29.0	13.7

Source: Bray et al., 1986; National Institute on Drug Abuse, 1988

In the most recent study, nine percent of US military personnel reported using drugs in the last 12 months. The most commonly used drug continues to be marijuana, followed by cocaine. The change in the military use of drugs is almost certainly attributable to the widespread use of urinalysis and to a strict 'zero tolerance' policy instituted by the military in 1981 (Bray et al., 1989; Bray, Marsden & Wheeless, 1989).

The visible effects of drug use have also declined sharply (see Figure 1), with far fewer negative experiences in the military than in the civilian population (see Table 3a). In 1988, 1.8 percent of personnel reported 'serious consequences' and 2.1 percent reported productivity loss during the last 12 months. For the three lowest pay grades (E1-E3) these figures are higher: 5 percent each. Negative experiences from drug use included fighting, trouble on the job, unsafe driving, health problems and trouble with the police (Bray et al., 1989: p. 12; Bray, Marsden & Wheeless, 1989: p. 15).

In contrast to the decrease in drug use, alcohol continues to be a major problem among military personnel (see Table 3b). (Bray et al., 1989: p. 46).

Figure 1. Drug Use Negative Effects, Total DoD, 1980-88

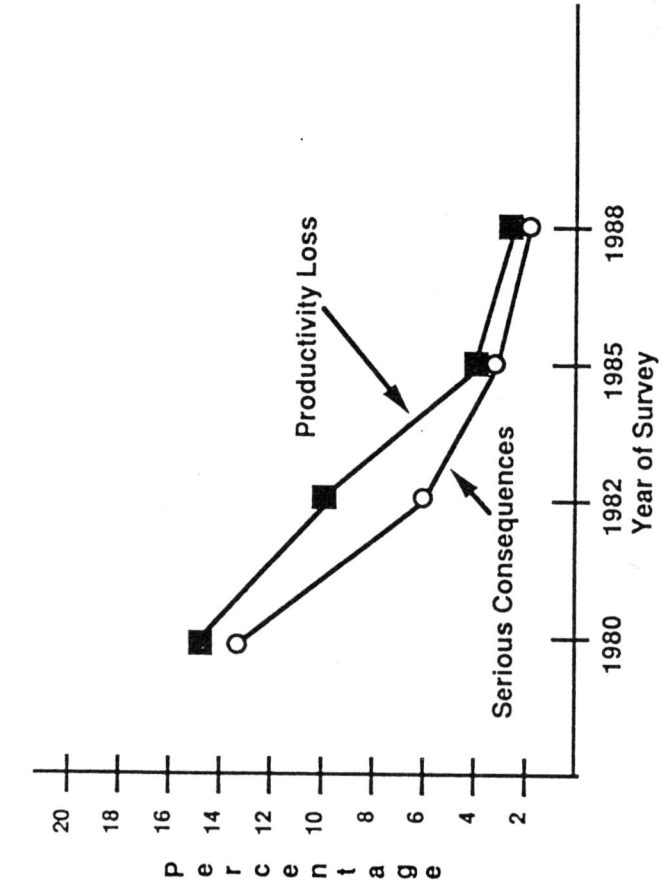

From: *Bray et al., 1988*

82

Table 3a
Percentage of negative experiences, 1985, past 12 months, drug use, age 18-25.

CIVILIAN	MILITARY
30.9	5.6

Source: Bray et al., 1986; National Institute on Drug Abuse, 1988

Table 3b
Percentage of negative experiences, 1985, past 12 months, alcohol, age 18 - 25.

CIVILIAN	MILITARY
46.2	67.3

Source: Bray et al., 1986:p. 4; National Institute on Drug Abuse, 1988: p. 5

Military programs to reduce alcohol consumption - education, enforcement of rules against drunk driving, and regulation of the price and availability of alcohol on bases - appear to have had an effect. Between 1980 and 1988, the average alcohol intake among military personnel declined by about 35 percent. Nevertheless, alcohol dependence has remained relatively constant (Bray et al., 1989: p. 33). Furthermore, military personnel are more likely to drink and drink heavily than their civilian counterparts; in 1985 the military showed almost double the prevalence of heavy drinkers (defined as those who consume five or more drinks at a time at least once a week) (Bray, Marsden & Wheeless, 1989: p. 13, 22).

About 10 percent of military personnel report drinking *during* or *immediately before* work hours. In 1988, 22.1 percent of military personnel reported lost productivity in the last 12 months as a result of alcohol use. Six percent reported alcohol dependence and nine percent reported other 'serious consequences' (Bray et al., 1989).

*　　*　　*　　*

The evidence seems clear that while drug abuse remains an important problem in the military, its prevalence has gone down considerably. Alcohol use, however, is an intractable problem; it seems unlikely to yield to the kinds of measures employed to diminish drug use in the military.

1.4 The Personnel Reliability Program (PRP)
Inevitably, then, some individuals assigned to nuclear weapons duties
are unstable. The PRP is supposed to weed them out during the
screening process, or decertify and reassign them if the problem is
detected later. The reasons for decertification are:
- alcohol abuse;
- drug abuse;
- negligence or delinquency in performance of duty;
- court martial, serious civil convictions or behavior indicative
  of contemptuous attitude towards law and authority;
- aberrant behavior: mental, physical or character traits that
  would lead to unreliable performance;   .
- poor attitude or lack of motivation (Department of Defense,
  1981b).
The initial screening procedure includes a background
investigation, security clearance, medical evaluation, review of the
candidate's personnel files, and a personal interview advising the
individual as to the nature of the PRP.

The strengths and weaknesses of the Personnel Reliability
Program have been analyzed in detail (Abrams, 1986: p. 509-519). In
the past five years, a number of changes have been made, among
them:

1) Closer monitoring. If an individual is transferred to a new PRP
   position under the supervision of a new certifying official, he
   must undergo a new interview, similar to the initial one. If
   medical and personnel records are moved to a new location, they
   must be re-screened (Department of Defense, 1985b: enclosure
   5).

2) Definition of scope. As in the past, the PRP is applicable to all
   personnel responsible for operations of nuclear weapons. It is
   now described, however, as 'a peacetime program...adherence to
   PRP procedures during wartime may be impractical....'
   (Department of Defense, 1981b; Department of Defense, 1985b:
   part D). This addition makes clear that in wartime or crisis,
   nuclear weapons might come under the control of individuals
   who had never been screened or monitored by the PRP.

3) Disqualification. It has become easier to disaffiliate personnel for aberrant behavior. The certifying official can now determine whether the behavior requires disqualification, without substantiation by 'competent medical authority', as previously required (Department of Defense, 1981b: enclosure 4; Department of Defense 1985b: enclosure 4).

4) Exclusion of immigrant aliens. Controlled and critical positions must now be filled by US citizens or US nationals (Department of Defense, 1981b; Department of Defense, 1985b: part D).

A number of recommendations for improving the PRP have not yet been implemented (Abrams, 1986: pp. 517-518). These include:
1. Requiring a physician to examine all candidates, without exception.
2. Informing the physician of the nature of the candidate's work.
3. Including an interview designed to assess the candidate's emotional stability.
4. Utilizing standardized psychological testing.
5. More systematic monitoring.
Largely as a result of the Bangor incidents, PRP policies are currently under review at several levels in the US armed forces. Officials from the Department of Defense, the Joint Chiefs of Staff, the National Security Agency and the branches of the military recently met to consider updating and revising procedures.[7] While improvements are both desirable and feasible, it seems unlikely that these reviews will result in fundamental changes.

During the period from 1975 through 1984, 51,000 personnel - 4.5 percent per year on average - were decertified from the PRP (Abrams, 1986). Analysis of the corresponding data through 1989 demonstrates both a sharp decrease in the number of individuals in the PRP, and a simultaneous drop in the numbers and percentage decertified from the program (see Table 4; Figure 2). The large drop in number of PRP personnel, from 119,625 in 1975 to 76,588 in 1989, is probably attributable to the reduction in number of weapons and the consolidation of weapons storage sites, and to the increased use

---

[7] Department of the Navy, 1990. Colleen Crowley, Personnel Security Specialist, Office of Naval Operations, communication with author, May 4.

of automated security and surveillance systems (reducing the number of security guards needed).[8]

Table 4

PRP totals and decertifications (1975 to 1989).

YEAR	TOTALS	DECERTIFICATIONS	%
1975	119,625	5,128	4.3
1976	115,855	4,966	4.3
1977	118,988	4,973	4.2
1978	116,253	5,797	5.0
1979	119,198	5,712	4.8
1980	114,028	5,327	4.7
1981	109,025	5,235	4.8
1982	105,288	5,210	4.9
1983	104,772	5,085	4.9
1984	103,832	3,766	3.6
1985	101,598	3,293	3.2
1986	97,693	2,531	2.6
1987	94,321	2,524	2.7
1988	82,736	2,294	2.8
1989	76,588	2,392	3.1

Source: DOD, OSD, 'Annual Disqualification Report, Nuclear Weapon Personnel Reliability Program,' RCS DD-COMP(A) 1403, Calendar Year Ending December 31, 1975; 1976; 1977; DOD, OSD, 'Annual Status Report, Nuclear Weapon Personnel Reliability Program,' RCS DD-POL(A) 1403, Year Ending December 31, 1978; 1979; 1980; 1981; 1982; 1983; 1984; 1985; 1986; 1987; 1988; 1989

---

[8] Department of Defense, 1990. Colonel Robert E. Pike, Assistant for Nuclear Matters, Office of the Undersecretary of Defense, communication with author, June 8.

Figure 2. Total in PRP and Total Decertified

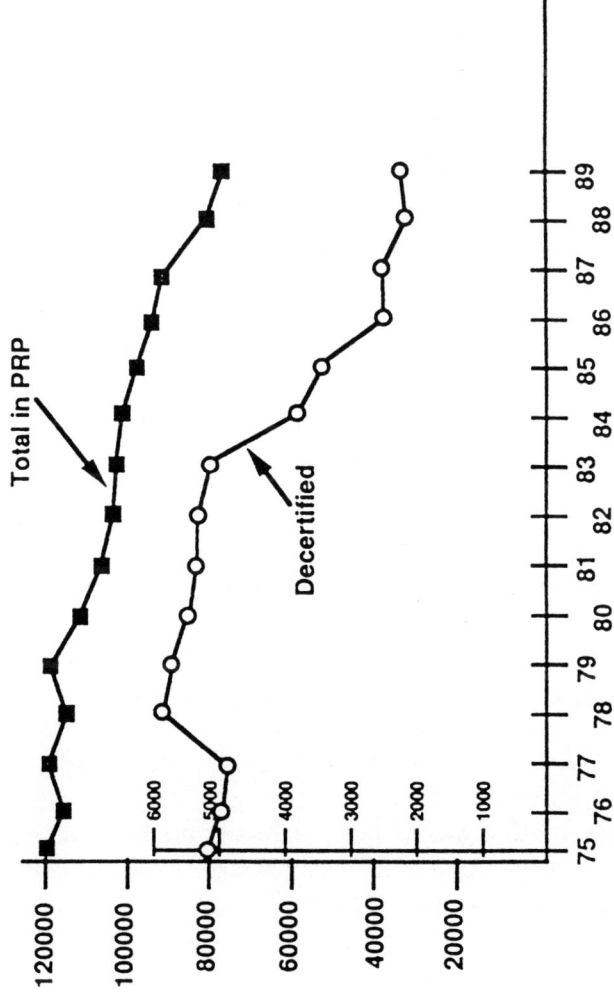

Source: See table 4.

The decertification rate has moved from a level of four to five percent during the period 1975 to 1983 to a current level of about three percent. This decline might be interpreted as an indication that the monitoring and enforcement processes have grown more lax, but there is no evidence to support this supposition. Alternatively, it might suggest that the initial screening has improved. In fact, the most important factor in the decline appears to have been the introduction of drug testing and 'zero tolerance' in 1981. Both the number of individuals and the percentage decertified because of alcohol abuse have increased, while the number and percentage related to drug abuse have gone down considerably (see Tables 5 and 6). Meanwhile, the percentage caused by psychiatric or behavioral problems has decreased slightly from about 24 percent in 1975 to 20 percent in 1989 (see Table 6).

In spite of the recent decrease in drug abuse, over the entire period from 1975-1989, it was the major cause of decertification (31 percent) as compared to alcohol use (10 percent) (see Table 7). Data on the Air Force (Tables 8 & 9), the Navy (Table 10 & 11), and the Army (Table 12 & 13) reveal trends that are quite similar, except for the lower incidence of drug abuse in the Air Force.

*   *   *   *

Despite the measurable decrease in disaffiliated personnel during the past six years, there are still on average at least 2400 unstable individuals in our nuclear weapons forces at any one time. Such personnel must be considered unpredictable in their behavior, especially during periods of heightened tension.

*   *   *   *

The information available on human reliability screening in other major nuclear powers is fragmentary. Nevertheless, the problem deserves our attention.

Table 5

PRP totals and decertifications by reason (1975 to 1989).

REASON	1975	1976	1977	1978	1979	1980	1981	1982	1983	1984	1985	1986	1987	1988	1989
Alcohol abuse	169	184	256	378	459	600	662	645	621	545	500	395	415	388	365
Drug abuse	1970	1474	1365	1972	2043	1728	1702	1846	2029	1007	924	555	477	257	363
Negligence or delinquency	703	737	828	501	234	236	236	252	220	160	365	170	158	103	113
Court-martial or civil conviction[a]	345	388	350												
Behavior contemptuous toward the law[a]	722	945	885	757	747	694	560	605	607	580	327	447	473	451	437
Physical, mental, or character trait or aberration	1219	1238	1289	1367	1233	941	1022	882	704	646	550	408	437	486	481
Poor attitude[b]	- -	- -	- -	822	996	1128	1053	980	904	828	627	556	564	609	633
Total decertifications	5128	4966	4973	5797	5712	5327	5235	5210	5085	3766	3293	2531	2524	2294	2392

[a] Classification of decertification changed in 1978, and the categories 'Court-Martial or Civil Conviction' and 'Behavior Contemptuous Toward the Law' were combined.
[b] Category not applied until 1978.

Source: DOD, OSD, 'Annual Disqualification Report, Nuclear Weapon Personnel Reliability Program,' RCS DD-COMP (A) 1403, Calendar Year Ending December 31, 1975; 1976; 1977; DOD, OSD, 'Annual Status Report, Nuclear Weapon Personnel Reliability Program,' RCS DD-POL(A)1403, Year Ending December 31, 1978; 1979; 1980; 1981; 1982; 1983; 1984; 1985; 1986; 1987; 1988; 1989

Table 6

PRP decertification percentages by reason for each year (1975 to 1989).

REASON	1975	1976	1977	1978	1979	1980	1981	1982	1983	1984	1985	1986	1987	1988	1989
Alcohol abuse	3	4	5	7	8	11	13	12	12	15	15	16	16	17	15
Drug abuse	38	30	27	34	36	32	33	35	40	27	28	22	19	11	15
Negligence or delinquency	14	15	17	9	4	4	5	5	4	4	11	7	6	4	5
Court-martial or civil conviction	7	8	7												
Behavior contemptuous toward the law	14	19	18	13	13	13	11	12	12	15	10	18	19	20	18
Physical, mental or character trait or aberration	24	25	26	24	22	18	20	17	14	17	17	16	17	21	20
Attitude[a]	--	--	--	14	17	21	20	19	18	22	19	22	22	27	26

[a] Category not applied until 1978.

Source: DOD, OSD, 'Annual Disqualification Report, Nuclear Weapon Personnel Reliability Program,' RCS DD-COMP (A) 1403, Calendar Year Ending December 31, 1975; 1976; 1977; DOD, OSD, 'Annual Status Report, Nuclear Weapon Personnel Reliability Program,' RCS DD-POL(A)1403, Year Ending December 31, 1978; 1979; 1980; 1981; 1982; 1983; 1984; 1985; 1986; 1987; 1988; 1989

Table 7
Summary: PRP Decertifications (1975-1989).

REASON	Total Number Decertified	Percent
Alcohol Abuse	6,582	10
Drug Abuse	19,712	31
Negligence	5,016	8
Court Martial	10,320	16
Traits	12,903	20
Attitude	9,700 [a]	15
Total Number Decertified	64,233	

[a] Values are for 1978-1989.

Source: DOD, OSD, 'Annual Status Report, Nuclear Weapon Personnel Reliability Program,' RCS DD-POL(A) 1403, Year Ending December 31, 1975; 1976; 1977; 1978; 1979; 1980; 1981; 1982; 1983; 1984; 1985; 1986; 1987; 1988; 1989

Table 8

Air Force PRP totals and decertifications (1977 to 1989).

REASON	1977	1978	1979	1980	1981	1982	1983	1984	1985	1986	1987	1988	1989
Alcohol abuse	52	129	303	415	536	524	452	391	313	267	285	281	257
Drug abuse	340	642	1020	964	956	848	988	471	472	245	224	113	110
Negligence or delinquency	656	335	81	91	103	111	76	36	255	46	27	34	36
Court-martial or civil conviction; behavior contemptuous toward the law	588	352	417	371	303	290	317	325	62	257	284	311	298
Physical, mental, or character trait or aberration	594	714	809	752	793	699	496	466	354	268	305	376	297
Poor attitude	-	508	822	908	884	865	764	704	521	445	478	555	551
Total decertifications	2230	2680	3452	3501	3575	3337	3093	2393	1977	1528	1603	1670	1549
Total in PRP	55751	53650	53524	53353	52164	52826	55481	53255	51955	51225	50177	45724	43540

Source: Ronald W. Shealy, Lt. Colonel, USAF, Chief, Civil Affairs Branch, Community Relations Division, Office of Public Affairs. Mimeograph sent January 7, 1985. DOD, OSD, 'Annual Status Report, Nuclear Weapon Personnel Reliability Program,' RCS DD-POL(A)1403, Year Ending December 31, 1984; 1985; 1986; 1987; 1988; 1989

Table 9
Summary: Air Force PRP decertifications (1977 to 1989).

REASON	TOTAL DECERTIFICATIONS (1977-1989)		PERCENTAGE
Alcohol abuse	4205		13%
Drug abuse	7393		23%
Negligence or delinquency	1887		6%
Court-martial or civil conviction; behavior contemptuous toward the law	4175		13%
Physical, mental, or character trait or aberration	6923		21%
Poor attitude	8005	(1978 to 1989)	25%
Total decertifications	32,588		

Source: Ronald W. Shealy, Lt. Colonel, USAF, Chief, Civil Affairs Branch, Community Relations Division, Office of Public Affairs. Mimeograph sent January 7, 1985; USAF Military Personnel Center, Office of Public Affairs, Washington, DC, data provided March 1990 in response to Freedom of Information Act request.

Table 10

Navy PRP totals and decertifications (1980-1989).

REASON	1980	1981	1982	1983	1984	1985	*1986	1987	1988	1989
Alcohol abuse	44	39	55	66	82	82	90	90	69	80
Drug abuse	337	377	603	481	297	224	204	193	110	204
Negligence or delinquency	81	69	68	44	53	34	91	97	53	58
Court-martial or civil conviction; behavior contemptuous toward the law	72	80	96	99	95	115	146	150	85	107
Physical, mental, or character trait or aberration	110	71	84	67	76	69	102	97	84	158
Poor attitude	56	69	56	49	57	37	80	51	35	66
Total decertifications	700	705	962	806	660	561	713	678	436	673
Total in PRP	29,821	28,915	29,510	29,042	31,004	29,317	33,200	30,913	25,340	22,758

* 1986 is first year that Navy PRP figures include Marine Corps.

Source: Naval Investigative Service Command, Washington, DC, in response to Freedom of Information Act request, March 1990

Table 11
Summary: Naval PRP decertifications (1980 to 1989).

REASON	TOTAL DECERTIFICATIONS (1980-1989)	PERCENTAGE
Alcohol abuse	697	10
Drug abuse	3030	44
Negligence or delinquency	648	9
Court-martial or civil conviction; behavior contemptuous toward the law	1045	15
Physical, mental, or character trait or aberration	918	13
Poor attitude	556	8
Total decertifications	6,894	

Table 12
Army PRP totals and decertifications (1978 to 1989).

REASON	1978	1979	1980	1981	1982	1983	1984	1985	1986	1987	1988	1989
Alcohol abuse	142	109	118	63	42	67	42	71	39	40	39	27
Drug abuse	703	471	302	217	199	412	172	187	104	59	33	48
Negligence or delinquency	31	23	25	33	33	39	39	38	33	34	15	19
Court-martial or civil conviction; behavior contemptuous toward the law	152	83	105	75	79	62	62	71	46	38	55	32
Physical, mental, or character trait or aberration	327	294	46	127	68	84	61	102	37	35	26	23
Poor attitude	111	75	140	56	43	58	37	42	33	35	19	16
Total decertifications	1,466	1,055	736	571	464	722	413	511	292	241	187	165
Total in PRP	22,666	26,611	25,108	22,133	16,733	14,103	13,896	14,931	11,619	12,188	10,502	9,190

Source: US Army, 'Annual Status Report, Nuclear Weapon Personnel Reliability Program,' RCS DD-COMP(A) 1403, Year Ending December 31, 1978; 1979; 1980; 1981; 1982; 1983; 1984; 1985; 1986; 1987; 1988; 1989

Table 13
Summary: Army PRP decertifications (1978 to 1989).

REASON	TOTAL DECERTIFICATIONS (1978-1989)	PERCENTAGE
Alcohol abuse	799	12
Drug abuse	2,907	43
Negligence or delinquency	362	5
Court-martial or civil conviction; behavior contemptuous toward the law	860	13
Physical, mental, or character trait or aberration	1,230	18
Poor attitude	665	10
Total decertifications	6,823	

Source: US Army, 'Annual Status Report, Nuclear Weapon Personnel Reliability Program,' RCS DD-CO-MP(A) 1403, Year Ending December 31, 1978; 1979; 1980; 1981; 1982; 1983; 1984; 1985; 1986; 1987; 1988; 1989

*　　*　　*

The Soviet Union. Although the Soviets are obviously concerned about the safety of their nuclear weapons, their practices are difficult to assess.

The current instability in the Soviet Union has helped push the military into a period of great uncertainty. Soviet officers and politicians now speak openly about deteriorating discipline among the troops (Fox 1990).

Morale is poor, and the endemic problem of alcoholism in the civilian population is also reflected in the armed forces (Gabriel, 1980:, Cockburn, 1983: p. 298; Tarasulo, 1985; Wimbush, 1981). The Soviet officer corps and non-commissioned officers may 'account for more than three-quarters of alcoholics and heavy drinkers' (Davis, 1985: pp. 403-404).

The anti-alcohol campaign initiated in 1985 has not reduced consumption measurably, but instead has stimulated the black market trade (Aslund, 1989: pp. 75-76). Soldiers now participate in biannual training sessions on the dangers of alcohol abuse. Personnel with drinking problems are subject to strict observation and treatment, and possible discharge from service (Lazarev, 1986).

Drug abuse was not considered a major issue in the past, but in the last several years its presence has been well documented. Drug addiction has become a problem, and drug-related crimes and medical emergencies are widespread (Cooper & Strasser, 1986).

Drug importation from abroad is less the supply route than the vast hemp and poppy growing territory that extends across Soviet central Asia and southern Russia. In Afghanistan hashish and opiates were readily available to many soldiers. The precise extent of drug use in the military has not been reported, but a survey in Georgia disclosed that drug addiction was present among soldiers as well as civilians (Kramer, 1988).[9]

A written description of the guidelines for assuring nuclear personnel reliability is not available. Initial allocation to training programs is based on a review of a candidate's dossier, so that only intelligent recruits with good political backgrounds are designated for demanding duties such as the air force and strategic rocket forces (Cockburn, 1983).

Nuclear personnel are also selected for ethnicity. Russians, who comprise barely half of the Soviet population, occupy most of the sensitive nuclear weapons positions (Broad, 1990).[10]

Screening and monitoring similar to the US PRP are probably in place for personnel assigned to nuclear weapons duty. There is certainly awareness of and concern about the psychological-physiological stress to which these personnel are subject (Gorokhov,

---

[9] One report said 40,000 crimes 'stemming from drug addiction' are committed each year. By 1988, medical authorities had registered 52,000 drug 'addicts' and an additional 80,000 users of 'narcotics'. Kramer (1988) notes that the terms 'addict' and 'narcotic' are used somewhat loosely in the Soviet Union. 'Addict' refers to those whom 'doctors officially consider sick', while 'narcotic' refers to any of a wide variety of substances.

[10] Anderson, Richard D. 1985. Department of Political Science, University of California, Los Angeles. Communication with author.

1985). The importance of psychological testing in an era of complex military technology has been emphasized (Bodrov, 1984). Data on disaffiliation rates from the nuclear weapons corps have not been published or made accessible.

France. French military recruits undergo a variety of physical, mental and psychiatric examinations upon enlistment, including written tests and interviews by psychologists or psychiatrists. These tests are designed to detect unstable personnel and to determine whether individuals are suitable for particular kinds of duty.[11]

There is no evidence that a complete survey of drug use in the French military has been performed. In 1980, over 2000 instances of drug abuse had come to the attention of the army health services, as compared with 880 in 1975 (LeFebvre, 1981: p. 669) out of an army population of about 330,000 (Martin, 1981). Seventy percent of those identified are dismissed from the military. Others are apparently given professional counseling and may be suspended temporarily from duty (LeFebvre, 1981: p. 671)

Nuclear weapons personnel are further screened and monitored in an effort to assure stability. They receive specialized training, after which they are subject to a security clearance investigation, a physical examination and a written psychological test. They are re-examined twice a year.[12] Launch officers for land-based missiles (which are under the control of the strategic air force) are volunteers who possess good records, a minimum of 4 years experience, and the rank of at least senior lieutenant. For command positions and aviators, applicants must have high professional qualifications, and hold the rank of senior captain or major.[13] Nuclear submarine personnel are selected on the basis of mental, psychological and physical criteria

---

[11] Degrais (1971) has provided a description of procedures employed in the navy. Similar sorts of preselection and screening are apparently conducted in the other branches (Vauterin, 1970: p. 455).

[12] Fleury J., General d'Armée Aerienne 1989. Interview with author, Paris, April 1 - French Armed Forces Staff, 1987. Correspondence from Division Relations Exterieures to Brigadier General Roland LaJoie, Defense Attache, US Embassy, Paris, June 4 - French Army Office, 1987. Correspondence to Brigadier General Roland LaJoie, Defense Attaché Office, US Embassy, Paris, April 1.

[13] French Armed Forces Staff, 1987. Correspondence from Division Relations Exterieures to Brigadier General Roland LaJoie, Defense Attache, U.S. Embassy, Paris, June 4.

designed to determine their capacity to serve in a stressful environment.[14]

Great Britain. Britain does not employ any special screening of nuclear weapons personnel beyond the normal procedures used to determine fitness for service in the armed forces (Gregory, 1988: pp. 79-80). In response to a perceived increase in drug abuse, the British Army introduced urinalysis for those suspected of drug use in 1986 (*The Times*, 1986). Officials estimate that one third of the 30,000 annual recruits have used drugs before entering the service (Beeston, 1986), but there are no comprehensive surveys of incidence.

Alcohol abuse affects all ages and ranks. The military has instituted preventive education programs and alcohol treatment units (Hiles, 1980 & 1981), but is still ambivalent on the subject, reflecting the availability and widespread use of alcohol (Wood, 1980).

Clearly, both drugs and alcohol take their toll. In the period 1971-1983, 17 service members died from abuse of volatile substances such as glues and fuels (Anderson, MacNair & Ramsey, 1985).[15] Between 1968 and 1977, at least 203 off-duty soldiers and 11 on-duty soldiers died in alcohol-related incidents (Lynch, 1987).[16] If the British take steps to control or measure the extent of such incidents among nuclear weapons personnel, they have not made this information public.

Other nations. The Chinese military is concerned with the political reliability of all its recruits, and especially so for nuclear weapons personnel. For positions not requiring a great deal of technical skill, this goal can be furthered somewhat by recruiting preferentially from the more politically orthodox rural population. Officials examine the background and record of an individual before assigning him to

---

[14] French Armed Forces Staff, 1987. Correspondence from Division Relations Exterieures to Brigadier General Roland LaJoie, Defense Attache, US Embassy, Paris, June 4.

[15] This represented a higher rate of incidence than in the civilian population at large.

[16] The actual numbers may be higher. The figure of 203 off-duty deaths is based upon an initial pool of 1,723 male service members who died during the period. Of these, only 931 were examined for blood-alcohol level, of whom 203 had concentrations in excess of 0.08 g percent (the legal level of intoxication for automobile drivers in the State of California).

sensitive duties.[17] Neither drug addiction nor alcoholism appear to be a significant problem in the military.[18]

Of particular concern is the question of whether new nuclear powers will develop screening programs that decrease the risk of unstable people gaining control of some weapons. If the United States took twenty years to develop its present imperfect screen for stability, what can we anticipate in developing nations with ballistic missile technology and potential nuclear capability? Controls may be far looser, and the potential for unauthorized use far greater.

2. Safety procedures: guarding against unauthorized use

Even if unstable individuals are 'minding our missiles', the danger will be slight if it is physically impossible for them to effect the detonation of a nuclear weapon. There are unverified reports of accidental nuclear explosions during the early development of the US nuclear program (Babst, 1989). Accidents involving chain reactions occurred at Los Alamos in 1945 and 1946 (Masters, 1955). There has been some speculation that China's second H-bomb exploded accidentally (Spector, 1987: pp. 32-36).

Although the precise number is unknown, it is clear that there have been hundreds of nuclear weapons accidents (Gregory & Edwards, 1988: pp. 104-160; Hansen, 1990). Several have involved the accidental dropping of bombs, the detonation of the weapons' non-nuclear explosives, and/or the release of nuclear material (Gregory & Edwards, 1988: p. 164, 180; Abrams, 1987).

2.1 The United States

Most nuclear weapons are now fitted with sophisticated safety devices to prevent accidental detonation, or purposeful use by individuals outside the chain of command. Growing concern over the possibility of unauthorized use led the US military to develop safety procedures such as the 'two-man rule' in the late 1950s. The execution of each critical link in the chain of events involved in the launch of nuclear

---

[17] Xue Litai, 1990. Research Assistant, Center for International Security and Arms Control, Stanford, California, June 12. Communication with author.

[18] Hua Di, 1985. Visiting Fellow, Center For International Security and Arms Control, Stanford University, June 20. Communication with author.

weapons requires the cooperation, often simultaneously, of two or more individuals (Ball, 1981: p. 4).

The two-man rule may not always provide a great deal of safety by itself. In 1978, a Minuteman launch control officer claimed that the mechanism requiring the simultaneous turning of two keys to launch a missile could be foiled by rigging up one of the keys with a spoon and a piece of string (Gregory & Edwards, 1988: p. 74). But the safeguard had already been supplemented by Permissive Action Links (PALs) in the 1960s, after serious security lapses were discovered in Europe (Stein & Feaver, 1987). PALs 'decouple control from possession so that the code-holder can be assured that his control of the weapon is not preempted by the person who has possession' (Stein & Feaver, 1987: p. 92). They consist either of combination locks that mechanically inactivate the weapon, or coded switches that electrically disable the device. The most modern American PALs have self-protective features that prevent tampering or disassembly (Caldwell & Zimmerman, 1989: p. 159). They also allow the code-holder to protect the weapon by entering a disabling command. Some have a 'limited try' feature that incapacitates the weapon after a certain number of erroneous codes have been attempted (Johnson, 1989: p. 145). Others have a split-code configuration, so that more than one individual may be required to enter separate codes to unlock the weapon (Stein & Feaver, 1987: p. 58, 63-64).

Release of US nuclear weapons requires both voice and written commands (over teletype) that are validated by codes and authenticator devices (Stein & Feaver, 1987: p. 65, 70; Bracken, 1983: pp. 168-169). In other respects, the safeguards for nuclear forces vary, depending on the branch of the military and the nature of the weapons. In the Strategic Air Command (SAC), all nuclear weapons utilize coded locks of some kind, as well as environmental sensors and other safety devices. Operation of ICBM launch controls requires the use of PAL-like codes; the warheads themselves are protected by devices which inhibit detonation unless the missile's prescribed trajectory has been followed. In strategic bombers, individual warheads do not have PALs: one PAL in the cockpit unlocks all warheads in the payload (Stein & Feaver, 1987: p. 60, 65, 68).

With some exceptions, the Navy does not use PALs (and has resisted their implementation) on the 3,715 tactical and 5,632 strategic warheads it deploys. This is partly because of the strong

Naval tradition of giving local commanders a great deal of authority and autonomy; the Navy rejects the idea that its commanders cannot be trusted with unlocked nuclear weapons (Stein & Feaver, 1987: p. 70, 72; Caldwell & Zimmerman, 1989: p. 161). It also contends that the need for PALs is less for Naval vessels. (Some weapons have coded use control devices, but the codes are carried on the vessels, immediately accessible to the captains (Zimmerman, 1989).) The crew of a submarine is not under pressure to launch quickly in an emergency, perhaps reducing the risk of unauthorized launch. The weapons on board a ship at sea are not vulnerable to attack by outsiders, and the Navy already has procedures in place to protect against unauthorized use by crew members (Stein & Feaver, 1987: p. 71, 75).

PALs on ships, especially submarines, might render the weapons unusable, it is said. This danger is supposedly compounded by the vulnerability of communication links with vessels at sea. Hence, transmission of PAL codes to a submerged submarine in crisis might be delayed. But the severity of the gap between land and sea communications may be exaggerated (Caldwell & Zimmerman, 1989: p. 163, 165-166; Stein & Feaver, 1987: p. 74, 76). The code could readily be transmitted along with launch orders, without which commanders are not allowed to launch their nuclear weapons (Carter, 1987: p. 593; Caldwell & Zimmerman, 1989: p. 166, 174).

Another category that may lack PALs are strategic weapons in storage in the United States. Warheads destined for deployment abroad by the Army and Air Force have PALs in place. Navy weapons and SAC missile warheads probably do not, since they do not require them when deployed (Stein & Feaver, 1987: p. 77).

In addition to PALs, the US has developed Environmental Sensing Devices (ESDs), which are supposed to prevent detonation until the weapon has sensed appropriate environmental conditions (such as temperature, spin rate or acceleration) (Johnson, 1989: p. 142).

Modern US weapons are considered safe from nuclear explosion even if the high-explosive charge is accidentally detonated. The 'one-point safety' feature is supposed to ensure that a detonation initiated at any point in the high explosive system has no more than a one in a million chance of producing a nuclear yield in excess of 4 pounds of TNT. In newer weapons, insensitive high explosives (IHE) are used to reduce the chance of detonation further (Julian, 1987).

But the most sophisticated safety devices can fail. In 1980, two launch control officers were asked to carry out a simulated launch drill of a Titan II missile. When they turned their keys, they discovered that their control panel was displaying a launch sequence rather than the expected test indications. They quickly shut the system down; one officer later claimed that this was the only way to prevent the missile from being launched. Some SAC commanders disputed this interpretation, claiming that the launch officers misunderstood the indications of a normal test procedure (Gregory & Edwards, 1988: p. 90).

PALs may be circumvented by the distribution of the codes to increase readiness. Theoretically, the codes physically validate the president's sole authority to release nuclear weapons for use. But the release of 'enabling' codes must be accompanied by an 'authentication' code that assures the direct participation of the National Command Authority in the decision. This is complicated by the fact that the president may legally delegate his powers to subordinates virtually without limitation (US Congress, 1975: p. 1). In an emergency, launch authority might spread down through the ranks (Bracken, 1983: pp. 196-204). Such decentralization of authority would necessitate dispersal of PAL codes before hostilities begin, in order to prevent the weapons from sitting locked and unusable during a conflict (Arkin & Fieldhouse, 1985: p. 84).

In summary, the US military has had a major commitment to guarding against unauthorized or accidental explosion of nuclear weapons through the development of PALs, the two-man rule, and anti-detonation precautions. Nevertheless, the risk of malfunctioning components or systems, as well as of loss of central control, is inherent in the complex weapons and in their command and control systems and requirements.

2.2 NATO

The United States was the first country to station nuclear weapons on foreign soil. Nuclear weapons are now stationed in Guam, South Korea and Europe (Arkin & Fieldhouse, 1985: p. 38). All these weapons - Army and Air Force tactical weapons, as well as Naval nuclear weapons stored on land - have some form of PAL or mechanical use-control device. Some are rather antiquated, consisting of mechanical combination locks external to the warhead, allowing some possibility of unauthorized detonation (Stein & Feaver, 1987: pp. 63-64; Kelleher, 1987: p. 449).

By 1992, the number of US nuclear warheads in Europe will be down to about 3,200 (SIPRI, 1989: p. 14). The weapons are stored at about 100 sites, each consisting of a number of storage igloos behind a heavily guarded defense perimeter. Access is limited to selected European and American personnel. Any handling of weapons is subject to the two-man rule, and the warheads are continuously monitored. Weapons on quick reaction alert (usually aboard aircraft) are kept at military bases in special areas cordoned off by double guarded barbed-wire fences, whose gates require two keys to open. Orders to launch must be received and authenticated by two officers.

PALs are especially crucial to secure control of NATO weapons, which are widely dispersed on foreign soil. It might be difficult to prevent premature use of the weapons if Europe were threatened with war. The weapons could be overrun or destroyed, providing an incentive for early use. Furthermore, NATO doctrine has emphasized attacks on the enemy's rear areas before or in the first phases of conflict, requiring rapid, coordinated action (Kelleher, 1987).

The final release of nuclear weapons for use must be authorized by NATO and the US government, but the process can begin with a request from a local commander, which is passed up the chain of command. The nuclear release authentication system then comes into play, with its system of guidelines and sealed code books. Consultation among the allies is unlikely to be widely or smoothly carried out in actual conflict, and is only required 'time and circumstances permitting.'

Under the best of circumstances, a request to use nuclear weapons can take from 24 to 60 hours to elicit a response. The complex, potentially uncontrollable command structure for NATO nuclear forces services may make it a 'regional doomsday machine'; 'national leaders would exercise little practical control over' it in wartime (Bracken, 1983: p. 163). By the same token, the risk of unauthorized use may be augmented if devolution of control becomes a reality.

2.3 Russia
The Russian political leadership attempts to keep tight, centralized control over their nuclear forces, and does not delegate any independent authority to military leaders to release the weapons for

use. Nuclear authority was apparently not delegated to any single person in the past, but would have been governed by consensus within the Politburo (Meyer, 1987). This arrangement was changed in April 1990 in the Law on Defense, which stipulated that the President of the USSR, as Supreme Commander in Chief, was directly in control of nuclear release orders. He had the authority to decide on retaliatory measures, to convey orders to the armed forces on the use of nuclear weapons, and to approve nuclear tests (Strekozov, 1990). Since then, that authority has passed to the President of the Russian republic, together with the Minister of Defense and the Chief of the General Staff (Blair, 1993).

The system allows autonomous use of nuclear weapons by the military only when the lower commands receive authorization from above.

Until the late 1960s, strategic warheads were kept separate from delivery vehicles and under the physical control of the KGB. With the decision to deploy ballistic missile submarines and to develop a launch under attack capability, this policy was abandoned. In the case of land-based ICBMs, faster and safer launch technology led to the arming of the missiles, which were placed under the dual control of the KGB and the Strategic Rocket Forces (Meyer, 1987: pp. 490-491).

In the early 1960s the United States provided the USSR with information on PALs (Caldwell, 1986: p. 10). Their entire strategic arsenal is thought to be equipped with use-control devices, probably, but not certainly, PALs (Stein & Feaver, 1987: p. 85). Older weapons may lack the most up-to-date safeguards,[19] and some ICBMs may rely on multiple-key systems. SLBMs may have some sort of external control mechanism to prevent launches not sanctioned by the political leadership, but their exact nature is not known. With the exception of land-based ICBMs and SLBMs, nuclear warheads are thought to be routinely kept separate from their delivery systems. There have been indications that tactical warheads lacked PALs (Meyer, 1987: pp. 491-493; Cochran et al., 1989: p. 16), but recent information suggests otherwise (Blair, 1993).[20]

---

[19] Blair, Bruce 1990. Communication with author, May 23.

[20] Blair also believes that Soviet submarines may have the functional equivalent of PALs through safety mechanisms requiring codes transmitted from higher authorities. He contends that non-strategic naval weapons have PALs.

KGB officers have shared custody of strategic weapons with officers of the Main Political Administration, both of which were separate from the military chain of command (Cochran et al., 1989: p. 16). Missile silos contain two KGB soldiers, who must arm the warhead before the two regular servicemen in the silo can carry out a launch (Cockburn, 1983: p. 298). KGB agents guard strategic installations and man or supervise warhead storage sites. Tactical warheads are stored separately from delivery systems and under the physical control of KGB personnel.[21] The KGB also has responsibility for maintaining secrecy and security in organizations connected with weapons development and production (McLean et al., 1986: pp. 13-14).

2.4 France
Control of nuclear weapons is highly centralized in France. The president has sole authority to order their use, and he may have sole possession of the enabling codes. This authority is reportedly delegated to the prime minister only if the president dies (Stein & Feaver, 1987: p. 87).

Tactical warheads are protected with PALs and stored separately from their launchers (Caldwell, 1986: p. 9; Kelleher, 1987: p. 468), and bombers do not carry nuclear weapons in peacetime.[22] In a state of heightened readiness, their short range missiles can be loaded onto launchers, mated with warheads and fired within 15 minutes (Defense Intelligence Agency, 1989: p. 3).

France employs the two-man rule in the handling of nuclear weapons. Two officers must separately receive coded orders to fire and then act simultaneously for a nuclear weapon to be armed and launched (Caldwell, 1986: p. 8). In the case of Mirage IV aircraft, there are two distinct command chains between the president and the pilots to convey these separate sets of orders (US Congress, 1975: p. 17). Some, perhaps all, bombers apparently also carry radio receivers allowing deactivation of their payload from the ground (Kohl, 1971[23]; Stein & Feaver, 1987: p. 87; Caldwell, 1986: pp. 8-9). It

---

[21] Blair, Bruce 1990. Communication with author, May 23.

[22] Fleury J., General d'Armée Aerienne 1989. Interview with author, Paris, April 12, p. 5.

[23] As quoted in US Congress, 1975: p. 17.

appears likely that all French nuclear weapons are equipped with PALs.

2.5 Great Britain

Although Parliament is Britain's ultimate political authority, the prime minister is 'solely responsible' for the decision to use British nuclear weapons. Once the decision had been made, the actual use would be initiated by the prime minister together with the chief of the defense staff, in the presence of both a civilian and a military assistant (Kelleher, 1987: p. 466).

Those in physical possession of British nuclear weapons usually have the capability to use them without higher approval. While the United States has evidently provided information on PAL technology to the United Kingdom, submarines and planes do not use them. There is also evidence that PALs are not deployed on land-based weapons (Gregory, 1986: p. 24).[24] All British nuclear forces employ complex launch procedures involving both coded orders and the two-man rule, which extend all the way from the prime minister (who does not have a set of launch codes) to the soldiers in the field. For example, the crew on each of Great Britain's 4 Polaris subs can launch its 16 missiles on its own volition. The two-man rule at each step in the launch procedure is supposed to ensure that about 12 crew members cooperate in authenticating the coded order and carrying out a launch. Reflecting official acceptance of the fragility of command and control, Polaris crews are authorized to launch without higher orders if they believe that the United Kingdom has been destroyed and that no one is able to transmit orders to them (Gregory, 1986: p. 21, 24, 25, 63-72).

British nuclear weapons are committed in principle to NATO. Aircraft carriers, destroyers and frigates routinely carry nuclear-free fall bombs and depth charges in peacetime. Once the ships leave the NATO area, command and control may be almost totally absent, as it was in the Falklands, where the British relied heavily on US

---

[24] Stein and Feaver surmise that these weapons have PALs because they are jointly operated with the US, which has PALs on all its weapons in the NATO arsenal (Stein & Feaver, 1987: p. 87). Caldwell writes that 'interviews with a number of former government officials indicate the United States provided PALs to Great Britain for its land-based nuclear weapons' (Caldwell, 1986: p. 7). Gregory, however, reports that while the US did provide information on PALs to Britain, 'she did not adopt the technology, preferring instead to rely upon organisational rather than mechanical means to maintain control of nuclear weapons' (Gregory, 1986: p. 24).

communications support (Gregory, 1986: p. 28, 29, 92-97; SIPRI, 1989: p. 18).

British officers in the RAF control the air force's 180-200 nuclear gravity bombs, but their authority over them is subordinate to that of NATO commanders (Gregory, 1986: p. 86, 88; SIPRI, 1989: pp. 18). Nevertheless, 'the RAF expects that in any major European conflict the degree of disruption and attrition to command and control systems will be so great that...squadrons (at base level) will be out of contact with higher headquarters for extended periods of time. Consequently, RAF procedures and training are based on the premise that central control will often be missing' (*RAF News*, 1983).

Officially, the British army's nuclear artillery and Lance missiles are completely integrated into NATO. The delivery systems are kept by the British, while the warheads are tended by American units that may be hundreds of miles away. If the warheads and launchers are coupled during a crisis, however, the British units may have full control of the weapons (Gregory, 1986: pp. 98-103, 117).

2.6 China

The Chinese have never given any indication that they have PALs, and it is uncertain whether they employ other forms of use-control technology or procedures (Stein & Feaver, 1987: p. 88). The Chinese apparently feel there is little danger of a deranged individual making an unauthorized launch because missiles are not prearmed with warheads: carrying out a launch would require two hours of effort by a missile crew. But the wide dispersal of weapons, poor communications, lack of safeguards, and the potential political instability may render the control of Chinese nuclear forces tenuous in the future.

2.7 Israel

Israel has never admitted to possessing nuclear weapons, although by 1988, it was thought by US officials to possess about 50-60 nuclear devices. Some estimates put the number at 100-200. The arsenal may include hydrogen bombs, and delivery systems include aircraft and missiles. In 1987, a missile with a range of 900 miles was tested. Such a missile could conceivably be targeted at and therefore pose a threat to the Soviet Union (Spector, 1988: p. 32, 164, 166).

The likely site for most of Israel's nuclear weapons production and storage is the large Dimona reactor, located in a remote region of the Negev Desert. Many of the weapons are thought to be kept in a disassembled state, requiring perhaps 78 hours of preparation to make them combat-ready. This would probably be the most plausible way of interpreting the Israeli government's claim that they do not possess nuclear weapons, but could acquire them 'in a short time - even a few days'. (Pry, 1984: pp. 80-82, 85). If Israel lacks PALs, they probably have the ability to develop them, given their advanced technology and access to US expertise (Caldwell, 1986: p. 16). Meanwhile, the danger of unauthorized use is reduced so long as the weapons remain unassembled.

2.8 Other Nuclear Capable Nations
In the not-so-distant future, the nuclear club will become an even larger and more diverse group. India, Pakistan and South Africa may have already joined. Several parties to the 1986 Treaty on the Non-Proliferation of Nuclear Weapons (NPT) are believed to be developing a nuclear capability: Libya, Iran, Iraq, and North Korea. A number of nuclear-threshold countries did not sign the treaty at all, including Argentina and Brazil (Goldblat, 1989: pp. 369-370). Brazil has had a 15-year old military program to make an atom bomb, and Argentina has declared its possession of the technology to enrich uranium. Both countries, however, have recently renounced the manufacture of nuclear weapons (Christian, 1990).

India and Pakistan appear to be embarking on a nuclear arms race. India tested an atomic bomb in 1974, while claiming that their nuclear program is for peaceful purposes. India has also tested a short-range nuclear-capable missile and has launched a satellite with a rocket which could carry a warhead over 1,000 miles. For its own part, Pakistan appears to have virtually everything it needs to fabricate four to six fairly advanced weapons (Spector, 1988).

South Africa is thought to have the capacity to build several atomic bombs annually. It may have an undeclared arsenal of about 10 to 40 bombs already, and could deliver them with aircraft (with a range of 2,000 miles) and possibly missiles and artillery (Ogunbadejo, 1989: p. 69; Spector, 1988: p. 286, 295; Walters, 1987: pp. 34-36).

It is unlikely that countries such as India, South Africa or Pakistan have PALs. In general, safety and control probably lags behind offensive capability as new nuclear forces are created. In these countries, 'command and control at the outset may be more capable for launching an attack than for effective control or restraint under crisis conditions' (Jones, 1984: pp. 24-25).[25]

*   *   *   *   *

A number of meliorative actions should be taken to diminish the possibility of unauthorized or accidental use:

1) Installation of PALs on all US nuclear weapons, including those in the Navy.

2) Provision by the US and other nuclear states of appropriate information on PALs to countries such as China, Pakistan and India (Caldwell, 1986: pp. 18-22).
   Supplying such information to countries outside the major nuclear powers may be hazardous. The assistance might be interpreted as de facto approval of their efforts to develop nuclear weapons (Caldwell, 1986: pp. 18-22). But it may well represent a pragmatic response to the failure of anti-proliferation regimes.

3) Exchange of information among all the nuclear nations on safety and security of nuclear weapons. This should broaden the 1971 Accidents Agreement between the Soviet Union and the United States to include all nuclear nations.

4) Development of a post-launch destruct system. If all precautions fail, and if unauthorized or accidental launch of a nuclear weapon occurs, a remote destruct capacity will guard against the destructive impact of the weapon. The Accidents Agreement of 1971 embodied a clear commitment on the part of its signators to make every effort to 'render harmless or destroy' an accidentally launched weapon. Such a commitment cannot be fulfilled unless a concerted effort to apply post-launch controls is initiated (Frankel, 1990).

---

[25] Caldwell and Zimmerman (1989: p. 170) advocate that the US share some PAL technology with other nations. Ogunbadejo (1989: p. 71) recommends that the superpowers assist South Africa and Israel in developing efficient command and control systems.

3. Instability in the nuclear world of the future

Terrorist groups, radical nations, or countries working in cooperation
with terrorists may attempt to obtain or build nuclear weapons. In the
last two decades, the frequency of reported terrorist attacks
worldwide has increased considerably.[26] These acts reveal a
developing sophistication in the use of technology, intelligence, and
communications systems, as well as a growing interdependence or
networking among terrorist groups in different parts of the world.
State support of international terrorism has grown. The placement of
nuclear weapons and facilities in regions where terrorists are active
may create the proper conditions for terrorist nuclear acts (US
Congress, 1977: p. 125).

In 1979, documents discovered after the downfall of Idi Amin
disclosed that he was recruiting help and expertise from terrorist
groups in a plan to build nuclear bombs small enough to fit into
suitcases, which could then be carried worldwide into Ugandan
embassies by teams of diplomats (Kellen, 1987: pp. 125-126). This
apparent science fiction plot, code-named 'Operation Poker', was
unlikely to be realized outside of Amin's mind, but it suggests the
kind of nuclear risk-taking and adventurism that might occur with the
spread of nuclear weapons.

Beyond skill, planning, and technical support, bombs require
fissionable material, about 5 or 6 kg of plutonium or 25 kg of very
highly enriched uranium (Mark et al., 1987: p. 58). But the amount
of highly enriched uranium or plutonium missing from nuclear
facilities in the United States is sufficient to fabricate hundreds of
bombs (US Congress, 1984: p. 246).

Internationally, the control of nuclear materials is often weak. A
nation can sign the Nuclear Non-Proliferation Treaty, receive nuclear
technology and assistance, and then, after all the materials have been
gathered, withdraw from the treaty and its safeguards with 90 days
notice. International Atomic Energy Association (IAEA) inspectors
are forbidden in many cases to look for or report clandestine nuclear
activities. If misuse or diversion occurs, there is no guarantee that
effective international sanctions will be imposed (Willrich & Taylor,
1974: p. 87).

---

[26] 'In 1970, 293 terrorist attacks were reported worldwide. During 1985, the figure
was 3,010' (Mastrangelo, 1987: p. 134).

Romania, for example, diverted a shipment of heavy water from Norway - supposedly destined for their own nuclear energy reactors - to India (Hart, 1981: p. 9). The United States is prepared to ship large amounts of fuel to Japan for their reactors seven times yearly, with the attendant potential danger of piracy or hijacking. Either terrorists or a state intent on developing its own nuclear arsenal might obtain necessary plutonium in sizable quantity from such shipments (Gordon, 1990).

In view of the resources needed to build a bomb, stealing or seizing one might be considered an attractive alternative. Adequate security for nuclear weapons is difficult and costly. The deployment of mobile basing systems will pose greater challenges for security: fences will be remote; sensors will have to be more portable and versatile; and the number and location of security teams will have to be greatly increased (Turner & Davies, 1990). While the newer members of the nuclear club have not been reckless extremists, the existence of their weapons provides new targets for terrorist groups.

Concern over security and terrorism prompted the US to begin upgrading security at NATO bases, so that all weapons would be protected by multi-layer systems including improved fencing, lighting and guard facilities, as well as electronic sensors and physical barriers to delay access (Golden, 1985: pp. 14-15). The Army may begin replacing storage igloos with a new kind of underground storage in the next decade (Julian, 1987: p. 175). Great Britain also has begun an effort to strengthen security, prompted by a House of Commons recommendation to spend millions of pounds to improve fencing and alarm systems at nuclear bases (Evans, 1984 & 1985).

Previous breaches of security indicate how difficult protection may be. A reporter, posing as a fencing contractor, was able to enter two SAC nuclear weapons depots, where he was shown gaps and weaknesses in the security systems and methods for disabling alarms. He came within a stone's throw of four hydrogen bombs, guarded by only one man. He also obtained blue-prints showing the layout of nuclear weapons compounds and the alert areas where B-52s carrying nuclear weapons were parked (US Congress, 1978).

Peace protesters in Europe and the United States have gained access to and tampered with Trident submarines, as well as MX, Pershing II, Cruise, Minuteman, and Trident II missile components (Laffin, 1984; Associated Press, 1984; Arkin & Fieldhouse, 1985: p. 145). Vehicles carrying cruise missiles in Britain and Pershing IIs in

West Germany have been obstructed or interfered with, sometimes causing accidents (Gregory, 1988: p. 73).

Smaller, newer nuclear nations will be vulnerable in that they will generally lack PALs and other sophisticated safeguards. Moreover, radical changes in leadership may occur in emerging nuclear powers. Among these states, only India and Israel have well-established traditions of constitutional succession. The coming government in South Africa or Pakistan might well ascend to power through violent means. Political change or instability could also threaten US weapons stored abroad. Nuclear states in crisis also represent a potentially serious risk if changes in control of weapons are imminent.

Most recently, internal instability has threatened nuclear weapons in the former Soviet Union itself. Stockpiles are located in dissident republics such as Lithuania, Latvia, Estonia and Azerbaijan. As various republics attempt to break away, and the military itself faces deep internal divisions, the control over nuclear weapons might become tenuous (Fox, 1990; Gertz, 1990a).

During the Azerbaijani uprising in 1990, Muslim separatists armed themselves with captured weapons including machine guns, helicopters and rockets, and clashed with Soviet troops. The Soviets perceived a threat to their nuclear weapons stockpiles near the Azerbaijani capital of Baku, and dispatched additional troops to protect them.

In or around early February, the Soviet fears were confirmed when the rebels stormed a nuclear weapons storage facility armed with automatic weapons. The sites are protected with special lighting, fences and barriers, and guarded with elite, non-Azerbaijani troops. Nevertheless, reportedly a nuclear weapon was almost captured by armed nationalists before being repulsed in a battle with Soviet troops (Gertz, 1990b; Fox, 1990).[27]

As a reflection of their concern about this issue, the Soviets have been evacuating nuclear weapons from potentially dangerous areas of Europe and border regions such as Baku, and moving them to storage bunkers in the Russian interior. The transport of the weapons complicates the task of protecting them, and heightens the risk of ambush.

---

[27] The unrest in Muslim areas of the Soviet Union has spilled over into Xinjiang, with violent clashes between rioters and Chinese troops (FBIS, 1990).

4. Conclusions

In large measure, the major Nuclear Powers have done their best to ensure that stable personnel operate their nuclear weapons installations. They have also developed technologically advanced safeguards and command and control systems designed to guard against unauthorized launch.

Even with the best methods of screening for stability, the evidence is unequivocal that many unreliable individuals remain in the nuclear weapons corps. The safeguards in the command and control system have worked thus far, but numerous instances of false warnings and potential breakdown in the control systems have occurred.

In a period of turbulence in the former USSR and Eastern Europe, the control over nuclear weapons may not remain as firmly in the hands of civilian leadership, and republics in the process of change might reasonably lay claim to weapons housed within their territory.

Perhaps the most important threat lies in the acquisition of weapons and missile technology by an increasing number of countries, some with radical leadership and apocalyptic visions. The control of the nuclear threat in such settings should be a continuing matter of concern for the developed nations.

Acknowledgement:
Dan Pollak played an essential role in data gathering and organization for this paper.

Chapter 7

Why We Cannot Rely on Decision-makers in Times of Crisis

Marta Cullberg-Weston

1. Introduction

In a book by the German psychoanalyst Horst E. Richter (1981), people from another planet arrive on Earth and find it destroyed by a nuclear catastrophe. They start to investigate what happened and they are very puzzled as they find evidence that the Earth people seem to have built up huge resources of nuclear weapons and then used them against one another. The only explanation they can arrive at is a hypothesis of collective suicide. Why collective suicide? From a rational standpoint you do not start a war which annihilates the civilization you want to defend, they reasoned. They believed too much in the authority of reason!

Another hypothesis, though, is that a nuclear war started by accident. As long as we live in the nuclear trap, we must find ways to minimize the risk of an accidental nuclear war.

There is vast consensus (Hellman, 1985; Intriligator & Brito, 1988; Petersen & Smoker, 1989; Ury, 1989) that the risk of an accidental nuclear war is much larger in a serious world crisis. Such a crisis might emanate from political tension in some of the 'hot' political areas of the world. Nuclear weapons have proliferated to politically conflictual areas and these weapons pose a great danger.

If multiple incidents (different sorts of false alarms occurring in close succession) happen at a time of crisis, or a terrorist launch is effected in a situation of high political tension, we have a dangerous situation. Consider the following scenario from the Cold War period (Allison & Ury, 1989, reported also in *Carnegie Quarterly*, Vol. 34/3-4, 1990):

> The headquarters of the United States military command in Europe has received a flash message that unidentified jet aircraft are flying over Turkey and that the Turkish air force has gone on

alert in response. There are additional reports of 100 Soviet
MiG-15s over Syria and further reports that a British Canberra
bomber has been shot down over Syria. (At this time, only Soviet
MiGs have the ability to shoot down the highflying Canberras.)

Finally, there are reports that a Russian fleet is moving
through the Dardanelles. The White House reaction is not fully
known, but reportedly General Andrew Goodpaster is afraid that
the events 'might trigger off all the NATO operations plan'. The
NATO operations plan calls for all-out nuclear strikes on the
Soviet Union.

Improbable as it may seem, these perilous interactions
actually occurred - in 1956, while the Hungarians were revolting,
the British and French were trying to take the Suez Canal back
from Egypt, and the Soviets were making veiled threats against
London and Paris.

The 'jets' over Turkey, it turned out, were a flock of swans
picked up on radar and incorrectly identified, and the 100 Soviet
MiGs over Syria were really a much smaller routine escort
returning the president of Syria from a state visit to Moscow.
The British Canberra was downed by a mechanical difficulty, and
the Soviet fleet was engaging in a long-scheduled exercise.

The international situation has undergone major changes during the
last few years affecting the nuclear weapons situation and making
nuclear proliferation the central issue. A panel of world experts
meeting in Stockholm 1992 summarized the changing perspectives in
a final document 'Towards a Nuclear Weapons-Free World':

> The Warsaw Pact and the Soviet Union have been dissolved and
> the communist regime is gone. The cold war is over. A period of
> confrontation, hostility and mistrust has been replaced by a spirit
> of cooperation that has enabled the United States and the
> Russian Federation to attain far-reaching disarmament
> agreements and increased mutual trust. This has permitted each
> of them to undertake unilaterally and bilaterally substantial
> nuclear disarmament measures. (Hellman 1992, p. 6)

However there are new risks for nuclear proliferation. For some
countries nuclear weapons are considered to be the ultimate tool
for securing national survival. Technological developments and

the increased availability of fissile materials make it easier for threshold countries to develop nuclear weapons. There have been several reports of attempts to smuggle fissile materials. (Ibid., p. 8)

If more countries develop nuclear weapons, the probability of heir use in war increases, as does the probability of their leak into unauthorized hands or to terrorist groups. (Ibid., p. 9)

Nuclear stability between the United States and the Soviet Union involved a long learning process. New nuclear-weapon-states might not be able to build weapons survivable enough to be confident of assured second-strike capability and this might increase the risk of preemptive attack by frightened neighbours. Few of the new nuclear powers could develop the elaborate system of command and control, the special safety devices or the satellite verification that reduced the risk of nuclear war between the superpowers. Threshold countries all live with the risk of being exposed to a strike against their nuclear facilities, intended to stop or delay their program. (Ibid.)

Russia is supposed to be the single nuclear successor of the USSR (recognized by the treads of CIS-states at a meeting in June 6, 1992) but Kazakhstan and Ukraine still keep their nuclear weapons for political power reasons and that presents the Start I and Start II treaties to enter into force.

The present adverse situation in the CIS countries creates concern about what will happen in case of a new turbulent period. (Ibid., p. 10)

There are also reportedly 3000-5000 persons holding sensitive information on design and operation of installations for plutonium production, uranium enrichment and weapons assembly. By international standards these persons are already very badly paid. Few of them will be able to find alternative employment on the market in their home country. (Ibid.)

These people already pose a real proliferation risk as threshold countries could buy them over to help in their programs.

The lack of effective security systems, the political unrest, the fanatic position of certain leaders especially when threatened and the lack of democratic institutional checks in new nuclear states increases the risk for a nuclear strike in a crisis situation and also the risk ofr a nuclear strike by mistake.

When the public refrains from engaging in the security problems of our nuclear world, they often rely on leaders they assume to be sane and rational. Their idea is that 'No one is so stupid as to start a nuclear war' or a notion that 'Our leaders know best what to do'. From a professional psychological viewpoint, we know that leaders may not at all behave rationally, especially not in situations of crisis. I will give a psychological overview of the decision-making process in times of crisis since it is of central importance to the question of accidental nuclear war. The main focus will be on the decisions taken by the head of state (or president) (and his advisory group) in the Nuclear Powers. In section 2, I will analyze the decision-making process in times of crisis from both cognitive and emotional aspects. This will give a psychological background to the decision situation which the president and his advisory group have to face.

In section 3, I will focus on the impact of group processes on the decision-making process. In the last section, I want to draw attention to a special decision-maker with potent power over our lives - the submarine commander. He has the possibility to launch nuclear weapons and is thus in a situation similar to the heads of states in the Nuclear Powers.

2. Cognitive and emotional aspects

2.1 Cognitive aspects of decision-making under stress
'Policymakers (like all human beings) are limited-capacity information processors, who resort to simplifying strategies to deal with the compexity, uncertainty and the painful trade offs with which the world confronts them', Tetlock & McGuire (1986) conclude.

Most studies indicate a curvilinear relationship between arousal and quality of performance. This means that some degree of stress may increase performance, but when the level of stress increases and rises to a higher level performance deteriorates (Frankenhaeuser, 1985).

In a crisis situation, the political leaders are subject to intense stress. They typically get very little sleep, they are bombarded by information from different sources and there are often very short deadlines for making decisions. This leads to the overloading of their cognitive systems. In such a situation there is also an increase in feelings of vulnerability, affecting the emotional climate. Even if expert decision-makers may have a greater stress tolerance, they are still human. Psychological research has given extensive evidence on how our thinking is affected in stressful situations (summarized by Holsti, 1972; Frankenhaeuser, 1988; Thompson, 1985; and Tetlock & McGuire, 1986). There is today impressive multi-method convergence in the research literature concerning how our thinking is affected by stress:

1. The area of attention becomes more limited (the tunnel phenomenon). This was originally described by Easterbrook (1959). In the Three Mile Island disaster, the staff was so busy trying to fix a minor problem that they did not discover the major problem evolving (Thompson, 1985).
2. Perceptual distortions may appear where messages/information are distorted in the direction of one's expectations. The Korean airliner incident (1983) and the Iranian airbus incident (1988), both illustrate how civil aircrafts were mistaken for military planes (on spy mission/attacking the US fleet) in situations of high tension in the area. 'They saw what they expected to see' (Petersen & Smoker, 1989).
3. The problems will be simplified. As thinking deteriorates, the possibility to keep a nuanced view of the problem or of the antagonist disappears. The tolerance for ambiguity is reduced and a black-and-white thinking dominates where calculations are made on an all-or-nothing basis.
4. Mental rigidity increases. When people are under strong emotional pressure, their cognitive processes tend to become rigid. One starts thinking in old patterns and cannot take into account alternative explanations to the problem. In such a situation it is easy to go for a 'worst possible scenario'.
5. There is a strong tendency to act. 'Nothing is harder under emotional stress than doing nothing', Frank (1986) concludes. The tolerance for ambiguity is reduced and as the stress

accumulates anxiety there is a strong pressure on the person to act in order to relieve the strain.

6. Long-term costs will tend to be neglected. Behavior will be dictated by a need to combat the immediate goals and this leads to a neglect of long-term interests.

The decision to use, or not to use, nuclear arms will most certainly be a decision taken under stress. In an accident situation, time is always short and decisions involve high stakes. This is quite serious when we summarize the above findings in relation to a nuclear decision.

The situation easily develops into a 'use them or lose them' scenario where other options will be harder to consider. There will be a strong tendency to act and the immediate goals of retaliation may override the long-term survival interest of the world population. Of course, simplification effects like these are not automatic, but it is quite normal that thinking changes in a crisis situation.

In essence, increased time for the decision process and carefully designed instructions are of paramount importance if we want to avoid defective decisions, even if there are still several other stressful factors as well in any accidental crisis.

2.2 Human beings and complex dynamic systems

A relatively new research field, concentrating on how people learn to control complex dynamic systems, suggests that we have considerable problems trying to establish a satisfactory control. A fundamental question about any system is whether it allows 'the operator' to develop a good model of the system. Technological systems are generally not designed with this in mind and we are left to develop our own models on the basis of our experience with the system.

If we consider the complex information systems which form the basis for the decision-maker in a global accident-related nuclear crisis, this research may give us some additional insights.

The complex dynamic systems research in Uppsala (Brehmer & Allard, 1985), Hamburg (Kluwe et al., 1984), Oxford (Broadbent & Aston, 1978), Bamberg (Dörner et al., 1980), and Austin (Kleinmuntz, 1985) reported by Brehmer (1987) suggest that people have considerable problems with time-dependent processes. They do not seem to develop predictive mental models of dynamic aspects of these tasks - they only learn to react by general heuristics. Feedback delay has disastrous effects on the ability to learn to control the system. If the task has a structure of a causal net, i.e. a structure where one variable influences another variable (in other words - there are side effects), it becomes very much harder to learn to control. In an accident scenario we may easily see a pattern of side effects.

There are wide interindividual differences in the ability to control a complex system. Dörner (1980) analyzes the reactions of people who fail to control a complex system. They may regress to:

1) Thematic vagabonding - i.e. they change their focus of interest from one aspect to another rather than concentrating on one strategy and trying to make that strategy work.
2) Encystment, where they concentrate on small details of the task and lose the overall picture. They become less and less willing to make decisions and tend to delegate the tasks and blame others for the mistakes. These phenomena from complex decision situations are very similar to those reported by Janis and Mann (1977) and Jervis et al. (1985), where it is called 'defensive avoidance'.
3) The intellectual emergency reaction is a still more risky aspect for the accidental situation (Dörner, 1980). The cognitive systems are organized to react quickly, but when the arousal level is too high an intellectual analysis is impossible. The emergency reaction thus leads to:
    *   a reduction in the level of reflection
    *   a reduction in the number of plans
    *   increased stereotyping of reactions
    *   decreased control over the execution of implementation of one's plans
    *   increased willingness to take risks and
    *   increased willingness to violate rules and regulations.

These emergency reactions are quite similar to the cognitive deterioration under stress reported in Section 2.1 above from another type of research.

Dörner (1980) concludes that subjects suffering from intellectual emergency reactions are more likely to destroy the system than to achieve control. The global system runs the same risk!

2.3 Decision rationality - action rationality/irrationality
Decision-makers in reality seldom use the 'rational actor model' which is assumed in international political models. Organization research can give some interesting views on this. Brunson (1985) claims that the business organization is not interested in decision rationality as their ultimate goal is action. Cooperative actions are easier to bring about if the actors are convinced that the action is positive. One should then avoid insecurity about which alternative is the best one. A rational decision-making process may be dangerous in a company as it may point to several alternative options.

The irrationality often found in the decision processes in companies are the result of the action orientation and the action goal. This may be called 'action rationality' (Brunson, 1985). Brunson states, however, that this type of rationality is not necessarily related to decision rationality at all.

Decision processes on the national policy level have many similarities to decision processes in companies as described by Brunson. The decision process will probably be action oriented and the process to arrive at a political decision may be quite irrational in relation to most criteria of rationality.

2.4 Pre-nuclear thinking in a nuclear world
Many researchers (Frank, 1986; Morgenthau, 1976; Jervis, 1984) have pointed out that people's images are still dominated by the thinking of conventional warfare. In effect, this 'conventionalization' is a form of escape from the realities of the nuclear revolution. But it is also an effect of perseverance in human thinking, a phenomenon well known in psychology (Ross & Anderson, 1982 summarize the experimental findings). This 'conventionalization' is also found in the policy-makers.

Kull (1988) interviewed 84 nuclear policy-makers in the US (and a smaller sample from the USSR) and his findings are quite serious. Conventional war models permeated the thinking of the policy-makers to a high degree. When challenged, the conventional war models were rationalized as necessary for the image of the policy in the eyes of the allies or the public, or they were motivated by the psychological needs of people. Rather than taking the painful path of realizing the realities of nuclear war, the decision-makers suggest new, dangerous and expensive devices to help the public (and themselves) deny nuclear reality.

A former Pentagon official pointed to an especially strong narcissistic resistance in the US to accepting vulnerability. He saw the Reagan Strategic Defense Initiative decision as an ingenious move to alleviate the fear of the population. 'Somewhere in the American viscera we do not want to believe that some son-of-a-bitch on the other side can destroy us and he [Reagan] is offering us a wonderful defense in the sky' (Kull, 1988).

But if we cannot accept being vulnerable, we cannot make rational decisions based on realistic facts. The SDI program will not make us less vulnerable; only measures to prevent an accidental nuclear war will serve this purpose. The military officers in the interview were especially prone to use images from conventional wars. To them, 'winning a war' was an indispensable model, which underscores the importance of the fact that the decision to use nuclear weapons is retained in political hands - even if it is not secure there either. This is also underscored by the process during the Cuban missile crisis (Holsti, 1972).

The tendency to use conventional concepts is understandable in terms of human psychological limitations - the nuclear effects are 'unthinkable' to the public. However, when this misconception is common in the minds of the men shaping nuclear policy it is a serious sign. In a crisis situation where the quality of human thinking deteriorates, these 'basic' concepts will gain a strong hold on the thought processes. In a crisis involving serious (accidental) launches, the tendency to retaliate will arise as part of the conventional syndrome. It may cloud the decision process where there is no time to investigate the background properly. This underscores the tremendous problem with the 'human factor' acting in a nuclear world.

2.5 Basic psychological needs in leaders activated in crisis situations
The decision-maker's perspective in a crisis situation is often deeply affected by past personal experiences. Our inner working models contain our basic assessments of the world and core beliefs will exert strong influences on our behavior in a crisis (Tetlock & McGuire, 1986; Rogers, 1989; Henricson-Cullberg, 1989). A decision-maker's blend of patriotism, political ambition and humanistic sensibility will be an important ingredient in the decision-making process (Rogers, 1990). Whether the decision-maker has a worldview in Hobbes'

zero-sum terms or an alternative conflict resolution approach will affect the choice of actions distinctly.

There are also personal differences in risk taking tendencies. Some presidents may even be seen as risk seeking, which will easily escalate a crisis.

In a crisis situation there is often a perception of threat to the political philosophy of the government or to the survival of the nation. This represents a threat to the inner narcissistic center. In such a situation, basic emotional needs will gain in strength relative to reason. This, of course, affects the leaders' decisions. Hidden stereotypes re-emerge easily and the antagonist is perceived as entirely evil and malicious.

Leaders in our countries are selected to represent the country's aspirations in central dimensions. Particularly in situations of crisis there is a request for a strong leader and in the back of the head of the decision-maker will be a fear of showing up as weak, as a coward. This will influence the decision-maker, in the direction of taking direct action - a dangerous policy in an accident scenario. Janis & Mann (1977) show that concerns about making a fool of oneself in the eyes of the public and about losing self-esteem if the decision works out badly, influence the decision process. Vital decisions always involve conflicting values - and this means that some ideals must be sacrificed. This further increases the already high anticipatory anxiety of the decision-maker. With lack of time there are great risks for hypervigilant reaction (see below) or for rage reactions with unwise decisions.

The hypervigilant reaction (Janis & Mann, 1977) is very similar to the intellectual emergency reaction (Dörner, 1980, see p.5): The decision-maker is unable to survey all available alternatives and narrows down the options. The least objectionable alternative may appear increasingly positive. The projective tendency is strengthened and information from the adversary is interpreted as a direct threat. Risk taking is increased.

This is, of course, a very dangerous reaction pattern in general, and it may be fatal if it appears in an accident scenario. Anger may also be precipitated by an accidental nuclear attack. Anger and especially narcissistic rage will arouse primitive reactions. When anger takes over the retaliatory impulse will not be hindered by more mature thoughts. Offensive rather than defensive actions are promoted and the possibility of understanding the opponent's perceptions and problems disappears.

Any antagonist action that threatens the important values of the country will be felt as a personal attack on the decision-maker and on his or her own inner identity (Wedge, 1986). This will arouse strong and powerful rage, which will influence the decision-making process strongly in the direction of retaliation.

A serious accidental launch against one's own country will arouse strong anger in the public and in the decision-making group, which will be difficult to control if the circumstances around the launch remain unclear for some time. The pressure towards immediate retaliation against the attacker might become too strong to resist. We also know that in stressful situations there may be an exaggerated reluctance to accept losses, even if they are small. Rationales like 'Our boys must not have died in vain' may occur, as Bradley (1988) reports.

The situation may naturally be still more serious when key decision-makers are influenced by psychological problems, by alcohol or by drugs, etc. I have intentionally not brought this into the picture, my point being that ordinary people are subject to all these psychological traps, which make an accidental nuclear crisis extremely serious. With complicating factors like psychological problems, alcohol intoxication, etc. the risks are enlarged considerably (Thomson, 1985; Kringlen, 1985; Abrams, 1988). (See also Chapter 6 above.)

3. Group processes

3.1 Decision-making in groups

It is generally recognized that a 'rational actor' model is inadequate as a description of human decision-making in stressful situations. There is a risk that the situation is not better if the decision is taken in a group.

The decision to launch or not to launch nuclear weapons will be the result of a group process in a 'war cabinet'. The classical study in this field was conducted by Janis (1972), who analyzed political fiascos and found them due to a collusive group decision process he called 'Group Think'. When the political crisis decision is formulated, it is in a highly stressful situation with great risks and high stakes involved. The group is then exposed to defective processes of the Group Think type. Janis describes six aspects of defective group functioning:

1) An illusion of invulnerability develops in the group, which will affect the decisions in the direction of risk-taking.
2) Information is discarded when it doesn't fit with the predominant policy plan.
3) Mind-guards help to keep the ideas in line with the general plan.
4) A false perception of unity in the group results.
5) The moral aspects seem clearly in favor of one's own plan. This is due to the projective tendency. It is also described by Nisbeth and Ross (1980), as 'the attribution error'. Actions of the antagonist are seen as due to characterological givens (dominance needs, aggressive imperialism, etc.) while their own actions are seen as a response to 'situational pressures' ('The US/the USSR must defend itself'). What is an accidental launch from the other side will easily be seen as an aggression within this frame of reference.
6) Stereotyped thinking makes the picture of the enemy all black and this further increases the tendency to perceive his actions as evil-minded.

In crises related to accidental launching of nuclear weapons, a collusive Group Think process will have catastrophic repercussions.

The quality level of the decision-making process will depend on many factors. Herek, Janis & Huth (1987) in a study of 19 US crises situations found large variations in the quality of the decision-making process in different crises even within the same presidential administration. For instance, the otherwise effective Kennedy administration decided upon the invasion at the Bay of Pigs, a fiasco studied by Janis (1972). In an accident-related crisis with its very limited time perspective, a defective Group Think pattern may evolve in one or both of the headquarters.

What can be done to decrease the risk? Knowledge of the Group Think pattern helps a bit to avoid the defective thinking. The most important preventive action is to reduce the stress by giving more time. The possibility of having people play 'the devil's advocate' may also break the group think tendency. But we can never be sure. The present nuclear arms system has several weak points due to human fallibility.

In democratic countries there are at least some institutional checks on the president and his advisors, but these are often non-existent in the new nuclear powers.

3.2 Group pressure

Knowledge of the strong impact of group processes have led to the suggestion of a 'devil's advocate' in the president's advisory group (Janis, 1972). This is theoretically a good suggestion, but it is very hard to make it work. It needs to be formally instituted, as it is extremely difficult to go against the group idea in emotionally charged situations.

Multiple experimental evidence shows the strength of the pressure to social conformity in a group. People will renounce their own view even of such reality aspects as the length of a line when in groups where their view deviates - the Asch phenomenon (Asch, 1956).

The person who deviates in a group will easily be driven out into the cold. Holsti (1972) reports about a former presidental advisor, Clark Clifford, who lost the President Johnson's ear when he offered advice against the escalation in Vietnam. In his salty language he describes the change in attitude towards him: 'The President was colder than a whore's heart'. Others were banned from top policy discussions for the same reason.

The pressure to conform can also be seen in bureaucratic systems where people obey orders and where they can disavow their personal responsibility - 'the Eichmann effect'.

Some of the classical experimental findings about the obedience pattern are pertinent to aspects of accidental nuclear war. Milgram (1968) made a series of experiments where he asked people to give electrical shocks to subjects when they failed to remember in a memory test. Sixty percent of ordinary people gave the subjects presumably deadly shocks - as indicated on a display panel - even if many were very disturbed by the task. This was an effect of the acceptance of the orders of a status person (the experimenter being a scientist).

From the Nazi period we have ample evidence of people carrying out apparently unimaginable actions (Lifton, 1986). Milgram's experiments further stress the strong submissive force in relation to an authority. In a group this is further augmented by the social conformity pattern.

I have focused on group processes and group pressure to give a background also to the decision situation in submarines. The following section illustrates how group pressure may operate in situations of crisis in the very special environment on board a submarine.

4. The submarine society

When PALs (electronic locks) were introduced on US nuclear weapons the weapons stationed at sea were not included. The security measures there are limited to the fact that several independent people should authorize the launch, using separate keys.

In the light of psychological knowledge of group processes, the separation of authority is no real safeguard. We know that the crew on the submarine has a strong solidarity with their captain and would certainly feel strong group pressure to accept his decisions. He will also be strongly influenced by unanimous crew demand.

In a crisis situation where communications to the submarine are broken, the crew is in a very difficult situation. If there has been an unspecified launch before the communication break, the stress and the pressure on the submarine will be very strong. In the fantasies of the crew the cities where their families lives might be under attack. This will form a strong motivation to retaliate.

A submarine community is a very special one. The crew lives in a very restricted space and is far away from home for long periods of time. Some persons may react with depressive reactions in such a situation, others with different forms of anxiety. Alcohol might be an easy way to sooth these feelings.

But we need not take alcohol or drugs into the picture. The stressful conditions of being cut off from information after (an accidental) launch will easily set into motion the defective group decision processes described as well as the obedience pattern towards the captain's decision. Primitive psychological reactions with retaliatory impulses will easily be triggered.

In conclusion, then, the separation of authority and the fact that there are others whose consent is needed is not a secure arrangement in the light of our psychological knowledge.

5. What can be done to reduce the risk?

Humans are fallible. All man-machine systems run into accidents sooner or later, as names like Chernobyl, Three Mile Island, Challenger, etc. remind us. We can never transcend our human limitations.

To go on stock piling nuclear weapons means denying the psychological reality of mankind. Until we have managed to realize that nuclear weapons are our worst enemy, we must avoid an accidental nuclear war. I will just point out a number of possible preventive measures:

- PALs need to be installed on all nuclear weapons - also those at sea - and in all Nuclear Powers. Today the fate of the earth may be in the hands of a single submarine commander and his crew! Joint decisions are not acceptable preventive measures, as I have shown above.
- Nuclear weapons are also proliferating to new and politically unstable regions. We know very little about the security measures for those weapons, and no chain is stronger than its weakest link. The institutional checks are definitely less strong in these powers. Measures to restrict proliferation are important, while proliferation of security measures is to be stimulated.
- Increased efforts to solve protracted political conflicts are important to reduce the risks of regional conflicts as starting points for a world crisis. This means finding ways of meeting pressing economic needs, humanitarian needs as well as the important identity needs in ethnic conflicts (Azar & Burton, 1986)
- Crisis diffusion measures, including crisis management training for key politicians and a development of crisis control centers.
- Strengthen the NPT-treaty, improve the IAEA safeguard system and create open skies agreements.
- All newly independent states should as soon as possible be parties to the NPT.
- Create agreements in advance among all states on how to deal with nuclear accidents and mistakes.
- Create nuclear-weapon-free zones in the Middle East, in South Asia, on the Korean peninsula and from the Baltic to the Black Sea as first steps toward elimination of all nuclear weapons.
- The Nuclear Weapon States should all reduce their arsenals drastically as no credible treat exists.
- Increased awareness of the nuclear realities and efforts to bring decision-makers out of pre-nuclear thinking.

Actually this all boils down to accepting our human limitations. We simply were not designed for handling threats such as those from nuclear weapons. We are not very rational and we are certainly not infallible. We cannot go on living with these nuclear systems which presume that we are rational and infallible!

Chapter 8

Preventing the Ultimate Disaster: Misperception at the Top

Frederick L. Shiels

1. Preventing the ultimate disaster

The idea of a nuclear conflict gives new meaning to the terms disaster and catastrophe. In comparison with the political and military disasters chronicled over the centuries, the scale of destruction and anguish unleashed by even a 'modest' atomic conflict would dwarf the former if not trivialize them. By any utilitarian measure of pain, even a relatively restrained 200 megaton exchange between the Soviet Union and the United States, or in a few years between India and Pakistan, claiming from half to most of the civilian populations (i.e. 200-400 million), would vastly outweigh the worst manmade disasters - World War I and World War II - which together took over 60 million lives. Postwar violence in Iran, Korea, Vietnam, and Israel, though highly traumatic for their populations - especially if one examines casualty data for the whole surrounding wartime period such as in Vietnam where there were possibly three million dead - are of a different order of magnitude, as are indeed all historical precedents with the possible exception of 'Noah's flood.'

There is little doubt then that slipping into even the most modest nuclear exchange would be folly and that this must be prevented as a *sine qua non* of future progress. What this chapter proposes to explore are some of the kinds of misperceptions among top officials that could prove exceedingly dangerous in the event of a serious crisis in which nuclear weapons might be used, including crises generated by or accompanied by nuclear accidents. What can we learn, if anything, from history that would help prevent such events and uses of atomic weapons? What could the consequences of misperception coupled with a false alarm or other accident be? And what are some concrete steps that could be taken to reduce the dangers posed by accidents, given the context that these misperceptions help shape?

Many of the proposals generated in this 'Accidental Nuclear War' symposium, similar conferences in the past few years, and works concerned with how nations control their nuclear weapons show considerable promise as risk reducers if adopted. What my own research tries to address, however, is some of the problems in the heads of leaders that would reduce the likelihood that such proposals would be adopted or that they would prevent disaster even if adopted.

Before looking at the specific proposals, existing beliefs about where a nuclear war, when or if it comes, will originate will be clarified. Four probable causes of nuclear war, each with variants, have been most widely mentioned: 1) premeditated, planned attack either in response to crisis or as a result of a determination that such aggression will pay; 2) crisis instability, resulting in an unplanned but deliberate escalation; 3) miscalculation; and 4) accident (Lebow, 1987). (It should be remembered that, judging from experiences in other wars, the predictable causes of conflict and then the course of the conflict itself may turn out very differently from *any* of the scenarios projected, e.g. World War I or the Russo-Japanese War.)

1.1 Premeditated attack
Although it is almost certainly true that a crazed or diabolical leader could initiate a surprise attack with the thought of surviving such an attack, particularly from Washington or Moscow, it appears increasingly unlikely and suicidal. Unless substantial advances in anti-submarine warfare are achieved, a first strike, even when the temptation to preempt is high, would be tantamount to self-extinction, as well as the extinction of the targeted Superpower. Strikes by Superpowers against other nuclear powers or exchanges between lesser nuclear powers are slightly more plausible but are still not probable because of the cost, either from minimum nuclear retaliation or from adverse world public opinion.

Consider the consequences of a Russian attack against China some years hence, for example, if only three or four Russian cities received a Chinese counterstrike with several million Russian casualties and if Russia managed to inflict casualties of some hundreds of millions on the Chinese (which would not be difficult). What would be the response among former Russian allies, Third World countries, and in the United Nations, not to mention the West?

If a *premeditated* attack is assumed unlikely, but possible, how might it be prevented? The conventional deterrence wisdom has been that assured response or second strike is the best prevention. This can be enhanced by reliable early warning systems.

A strategic defense system, such as that initiated by the Reagan Administration could lessen the effects of such an attack (yet not necessarily deter it), but with costs and unknowns serious enough to warrant considerable skepticism. Ultimately, in a future world with an unstable leader, most likely a Khomeini or Hitler who had abandoned survival goals, a desperate attack might not be preventable. The only mitigating options would be guaranteed second strike, strategic defense, or some kind of disarmament, build down, or other scheme to lessen the effects of such a nightmare.

1.2 Crisis instability
Some recent strategic theorists argue that crisis instability is the number one threat to peace and the likeliest cause of unintentional (but no less lethal) nuclear clashes. Such writers as Jervis (1984), Frei (1983), Lebow (1984), and McNamara (1987) have underlined the complexity of modern defense networks and the risks of miscommunication, not only between powers, but within them. Superpower leaders may draw on questionable lessons from past crises and wars in response to lower level threats (Jervis, 1976: Ch. 6). They may be enticed into conflict by the maze of formal and informal alliance networks, including connections in unstable regions of the Third World. Political considerations, such as those that drove Kennedy to extra toughness during the Cuban missile crisis may force leaders into more intransigent positions (Allison, 1971: pp. 187-188).

Organizational rivalries and rigidities may lead to posturing. In the case of Cuba in 1962, as close an example as we have to a full nuclear crisis, maneuvering and uncertainty occurred involving the Central Intelligence Agency, the US Air Force, and the US Navy both during and before the October showdown. This made both prevention of a bad situation and its resolution more difficult, as Allison notes (1971: Ch. 3). Crises such as the Arab-Israeli War of 1973 and the invasion of Afghanistan in 1979, as well as unstable situations in Poland, Nicaragua and the Persian Gulf force us to reflect on the potential for drawing an arrow from the nuclear quiver without necessarily having planned to do so. And always, the horrifying European experience of the summer of 1914 and subsequent locking in to inflexible war positions looms in the background. It is worth remembering that World War I broke out during a period in which there were some favorable trends occurring in the international system and a relative absence of tension in Europe in the months before the Austrian archduke's assassination.

1.3 Miscalculation

Next on the scale of diminishing purposefulness and related to unstable escalation is the threat of miscalculation, even where there is not an overt intentional show of force. A Superpower might mistakenly feel that its actions will not seem highly provocative toward the other and move unilaterally in a dangerous way. The Soviet Union badly underestimated the consequences of its support of North Korea, its move into Afghanistan, and particularly its construction of missile bases in the brush of northern Cuba in 1962. The United States and particularly its allies Britain and France did not fully appreciate the Soviet Union's commitment to Egypt in the 1956 Suez crisis. (The Americans did quickly pull the reins on their allies when this potential for high risk began to be apparent, as well as out of pique about not being consulted.) One might cite other errors of judgment, such as Britain's with Germany in Czechoslovakia in 1938, the USSR with the US and Korea in 1950, or the United States with the Japanese in 1941.

Overarching these occasional misjudgments, it must be recognized, are *structural* features which make worse miscalculation and crisis instability. The presence of strategically destabilizing weapons systems such as the powerful MIRVed SS-18 and MX heighten fears of pre-emption as would any credible strategic defense system. Launch on warning options that could make possible responses to attacks *perceived* by radar and computer-assisted warning systems before other evidence manifested itself are equally disturbing, although they would not necessarily be used.

1.4 Accident

Computer malfunctions, failsafe systems that might fail and unidentified flying objects that coincide with periods of tension present the potential for triggering nuclear measures. In spite of the fact that such accidental war scenarios are downgraded by some theorists as less probable than escalation and miscalculation, the possibility is not dismissed by many. As systems become larger and more complex, and as time passes there are certain probability factors that imply a false alarm, of which there have been several, coinciding with a malfunction and/or a hypersensitive crisis period leading to war or near war. Particularly unsettling is the possibility that a minor technical failure could call forth alerts that prompt snowballing counteralerts with the temptation to launch a preemptive strike.

Events have occurred in the past few years which both increase and decrease the probability of an accident occurring and of accidents turning into deadly exchanges. The potential presence, for example, of increasingly well equipped Russian missile submarines at some distance off of the American coastline effectively reduces the decision time any US President would have to react to *any* accident serious enough to be interpreted as a possible attack. Background political tensions would exacerbate this pressure. Moreover, the ever more tightly coupled strategic systems have made malfunctions in one segment prone to cause alarms in others (the *reverberation* phenomenon). Russia also has this coupling problem, as Bracken (1985: pp. 54-55) has observed.

On the positive side of the ledger, the probability of a climate of crisis from bad Russian-American relations appears to have lessened sharply as a result of the dizzying changes initiated by President Gorbachev and the devolution of power within Eastern Europe and now within the Soviet Union itself. Scenarios involving flashpoints of crisis in Central Europe that have served nuclear strategic gamesmen for nearly four decades (e.g. 'riots in East Germany leading to Soviet tank intervention and NATO alerts...') now appear ludicrously dated.

What is far less clear is whether or not the great shifts in the political tectonic plates of Europe will affect the Russian leaders' political stability. Especially disquieting is the potential for civil war or coups in Russia in the wake of secession movements or economic breakdown. The United States has shown considerable caution so far, although President Bush was able to refrain from statements of sympathy for minority peoples. If scenarios involving 'Brezhnev Doctrine' style invasions of East European reformist states or tactical nuclear weapons being rattled over Yugoslavia seem outdated, new scenarios of peril ultimately deriving from the improvisational, gambling nature of the Russian regime may have to be taken seriously.

Even had the political uncertainties of Eastern Europe not occurred, the opportunities for failures and emergency plans not measuring up are legion. Following are just some of the ways in which an accident-generated nuclear exchange might begin, particularly if coupled with a political crisis:

1. Computer failure contributing to false indication of attack.
2. Launch on warning after equipment failure indicating attack.
3. Launch on impact after accidental nuclear firing (although the launch might be very limited).
4. Human error advising an attack from radar indications.
5. Launch on warning through the recommendation of a secretary of defense who is preoccupied, overwrought or deranged and who believes an attack may be imminent.
6. Launch on warning through the recommendation of a secretary of defense who is badly advised or who panics after receiving faulty advice, believing an attack to be imminent.
7. Launch on warning through recommendation of a secretary of defense who is ideologically disposed to believe an intentional attack is possible.
8. Launch on warning because of catalytic (third party) attack.
9. Launch on warning through a president who is preoccupied overwrought or deranged, and believes an attack is imminent.
10. Launch on warning through a president who is badly advised or who panics because of bad advice.
11. Launch on warning through a president who is ideologically disposed to believe an intentional attack is possible.
12. Unauthorized launch through a rogue nuclear submarine commander.
13. Unauthorized launch through a nuclear submarine commander who is overwrought or under blackmail.
14. Accidental launch by the United States, combined with: a) ongoing crisis with Russia; b) Russian or CIS leadership problems/crisis; c) inability of President to communicate with Russian chief; d) temporary crisis among United States leadership; and e) Russian crisis with another country or catalytic attack.

Within the categories of Russian internal crisis in Russia (or Ukraine) complicating a nuclear system accident the following kinds of scenarios might be imagined:

1. *Deterioration* such as divisions within the government, or the military balking in handling an ethnic separatist crisis; civil conflict.
2. *Sudden death or incapacitation of the Russian head of state* leading to some breakdown of authority in Russia.
3. A *coup* in Russia.

As has recently become clear, such a possibility cannot be entirely dismissed, just as unprecedented or bizarre incidents affecting the American leadership cannot. In view of the strong tendency of American and Russian leaders to avoid interfering in the internal affairs of the other country, it might seem odd to consider the possibility of a kind of 'internal Serbia' pulling the United States unto a conflict with Russia over some serious threat by Moscow against a minority population. But in a time of fast breaking events and great fluidity in certain parts of the international system, such a case is not wholly inconceivable. As will be seen in the discussion that follows, one of the most dangerous misperceptions afflicting the Superpower leadership today is very likely to be that scenarios of the sort described above are impossible and, paradoxically, if possible, then difficult to do much about.

Thus, while many of these scenarios are thought to be extremely unlikely but in all hypothetical nuclear situations, the event for which the probability is so miniscule has potentially cataclysmic effects and the number of ways in which something might possibly go wrong, even at very small levels of likelihood, is disquieting. Such exaggerations as Murphy's Law - if something can go wrong, it will go wrong - need not predominate to make us uneasy about the status quo. Moreover, while a *large-scale* nuclear brawl occurring inadvertently or as a result of some technical mishap may itself be extremely improbable, a lesser exchange, say involving a few megatons on each side, is more probable and still catastrophic by historical standards.

When we attempt to guess about how likely the events leading to any number of historical occurrences was, we become amazed that so many seemingly improbable things have happened: the New York power blackouts of 1965 and 1977; the Three Mile Island and Chernobyl disasters; the Bhopal chemical plant tragedy; some of Hitler's aggressive moves, such as his 1938 Czech policies; US intelligence failures at Pearl Harbor and regarding the Chinese in

Korea in 1950, the Yom Kippur War, and the Iranian Revolution (1978); the background to the Cuban missile crisis, the 1968 invasion of Czechoslovakia, and the Falklands War, to name a few. Such cases involve varying mixes of human and machine error. But what must be remembered is that it would not take the triggering of an all out nuclear exchange for a nuclear weapons accident to be judged disastrous.

Any of the above listed accidental or inadvertent uses of nuclear weapons would pose a grave danger, even though the probability of their coming to pass might seem very small. Calculations have been done estimating that in spite of extensive post-mishap safety improvements, the likelihood of another Chernobyl or another Challenger-type disaster occurring eventually is quite high, and in the not-too-distant future higher than we would like. The same can be said for a nuclear weapons accident, with the consequences very probably worse than the Challenger and very possibly worse than Chernobyl. And if the time frame we are concerned with is the next thirty years, rather than simply one or two years, the possibilities are grim indeed.

Abrams (1988) has identified three major areas where 'accidents' might occur: failure of equipment, failure of the people operating systems, and situational variables (presence of terrorists, degree of proliferation, etc.). Most of the kinds of accidents we have listed fall into one of these categories. What is especially unsettling is that, although some of these accidents could be attributed to misperceptions (e.g. of a judgment-impaired president, secretary of defense, or submarine commander) there are other kinds of misperceptions that make *these* risk producers even riskier and more difficult to guard against. For the past eight years I have been doing research that pulls together many of the ideas on misperception advanced by Jervis, Janis, and others, applying them to historical cases, and advancing some new ideas on causes of error (Shiels, 1991).

These may be misperceptions stemming from: 1) the real nature of international politics; 2) the nature of the opponent; 3) the nature of the technology and safety of the system; 4) the nature of a crisis; and 5) ideological distortions ('Russia is willing to risk losing more lives than we.' 'China will back down before a threat to their communist system survivability.') What I want to do for the rest of the body of this analysis is outline five specific and representative types of misperception that seem to me particularly dangerous as catalysts of nuclear war.

Professor Cullberg's essay (Ch. 7) discusses a number of limits to rational behavior by leaders because of crisis stress and small and complex group organizational dynamics. My concern here is more with ongoing assumptions and misperceptions of leaders, and to a lesser extent societies, that interfere with preventing or coping with inadvertent nuclear war.

1. The assumption of rationality in an opponent or that the opponent has more information than is the case

We may reasonably assume from experience that the Russia's leadership will behave rationally in most cases and that it will be well informed in most cases (but not all). There are situations during leadership transition or illness that we cannot completely anticipate. Whether we regard the era in which the Soviets are thought of as adversaries to be over or not, there are still potential adversarial situations that could arise. And there are other countries besides Russia that the United States leadership could confront that might well be less rational or in possession of less information than the Russia (or the United States for that matter).

Although the ownership of nuclear weapons has been widely observed to have sobering, maturing effects on governments, the Indians, Pakistanis, Chinese, or later Israelis, Iraqis, North Koreans, South Africans or Iranians might well not have the inhibitions and safeguards on their nuclear systems that the Superpowers have had. Any government that sees its vital interests as threatened may be tempted to use its nuclear weapons, and the temptation may be higher if the weapons are much more limited in potential effect than those of the United States or the Soviet Union.

2. Underestimation or overestimation of hostility in another country

This misgauging of hostility levels presents a double bind to leaders and gives the critic the ability to 'damn them if they do and damn them if they don't.' It was assumed during the later, declining phases of the Cold War that great danger lay in overestimating the bad intentions of the Soviet Union (stemming from former President Reagan's image of the 'evil empire', for example). But the United States has also had *bad* experiences with failing to perceive the hostility and willingness to take risks of adversaries, either its own or those of allies. Japan (1941), North Korea and China (1950), the USSR and Cuba (1962), North Vietnam (1964-75), and Iran (1978) all in varying ways proved willing to throw down the gauntlet to the putatively mightiest power on the globe. The irony is that the lesson of such experiences - that surprise attacks can be quite successful and are to be expected - is probably exactly the wrong one to apply to nuclear preparedness (see below).

3. The assumption that the future will be like the past, that surprise attack must be avoided at all costs
The key phrase here is *at all costs*. A launch on warning or response to the wrong attacker could incur damage greater than the initial attack, even if real, would cause. The United States and the Soviet Union were damaged by surprise attacks in 1941. While the physical destruction wreaked by the Germans on the latter was incomparably greater than that by the Japanese on the former, the psychological effects of the assaults, in the minds of the Soviet and American military leaders, were not so different. It may be said that postwar world history has been shaped by the mindset created by these attacks as much as any single factor in existence. Trillions of dollars have been spent to insure that another surprise attack does not take place. This insurance has been purchased at a huge cost to the domestic development of both societies. The United States and particularly Russia have seen their living standards decline relative to Western Europe and Japan. The former spend about six and thirteen percent of their GNP on defense, respectively, the latter about three and one percent. Whatever the reality in 1950, in the 1990s the paramount danger to both sides is the existence of the complex and ferocious weapons systems themselves. One unsettling problem is that any response to *the perception* of an attack may be the wrong response. If one fails to respond to an actual attack, one has committed a Type I error (Intriligator and Brito, 1988: p. 15) If one responds with force to a non-attack or an accidental launch one has committed an even more tragic (Type II) error. To use any but the most minimal limited-objective tactical nuclear arms might may well be like fighting with hand-grenades in a telephone booth.

4. The assumption by leaders that they know what they need to know (and the same assumption by followers about leaders)
Scheer (1982) has reminded us that George Bush and Ronald Reagan have been quoted more than once as saying that under certain circumstances the use of nuclear weapons was more desirable than the alternatives. Both politicians are also on record as saying that the weapons must never be used. An illusion, but one that seems difficult to avoid, is thinking that competent leaders and well designed systems truly allow one to sleep soundly at night and to avoid peril by day. The United States 'learned' again and again after World War II that its leaders were inadequately informed and had inadequate means for dealing with big problems Cuba (1962), Vietnam (e.g. 1968), Iran (1978), the Middle East (1973), and deterrence in Korea (1950). The gravest aspect of the Cuban missile crisis was not the way in which American leaders reacted to the problem of the missiles, but the way that a series of errors and faulty assumptions allowed the problem to unfold in the first place.

5. The assumption by leaders that there are sufficient safeguards against accidental nuclear war or provocative accidental use of nuclear weapons
Abundant evidence has been provided by research that both strictly accidental and *inadvertent* nuclear weapons use, perhaps leading to war, are an entirely possible, if not highly probable occurrence. There is very little evidence, that leaders are aware of these dangers, perhaps because leaders are not likely to convey doubts about such things. Presidents, for example, like corporate CEOs and airline pilots seem almost programmed to project a public image of cool confidence about the potential dangers of their product or service. It is entirely possible that presidents themselves have been unaware or dimly aware of many of the safety aspects of the nuclear network including C^3I, the weapons systems and their operators. The essential and sobering difference to keep in mind is that while, for example, the explosion of a Ford Pinto on impact or a faulty Boeing 747 body may have been somewhat more likely than the misuse of an atomic weapon, the magnitude of the disaster that the latter could involve is incomparably greater.

The implication of these and many other sorts of misperceptions is grave as analyses by Betts (1982) and Wohlstetter (1962) suggest.

There are simply limits to leadership judgments and abilities to act quickly on the 'right' patterns of information out of the kaleidoscope which is presented to them in a crisis. In his concluding analysis in *Surprise Attack* Betts (1982: pp. 288-289) points out some of the limitations on preventing the unexpected:

> Inadequacies in warning are rarely due to the absence of anyone in the system ringing an alarm. Usually the problem is either that a conceptual consensus rejects the alarm for political or strategic reasons outside the framework of military indicators or that false alarms dull the impact at the real moment of crisis. The first problem cannot be averted by organizational change, because it is an intellectual and cultural phenomenon that transcends differences in structure and process. The second cannot be prevented because it occurs at the enemy's pleasure.

While this is not precisely the problem in preventing accidental warfare, it is very similar. Past false alarms may appear to increase vigilance and precaution, but in fact do not have that effect in specific situations. And if the political leaders of the Nuclear Powers do not see accidental war as a top priority threat, then suggestions about fine tuning the network of checks and precautions will not bear much fruit.

2. Conclusion

In my own research into what I call 'preventable disasters' and government leaders' readiness to deal with crisis, I use the analogy of a commercial airline pilot preparing for a flight. There are basically three categories of mishaps that can occur: 1) potential *natural disaster* causes such as clear air turbulence, wind shear, or fog that can only be prepared for in a limited sort of way; 2) *deep structural features*, not only within the aircraft itself ('hidden defects') but within the system in which the airplane will fly (such as poor location or condition of airports in foreign countries and officials' lack of success in rectifying this); and 3) relatively *preventable disasters* such as failure to go through careful pre-flight procedures, consumption of alcohol by crew members, etc.

The third group is clearly the area in which the pilot has the most control. So it is with the Washington and Moscow (and to some extent London, Paris, and Beijing) leaders' ability to prevent inadvertent nuclear war. It is very difficult in the short term to change givens such as the huge size of arsenals and numbers of fallible human beings and breakable machines that manage them. But it is possible to come to certain realizations and in turn put into practice procedures that will make flight through the next few years safer. Consider the following:

1. Nuclear Powers like the United States have long recognized that the sort of nuclear roulette played in the 1950s and early 1960s is no longer feasible. Opponents cannot be underrated and a range of sub-nuclear measures to counter threats should be available. It is essential that this sobriety and assumption that the atomic option is really not an option at all in Superpower relations - if in any relations - be institutionalized. The leaders of all the Nuclear Powers should make clear that the only conceivable use of the weapons is as a deterrent to a mortal attack.

2. It is tempting in the face of what seem to be abrupt, profound changes, to imagine that high-risk confrontations with Russia are obsolete. Both Yeltsin's position in Russia and that of the countries surrounding are not absolutely secure. There are also tinder boxes in the Middle East, which, if not as closely interwoven with Soviet-US relations as was the case twenty years ago, still have the potential for crisis. The most powerful factor going against the occurrence of another nuclear war is probably the lesson, learned in World War II and reinforced in Vietnam, that high cost conflicts have become unacceptable. This slow alteration of consciousness is profound and undergirds much of the movement toward minimum deterrence, that is that small numbers of terror weapons are more than sufficient to make purposeful war extremely unlikely.

3. Every incoming president should emphasize to the intelligence community and the strategic command and control network that any sign of weakness in the network should be reported as a top priority and errors should be on the side of caution. If this seems self evident, the surprises of the successful Soviet ICBM launches of 1957 as well as the 1962 Cuban missile emplacement

underscore the fact that Soviet advances are not always appreciated in a timely fashion.

More recently, the vulnerability of the system to false alarms and component failures, as well as the accidental silo explosion of a Titan missile in Arkansas point to the need for constant re-evaluation and the application of new sorts of evaluation with every incoming administration and perhaps in every year.

4. *Defensive avoidance* of incipient nuclear problems appears unlikely but multiple, competing intelligence sources, political as well as mechanical, need to be operating constantly.

5. A White House unit, formal or informal but with a clear sense of mission, should be detailed to be on the lookout for crises with nuclear potential and should go into a heightened state of readiness whenever the president is preoccupied with intensive negotiations such as Camp David and SALT or domestic political crises such as Watergate. It is essential that this group have nuclear crisis prevention as its central mission, and be independent of more general White House support duties. For example, if President Carter's pre-Camp David staff had also to deal with strategic preparedness in the broadest sense, it would not have been able to perform one task without jeopardizing the other and thus would not have been able to meet the standards we are asking for.

6. Governments must be especially cautious about reaction to nuclear yellow lights when there is a political crisis. There is the risk of a false alarm syndrome in which recent perceived threats which do not materialize lower a country's guard. This is unlikely in the case of nuclear preparedness, but should be watched for, as well as the opposite danger of overreacting (or, worse, launching on warning because of recent tensions). The suggestion made by Richard Betts (1985) and others (i.e. the Nunn-Warner study groups) of nuclear risk reduction centers within the Soviet Union and the United States that would specialize in warning each other about fears or possibly controversial intentions within the governments, seemed especially promising, although it has not yet been implemented in the way it was originally intended.

7. The capability of recalling or destroying nuclear missiles after launch should be added to every offensive missile in the Superpowers' inventory.

8. There should be a special unit within the CIA assigned to monitoring leaders of all important powers and any potential nuclear state for signs of instability, deteriorating health or irregular behavior. There is no guarantee, of course that such a unit will not miss the mark on occasion, it is again a matter of reducing the odds. There is also no guarantee that knowing a leader's condition will in any way lesson his ability to do harm, but at least it will provide a chance so to do.

9. United States pluralism is the best guard against ideology obscuring prudent nuclear decision-making. Ideologues such as Forrestal, Dulles, and Reagan have always been tempered by more circumspect voices along side of them. And in spite of national chauvinism and anachronistic jingoism, not to mention the military/industrial network, a number of sober arms control constituencies in the media, academia, the scientific community and elsewhere have built a broad enough base of support to insure that politicians will find nuclear arms control initiatives and crisis avoidance bring unambiguous domestic political rewards.

In spite of the wisdom of such general improvements in the process, they are offered with the knowledge that the irrational individual and group barrier to full preparedness makes implementation of most of them unlikely. The kind of dulled, repressed consciousness of most of the citizens of the world regarding the acute and unprecedented hazard of nuclear weapons described so well by Jonathan Schell (1982: pp. 148-156) is only very slowly being changed. The best we may be able to hope for is diligent work by the relatively more conscious on a number of fronts: in weapons system safeguards, in risk reduction strategies, in build down and weapons reduction efforts, in moves to reduce tensions and areas of conflict such as are sporadically occurring today, in improved processes for screening leaders and improving permissive action links.

It is daunting to realize that even if all of the recommendations of recent writers and conferences on this subject were adopted, the chance of a weapons-related accident occurring in our complex massive systems over time is a very real one and that there is a possibility, remote or otherwise, that such a failure could trigger a much wider unintended use of 'unusable' arms that we might or might not live to regret.

Chapter 9

The Time Factor

Francesco Calogero

Possession of the operational capability to respond to a nuclear attack in extremely short times (less than half an hour from first alert to final decision) is still deemed essential, presumably by both Superpowers. This causes a potential danger, of which the public and decision-makers are perhaps insufficiently aware; while the justifications for maintaining such an operational capability appear nowadays highly questionable.

In this chapter the following points will be discussed:

1. In the USA - and almost certainly, in the Soviet Union as well - a sophisticated and expensive system is maintained, to provide (at least in theory) the capability to decide and execute a large scale nuclear strike within an extremely short response time - of the order of half an hour or less.
2. The maintenance of such a capability is unnecessary, even if one believes that nuclear weapons are essential to deter war.
3. Such a situation increases the risk of a catastrophic use of nuclear weapons.
4. The public - and probably most decision-makers as well - are largely unaware of this situation. Once informed, they are likely to want to change it.

Of the three main components of strategic nuclear arsenals - submarine-launched ballistic missiles (SLBMs), long range bombers, land-based intercontinental ballistic missiles (ICBMs) - the most worrisome component from the point of view of quick launch are the ICBMS, followed by the bombers. The submarine-based missiles, both because of their essential invulnerability and because of the difficulty to communicate with them in real time, are not supposed to respond quickly in the case of a nuclear attack against their countries. The SLBMs now pose other serious risks relevant to the possible catastrophic use of nuclear weapons, inasmuch as the unauthorized launch of their nuclear missiles is not prevented by Permissive Action Links (PALs); but this danger could be eliminated by installing appropriate PALs on their missiles, suitable to exclude unauthorized use (even by a conspiracy of the complete crew of the submarine, or any group that might take over the boat), but adequate to guarantee that the missiles would be certainly capable to retaliate against a nuclear attack to their countries (this is *not* a time urgent task). It is important to emphasize that SLBMs provide by themselves a capability of assured destruction that is certainly more than adequate to underwrite deterrence.

For the bombers, a capability of quick response might have some justification - namely, be less risky - since it does not necessarily imply the initiation of a nuclear attack. The bombers now have the operational capability to get off the ground in a very short time (less than half an hour), but they would then go to preassigned destinations outside of the borders of the target country, and wait there in a flight pattern so as to minimize the danger that they be destroyed. Only after receiving an additional specific order from the National Command Authority, backed by appropriately coded signals to unlock the PALs installed on the nuclear weapons they carry, would they proceed to their assigned targets. Hence, for the bombers, the decision to be taken within an extremely short time (less than half an hour) would be only to get them in the air; the fatal decision to deliver the nuclear weapons to their targets could wait. However, just because of this, the decision to get them off the ground can be taken at a lesser level than the supreme one (in the USA, by the general in temporary command at the Strategic Air Command Headquarters in Omaha), and with less justification (just because the consequences would not necessarily be catastrophic; indeed, there are known examples when such a decision has indeed been taken, on the basis of false alarms); and thereafter the fatal decision - to end our civilization - would have to be taken within a short, if not extremely short, time (a few hours at most).

In the case of ICBMs, the situation is much more dangerous, since, once launched, they cannot be recalled or stopped. For this component of the strategic triad, which carries more than enough nuclear weapons to cause 'the end of civilization,' there is now the operational capability to bring about such a final catastrophe within a response time of less than half an hour. Indeed, an enormous investment of equipment and manpower is in place, precisely to maintain such an operational capability to launch within a time shorter than those taken by the missiles of the adversary to fly their course - or rather, shorter than the time that might elapse between the first warning of an attack and the actual impact of the attacking missiles - a time which is less than half an hour for incoming ICBMs, and may indeed shrink to a quarter of an hour or even less in the case of incoming SLBMs.

The maintenance of such a capability is unnecessary, even if one believes that nuclear weapons play an essential role in deterring nuclear war. Indeed the enormous destructive capabilities of nuclear weapons and the characteristics of the nuclear arsenals guarantee that, even after having absorbed a first strike by all the nuclear forces of the other side, it would still be possible to inflict on the society of the adversary an absolutely unacceptable damage by a retaliatory second strike, using only the forces that would surely have survived the attack (including most of the submarines). There is, therefore, no need to envisage a launch of missiles - or even to get the bombers in the air - within the extremely short time that might elapse between the first warning that a nuclear attack is on its way and the actual arrival of it.

A clear confirmation of this was provided some time ago by Robert McNamara, who stated publicly that he had advised both of the US Presidents under whom he served as secretary of defense - Kennedy and Johnson - that if they ever got the information that a nuclear weapon had been detonated on the territory of the USA (not just the news that a hostile missile was on its way!), they should authorize no action in retaliation without having waited at least 24 hours and having inspected personally the purported location alleged to have been hit by the nuclear weapon. This advice was presumably more symbolic than meant to be taken literally; it clearly implied the message to avoid by all means any hasty reaction. Evidently McNamara considered the danger implicit in the plan to make a hasty decision more risky than a policy to 'wait and see'. He, of course, knew that no adversary had in any case the capability to 'disarm' the USA. And it should be emphasized that such an assessment is as valid now - for both the USA and the USSR - as at the time when McNamara was serving as US secretary of defense; and it will remain true even after very substantial progress has been made towards nuclear disarmament - especially if such progress is made in the most reasonable way, namely giving priority to the elimination of the nuclear weapons more suited to a first strike role, such as highly MIRVed ICBMs.

Why then is such a major effort made - presumably by both Superpowers - to retain the capability of a quick response? Let me suggest one good reason, and two 'real' reasons.

A good reason is that retention by either side - at least theoretically - of the option to launch on warning or under attack, makes any plan by the other side to effect a disarming first strike even more impossible than it would be otherwise. This, of course, contributes - albeit only marginally; 'more impossible' is tantamount to 'impossible,' is it not? - to reinforce strategic stability, hence to lessen the risk of nuclear war. Whether the cost in terms of equipment and manpower - and especially whether the trade-offs in terms of increased danger of accidental nuclear war (see below) - justify the attempt to retain such an option is, however, questionable.

A reason that probably plays a much more important role (a 'real reason') in explaining why so much effort is invested in retaining a (theoretical) capability to respond in extremely short times to a nuclear attack is the ingrained tendency to plan for the last war rather than the next one (or, to put it more politely, to base one's planning on sound, verified, experience - even if in the meantime it has become quite obsolete). This reason is probably particularly relevant both for the US, because of the Pearl Harbor experience, and for the USSR, because of their disastrous lack of preparedness when they were attacked by Hitler's troops in 1941.

Another 'real' reason is the strong desire to retain an important strategic role for the ICBMs, and especially for the long range bombers, in spite of their vulnerability. The fundamental motivation for this wish can, in my opinion, be found in the rivalries among different sectors of the armed forces (typically, the Air Force versus the Navy), and also in the kind of sentimental/prestige attachment of Air Force generals - all of them pilots - for bombers (which are indeed - especially the very modern ones - wonderful toys!). But to mention such motivations is considered very bad form; so that they never receive the attention they deserve. The justification for retaining ICBMs and bombers - in spite of their vulnerability, which is clearly a liability with respect to strategic stability (the more so, the larger the number of nuclear warheads that each MIRVed ICBM, or each bomber, carries) - is rather framed in terms of such fanciful imagery as the notion that 'it is dangerous to put all one's eggs into a single basket.' (Incidentally, there is a simple way to maintain - if one deems this essential - a stabilizing deterrent role also for ICBMs, notwithstanding their vulnerability: an agreed transition to a universal regime of single warhead payloads - i.e. no MIRVs. In such a regime, no valid motivation would remain to maintain the capability to launch the ICBMs on warning or under attack, since a 'counterforce' attack aimed at the ICBMs of the adversary - even if it were 100 percent successful, i.e. no misses - would deplete the arsenal of *both* sides of the *same* number of warheads.)

The existence of an elaborate machinery having the purpose to provide to the top decision-maker - to the National Command Authority - in each Superpower the capability to decide and execute, in less than half an hour, a nuclear strike that would signify the end of our civilization, constitutes an evident danger. This should be rather obvious to any reasonable person. It is of course likely that, under normal circumstances - namely, in a situation of low international tension - such a capability would be more theoretical than practical; presumably if the top decision-maker were taken by a sudden fit of madness under such circumstances, he would not succeed in bringing about the end of our world even if he tried. There must be in place an adequate number of 'negative' checks to prevent this - one hopes. But the very fact that the theoretical capability to launch within extremely short times (minutes!) is nevertheless considered essential, and therefore must be kept (at least virtually) operational, implies that these negative checks cannot be too stringent. And human errors are always possible; indeed, in this very context, some are known to have occurred, many others have probably occurred which are not known. And in any case - most importantly - the situation becomes intrinsically much more dangerous in time of crisis, if the whole machinery is poised to respond in such short times.

It is of course possible to play down the risks on the basis of the record so far - no nuclear weapon has ever been accidentally launched nor exploded (we are told). But this argument is obviously silly; it reminds me of the story of the man who fell from the top of an 80-floor skyscraper, and as he was passing by the 30th floor was telling himself: 'so far, all is OK.'

A precise assessment of the probability that a catastrophe can occur is of course difficult. But there can be little doubt that such a probability is very much increased by any arrangement that envisages - and that maintains the operational capability - to decide the irretrievable launch of nuclear armed missiles in times as short as a few minutes. Moreover, this is surely a context in which 'worst case analysis' should be applied; and an assessment based on consistent use of this methodology - i. e. based on the assumption not only that anything that might go wrong will go wrong, but that surely there are many more things that might go wrong without anybody having thought of them in advance - would surely advise most strongly against the maintenance of any machinery poised to destroy our world within minutes.

The public - and probably most decision-makers as well - are unaware of this situation. A reason for this is, that the precise arrangements regulating the release procedures for nuclear weapons are classified. But this fact should not prevent the public from making its voices heard on these matters. In the first place, a discussion based on the kind of arguments outlined above (requiring no access to classified data) is quite adequate to arrive at reasoned conclusions. And secondly, the onus to convince us that the present situation entails no danger should be with those who know the details - with the clear understanding that no blank statement by them, to the effect that the present arrangements are sufficiently safe, should be considered sufficient (indeed, the more I am told that everything is safe, the more I worry...), unless it can be backed by a detailed description of the technical foundations for such a conclusion (at least by describing very explicitly the kind of independent review procedures and tests that have been undertaken by experts having a strong institutional interest vested in finding the system at fault rather than in pronouncing it safe).

In conclusion, I would like to suggest, as an important task for all of us who are concerned with the situation, to raise these issues again and again, and to disseminate as widely as possible the basic information on these matters; including the crucial role likely to be played by the *time factor*.

Every reasonable individual - I would think - will be shocked to know how things stand in this respect; and also to know how unjustified this situation is from a strategic point of view.

In countries ruled by decision-makers selected through a democratic process, the continual airing of these issues should force them to listen, and to act. Of course a major responsibility in this respect is with the citizens, and the rulers, of the countries that possess nuclear weapons, primarily the two Superpowers. But since a nuclear war would have catastrophic consequences for all humankind, - all citizens of the world, and all decision-makers worldwide, have a responsibility in this respect, to be exercised through the United Nations, through other international organizations (for instance, the military alliances), through grassroots initiatives, and in all other possible ways. Survival is at stake.

Chapter 10

The Psychology of Risk Compensation and its Implications for Accidental Nuclear War

Morris Bradley

This chapter focuses on a single issue: risk compensation and its implications. The probability of accidental nuclear war may be much higher than we have assumed because of psychologically induced risk compensation. There is new evidence that raises the question whether safety devices and procedures designed to reduce the probability of catastrophic accidents to extremely low levels could also have a contrary effect on the personnel involved, encouraging risk-taking. The second part of the chapter outlines the implications of this possibility.

In previous writing I have argued that psychology has a key role in many questions concerned with peace issues (Bradley, 1986a, 1986b, 1987a, 1987b, 1987c & 1988a). I have assembled evidence that human factors are an essential part of any attempt to understand the problems we face and that psychology can already offer many of the answers we need. In this essay I focus on risk compensation because it should make us reconsider both the deployment of nuclear weapons, and many other modern technological developments, that are based on the presumption that the probabilities of catastrophic accidents can be reduced to negligible levels. Notice how the word 'negligible' is commonly used as synonymous with a zero level of probability of accident - the word is apt because it is indeed negligent to disregard such risks.

1. The theory of risk compensation

In everyday life people constantly take risks, varying their behavior according to their perception of probabilities and consequences. The process is not limited to conscious decisions involving danger: almost everything we do or say involves subtle shifts of responsiveness to the

157

information and opportunities we encounter. The theory of risk compensation suggests that people behave as if they have an unconscious risk-setting scale, or adjustable reference point, representing the level of risk that they will tolerate in a particular set of circumstances. This setting is adjusted in accordance with information they receive from their perceptions regarding the risk, for example when they observe what happens when that risk is taken. Even at an unconscious level, the results of experience could make a subtle shift towards perceiving a particular risk to be greater, so that the appropriate risk-setting is then adjusted, as it were, to a new point. At any particular risk-setting, the theory predicts that a person will increase the risk taken until it reaches that point (since there are usually gains from this) and similarly, decrease risks being taken if they exceed that point. Hence, if a person perceives that the risk in certain circumstances has been reduced for some reason, the theory predicts that a compensatory increase in risk-taking will occur, in order to maximize gains, as if using a risk-setting reference point.

When this theory is presented, with its emphasis on the human involvement in risks, it may seem self-evident. So it is important to remember how little attention has been paid to this kind of human psychology when decisions have been taken to risk deploying nuclear weapons or developing modern technology. In the section below, the resistance of professional engineers and safety planners to the ideas of risk compensation is also discussed.

2. Evidence for risk compensation

It may help to begin with some illustrations of risk compensation that I hope will be memorable. In the 1970s, I was chairman of the Scottish Association for Public Transport, campaigning for a more enlightened transport policy because I was appalled by the simplistic assumptions on which government policies were based and the damage that was being done. I challenged the policy assumption that narrow, winding roads are dangerous and therefore widening and straightening them would result in fewer accidents. Psychologically this was simplistic because it assumed that drivers would not compensate for the changes by driving faster, or further, or more often.

John Adams,[28] a Risk and Transport Analyst at the Transport and Road Research Laboratory in the UK, pointed out that test crashes of cars containing dummies do demonstrate that seat belts offer protection in an accident but do not take account of the perception of greater safety which can lead to less careful driving through risk compensation. He argues that the most convincing interpretation of official road accident statistics is that they have varied with changes in economic prosperity, so that reductions in accidents following the introduction of seat belts by some countries shortly after the 1973 OPEC oil price rises were part of a previous trend and cannot be attributed to the use of seat beats. In fact, those countries which did *not* introduce belts at that time actually observed even greater reductions than those that did. Moreover, since the introduction of seat belts in the UK, accidents to cyclists and pedestrians have increased, including accidents to pedestrians when they are on pavements.

Risk compensation does not necessarily mean that drivers would begin to drive much more recklessly. Adams points out that at the time when it was claimed in Britain that the introduction of seat belts would save a thousand lives a year, drivers were travelling approximately 250 billion kilometres/year. So this saving in lives would require only one fewer fatal accident in every 250 million kilometres travelled. Conversely, risk compensation after the introduction of seat belts would only need to change driving behavior in a subtle, marginal manner to raise the fatalities an equivalent proportion.

Recommendations by Adams, based on risk compensation, were recently accepted by the planning authorities in Stroud, where a road 'improvement' scheme has been abandoned. It would have straightened and widened a road with a junction in a residential area, removing many mature trees to give better sightlines. He established that the accident record at this junction was no worse than at other junctions and that drivers typically exceed the statutory speed limit on the wide roads approaching this section, but reduce speed as they approach these bends. He argued that the trees and curve of the road were accurately perceived by drivers as increasing the risks so they compensated by slowing down. Without these features, the vehicles

---

[28] Adams, John 1990. 'Only Dummies Don't Take Risks'. *Antenna*, BBC 2 Television.

would probably not slow down and the danger of accidents at the junction could be greater than at present. Adams commented that 'Safety features can protect dummies but real people are not dummies. Real people are risk-takers and they respond to changes in risk. Safety planning that ignores this lesson will not only fail to achieve its objectives, it very often produces results which are not desired.'

There is an important qualification to be made to this argument. Many attempts to improve safety problems, such as redesigned road junctions, do reduce the number of accidents at a particular junction. This is probably because they eliminate some source of misinformation or misperception that causes an error of judgment. In these cases, the safety improvement is welcome and can be verified from the accident record at that junction.

However, it is still important to ask whether a compensatory increase in risk-taking can occur elsewhere, since the perception of the overall safety limits of the route as a whole will have been affected. Similarly, human errors caused by aircraft instrument panels can be identified and certainly accidents should be reduced by redesigning the panels, but there is also the problem that pilots may compensate for the perceived reduction in instrument error by being less careful in other ways.

Wiel Janssen at the TNO Institute for Perception in the Netherlands has tested the risk compensation theory experimentally and claims that it can produce quite substantial effects. He invited drivers who habitually do not use seat belts, to drive a test car equipped with sophisticated recording devices. They were asked to drive on a section of motorway and ordinary roads, and then through a slalom type of test, and finally they were asked to drive as fast as possible towards an imitation stationary vehicle, braking just in time to avoid hitting it. The drivers undertook the task twice, without a seat belt and wearing one. The sample tested so far is small but significant differences were found. Although these drivers did not habitually use a seat belt, when they were tested wearing one, they drove on average three kilometers per hour faster, braked later, and displayed more aggression. This is compatible with the hypothesis that they perceived the seat belt as decreasing their risks and that they compensated by increasing their risk-taking proportionately. There are more complex interpretations of the results that have to be eliminated but this indicates how research can test the theory of risk compensation.

There has been a vast amount of research in psychology based on the concept of optimal arousal systems and the psychological means of increasing arousal, including risk-taking. Zuckerman (1971, 1978 & 1979) investigated sensation seeking and identifies four types: thrill and adventure seeking in dangerous sports; experience seeking which can lead to unforeseen dangers; disinhibition or the need to act freely in social settings such as drinking, parties, changing sexual partners; and boredom susceptibility- restlessness and aversion when there is no variation of experience.

Berlyne's classic psychological research (1970) explored the motivation to seek excitement, or arousal, in risk-taking, for example in the voluntary risks taken by rock climbers. He suggested that people react to monotony and boredom by seeking to maintain an optimal level of arousal. People may even seek danger as an arousal-jag: a form of psychological stimulant. Experiencing extreme surrogate dangers through the entertainment media, which is so universally popular, may serve this purpose without involving real risks. This approach is shared by Michael Thompson (1980 & 1983), an anthropologist at the Musgrave Institute who is also a rock climber. He has pointed out that there have been many improvements to equipment, making climbing much safer, but the climbers have probably made risk compensations by attempting more dangerous rock faces and indeed, the accident rate has remained about the same as before.

The question whether there are personality differences so that some people are inclined to take much greater risks than others, is complicated by the ease with which we all switch between high and low risk behavior as circumstances seem to dictate (Douglas, 1986). What is clear from countless examples, is that in certain circumstances, some people who may not have given any previous indications of this tendency, can take actions that place themselves and many other people at extreme risk (Dickerson, 1984 & 1987; Dixon, 1976 & 1987). So it would be a mistake to conclude from the theory of risk compensation that we can depend upon people to become cautious whenever risks seem to be very great.

3. Resistance to the theory of risk compensation

At this stage there is enough evidence to warrant risk compensation being taken as a serious possibility because, if it is substantiated, it will invalidate the assumptions underlying many human enterprises that could have profound long-term consequences. Risk-taking in the broadest sense of subtle behavioral changes mediated by shifts in perceived probabilities and pay-offs (of which we may not be aware), is ubiquitous in human behavior and that of many other species. For many years, developments in psychological research have revealed more and more complex brain functions and it would be no surprise if risk compensation is found to be among them, since it would enhance survival chances during evolution. Of course, risk compensation may vary in magnitude depending on differing circumstances and individuals but the phenomenon would be expected to be a general one emanating from fundamental brain capacities rather than a quirk of behavior, only appearing in certain contexts.

Most safety engineers and planners have been hostile to the theory of risk compensation. Thompson says that this is because 'if it were true it would completely destroy the whole framework, the whole theory, on which they are basing and justifying their decisions.'

This is very significant with regard to accidental nuclear war and other modern technological developments which are justified on the basis that there is no risk involved.

4. Risk compensation and accidental nuclear war

To establish that risk compensation does increase the risks involved in accidental nuclear war, we have to establish ways in which humans can influence the probability of its occurrence. Few people would be happy to make the massive nuclear retaliation upon which deterrence theory is based, a fully automated, launch on warning system. Even if it were, humans would be involved in design, manufacture, deployment, testing, and maintenance. At present, human error is possible in the command structures and at the interface with nuclear weapons, where safety procedures, maintenance, testing, and checking, etc., could allow opportunities for people to take psychologically induced risks. In practice, many of these procedures involve monotony and boredom. The greater the emphasis on multiple checking procedures, designed to try to reduce the risks to zero, the greater the probability will be that those procedures will be perceived to be highly redundant, unnecessary, and costly by the people who have to carry them out. Human ingenuity is never used to better effect than when devising means of avoiding long hours of tedious and apparently pointless work.

It takes little imagination to realize that all safety systems or procedures involving people are vulnerable to subversion and so in practice the risks involved must always exceed those derived from theoretical assumptions. These are not necessarily conscious, extravagant risks, but may be marginal lapses, short-cuts, etc. which seem insignificant, given the high overall perception of safety and risk compensation. In theory, the risks of accidents with nuclear weapons have been presumed to be negligible because it has been assumed that all the procedures were infallible and would be followed meticulously, though such perfection would be historically unique. In reality, of course, it is apparent that errors are possible and malpractices can develop. In complex systems, unpredictable circumstances can arise in which apparently trivial lapses and deviations from perfection can act synergistically, perhaps through extraordinary coincidences, and increase the risks very greatly. If risk compensation theory is valid, human fallibility is likely to create far greater risks than was previously thought and the probability of accidental nuclear war can no longer be considered negligible.

The question should also be asked as to how could such an implausible assumption, that the safety systems offer perfect protection, have received official approval. Perhaps the public in general is capable of believing anything that they wish to be true, shutting out of consciousness what they fear, by psychological denial. Are we to conclude that this also applies to the most senior decision-makers? If so, what does that imply for planning the future of our planet?

5. The implications of risk compensation

The possibility of risk compensation reinforces the conclusion that the risks associated with the technological developments of the second half of the twentieth century - epitomized by accidental nuclear war - are not only quantitatively greater than the risks of previous decades, but are also qualitatively different. The unprecedented increase in the severity of the consequences of these risks, goes far beyond everyone's experience and beyond most people's powers of imagination. Not surprisingly, adequate words to express such horrors are not available but I will call them *planet-critical* consequences, to try to emphasize that they could take civilization, as we know it on this planet, past the point of recovery. Since these challenges are qualitatively different from anything in our past experience, the appropriate human responses must also be qualitatively different from the ways in which we have responded in the past.

6. The need for a qualitative change in risk perception

We need to recognize how ill-equipped we are as a species to make the necessary changes. The biology of subhuman species shows how risk-taking is highly rewarded for the successful. Our own evolutionary history makes us as a species highly adapted to a life of constant risk-taking. Sometimes we are more cautious, but only to a degree: young or old, habitual risk-taking is the universal experience we share, at work, at play, and in all areas of human relations. As individuals we seem to use risk-taking as a means of testing our competence, a process we can see developing in children from the earliest age. Have we perhaps endangered the future of the planet simply through displays of virility? Daring risk-takers are highly rewarded and admired in most cultures but cautiousness certainly does not have a sexy image. How then can we respond appropriately to modern technology which has created such unprecedented risks? Collectively, we have to understand that certain types of risk can be rejected completely: it is at least theoretically possible to dismantle weapons systems and industrial processes. This may precipitate crises and may be very threatening to many people. However, the question at issue is, do we make the appropriate response to planet-critical risks our imperative and then tackle the problems of human adjustment, or do we let the human difficulties take precedence and fail to eliminate the planet-critical risks? The choice depends on our attitudes and values.

7. A formula for constructing a new attitude

To respond appropriately to risks such as that of accidental nuclear war, we need to construct a totally new attitude: to find a way of thinking that we have not known before. I wish to propose a formula for constructing this new attitude. We should examine each example of modern technology - nuclear weapons are by no means the only ones we need to examine - and ask the question, what is the *worst consequence* that could possibly happen as a result of this technological process or product, if everyone concerned with it, or able to help in such an insane task, were to *devote their best efforts to making that catastrophe happen*? Then we have to make ourselves imagine and examine that catastrophe in its fullest manifestation and with all its repercussions and ask ourselves whether this possibility is acceptable and whether it cannot be compatible with a viable future for humanity. If it seems excessive to postulate the worst case outcome we should question whether our judgment is subject to risk compensation in this instance too, because an understanding of human fallibility should force us to recognise that the worst case could occur.

If the answer is *yes*, then we can begin the traditional discussions which attempt to balance the advantages of that product of technology, against the costs of such a catastrophe, taking into account the probability of occurrence.

But if the answer is *no*, then we must recognise that this is a case where the traditional analysis cannot be used. If any of the products of modern technology is identified as capable of producing a catastrophe which cannot be acceptable, then we must adopt a new attitude and make a new response to it. The temptation will be to reassure ourselves that the risk is negligible because there are so many ample safeguards. But that is precisely the error that we should identify from the lessons of risk compensation. The risk may seem small, but compensation will constantly act in ways that increase it. The conclusion is inexorable, such an example of modern technology, no matter how attractive its advantages may be, cannot be acceptable. There is only one way to try to reduce an unacceptable risk to zero and that is dismantling and dispersing the materials involved.

This formula requires great courage because we have to imagine and admit the most appalling future possibilities, and in doing so, recognise our own weakness and vulnerability. Undertaking the task of removing and preventing these unacceptable risks, in the face of widespread hostility, requires confidence combined with realism. Without confidence we will despair, without realism we will lose the sense of urgency. To gain confidence we need to explore the cooperative processes by which we may be able to succeed (Bradley, 1989a & 1989b; Bradley & Smoker, 1988).

8. Helping the attitude change

To communicate these ideas and help a new attitude to evolve, we need to offer people the most vivid analogies. One way of illustrating the plight of humanity, can be found in the way that insects become caught and pollinate the plant *Arum Maculatum*. This has a specialized trumpet-shaped corolla or flower, called a spathe. Insects land on the relatively flat, slippery lips of the spathe, which curve inward and downward. As the insect moves around on the gently increasing slope of the surface, a position can be reached where the slope has become just too steep for recovery. Inevitably the insect will then drop down into the inner parts of the flower, brushing through a screen of interior hairs that prevents return. Happy for the insects, by the time that their pollen has been dislodged and the flowers own pollen has taken its place, the hairs have withered and the insects do finally escape.

We are behaving in an analogous way to these insects. Our confidence in our ability to take risks is confirmed by our daily experience. Self-esteem and competitiveness are involved. We feel able to put right any damage we may cause accidentally. What we are failing to see is that there has been a gradual, hardly perceptible change in the nature of the risks we have taken with modern technology. The new planet-critical risks we face are analogous to the steepening slopes of the spathe on which the insects move prior to the sudden drop down into the plant. Scientists who are familiar with systems theory (Damgaard, 1987; Wooldridge, 1980), and especially catastrophe modelling are aware of more complex hazards. For example, the possibility of starting a positive feedback process whereby hidden effects of our maltreatment of the planet may reach a planet-critical point of no return, before we become aware of the dangers. Just as the scientists and engineers who produced the apparently safe CFCs did not anticipate that they could damage the ozone layer.

Not every story ends with the insects escaping. If we intend to deal with the condition of our planet seriously, we need to face the necessity for extremely onerous decisions, based on the imperative that decisive actions on many issues cannot be postponed. Since these actions are very likely to be incompatible with current levels of consumerism, and certainly not with the aspirations of the rapidly growing world population, implementing them will mean a major crisis for democracy. I can only imagine one condition, in which the whole of humanity might be able to accept such stark decisions, and that is through the recognition that the costs must be shared equitably so that the burden can be borne cooperatively. The reward we can offer, if we succeed in this task of apparent sacrifice and loss of material prosperity, is that successful cooperation and equity can transform human relations, so we may witness the evolution of a new culture which surpasses materialistic values.

The most obvious characteristic of our age is the exponential speed of change. Humans attitudes have typically reflected rather slow adaptation and indeed, resistance to changes of the cooperative kind I am proposing. Can we discover, in the few years we may have left, the new attitudes needed to take us beyond this age of confrontation, risk of accidental nuclear war, environmental destruction, and violence within and between nations? We also know that humans can adapt very rapidly when self-interest is awakened. As I have argued elsewhere (Bradley, 1990), the task is one for which psychology is highly relevant: presenting cooperation and shared responsibility for the planet's future, to the world community, in such a way that they elicit enlightened, or even a self-interested, agreement.

PART IV

Organizations as Solutions
and as Problems

Chapter 11

The Security Paradox and the Fear Trap

Ib Damgaard Petersen

Paul Smoker

1. The security paradox

1.1 The traditional paradigm

Ever since the days of Macchiavelli the use of violence has been a corollary to what he termed 'the liberty of a state,' the non-interference by external powers with the territory of the state and its state affairs, and what we may call 'state sovereignty.' Preempting Hans Morgenthau's 'realistic' theory of politics among nations he advised that the best way of securing the state was continually to expand its might and territory and ruthlessly to suppress any internal disturbance threatening the existence of the state or the overthrow of the ruler (Held, 1987: p. 46). From this emerges some of the most tenacious assumptions about state life and international politics to this very day, the assumption about the anarchical nature of international affairs and the state as a unitary actor implying the undisputed freedom of the ruler to use the resources of the state in an international power game unbound by internal considerations other than the protection of citizens and the expansion of the might and territory of the state. As the executor of the national interest the ruler is also unbound by everyday moral codes of conduct. Only the *raison d'état* counts. This is as close to Morgenthau's prescription for the foreign policy decision-maker, 'to act in the interest of the state defined as power,' as one could wish (Morgenthau, 1954).

The power game presupposed the possession of military forces. Part of the game was to form a winning coalition with other states or to form an alliance to guard against a threat from some other state. By making clever use of the balance of power by quick alignments and realignments in the interest of the state, its power and status could be enhanced. Whereas the state was ordered and under control, the international scene was anarchic, the war of all against all.

Ideas like these have held sway ever since the Renaissance occasionally in competition with other ideas like the Grotian perspective of international affairs in the seventeenth century which denied the basically anarchical nature of the international system and found grounds for the introduction of international laws (Lijphardt, 1974); the 'modernist' position of Norman Angell before World War I, which postulated a fundamental change in world society following the Industrial Revolution, based on mutual interdependence and cooperation (Angell, 1908; Navari, 1989); or the utopian idea of a legally ordered international system based on the League of Nations in the aftermath of World War I (Lijphardt, 1974). After the first Cold War ended in 1954 similar ideas about an ordered international system were set forth in the more elaborated theory of interdependence or globalism in the 1960s and early 1970s (Leurdijk, 1974) only to be refuted by 'neorealism' in the late 1970s and 1980s (Keohane, 1986).

The basic idea in the traditional conception of security was that the possession of military might and the clever use of the balance of power could ensure the safety of a state.

1.2 The limits of the traditional paradigm

Since the creation of a terror-balance in the late 1950s this has no longer been possible. No state could in principle any longer rely on its own forces or those of its allies to ensure its safety. No victory in any conventional sense of the word was any longer possible between Nuclear Powers with a second strike capability. The Superpowers could *deter* each other but they could no longer protect themselves solely by their own means. *Their security, or indeed survival, was dependent on decisions taken by the opponent.* Interdependence thus was introduced into a paradigm that basically rested on the assumption of in principle *independent* nation-states.

1.3 The challenge

This clearly was a challenge to the old paradigm of realism and a strong argument for the adoption of an at least minimal version of the paradigm of interdependence with its corollary of an international order in stead of international anarchy. The German-US political scientist Karl Deutsch already in 1957 had pointed to the historical development of *security communities* in England, Scandinavia and between USA-Canada as a consequence of specific historical processes that were to be repeated in the creation of the EEC. A traditional way of thinking, however, is difficult to uproot and in the heated atmosphere of ideological conflict during the first Cold War and its aftermath, accommodation seemed to be almost impossible, even if it would have been a logical consequence of the new situation. Stated in game-theoretical terms, both Superpowers were at this juncture unable to make any move to improve their positions within the power game. Only a bargain, changing the rules of the game would have made it possible to continue the game and find better positions for both. Such a change of the game might have been the creation of a 'security community' (Wiberg, 1989: note 30).

1.4 Trying the impossible

It can be argued that rather than create such a security community statesmen tried to refute the lesson through an arms race to get the upper hand in a military competition which had lost its very meaning, seeking in vain to restore violence to its old status of final arbiter in the world of states and final protector of sovereignty. The last such attempt was the so called SDI initiative launched by President Ronald Reagan in 1983, a 'shield' against intruding missiles and, if successful, an eminent instrument of attack.

Neo-realism could incorporate interdependence and linkage-processes in its power game and ideological armor without apparently having to learn its corollary of international order which alone would have been able to abolish the terrifying destructive prospects of the new nuclear situation.[29]

Every time a technological breakthrough occurred and more sophisticated weapons were introduced, the power of destruction was enhanced, the available decision time tended to shrink and the instability of the deterrence system became more precarious. In the end, despite the costly efforts, the security of both parties had diminished. As both Superpowers developed roughly the same types of new weapons, the means of creating protection against enemy attack and restoring the usefulness of nuclear weapons through first strike capabilities and conceptions of limited nuclear war, by necessity led to diminished security on both sides. The reasons for which these

---

[29] An attempt to use a diacronic and quantitative approach to the study of long-term effects of growing interdependence can be found in Dean Babst, *Global Security Study no 9*, Nuclear Age Peace Foundation, September 1990.

weapons were created were sacrificed by their coming into existence, the means defeated the ends. This is *the security paradox* which has developed within the traditional or realist paradigm, a puzzle that can only be solved by a change of paradigm: the more the Superpowers invest in national security in terms of military capabilities the less the security of both parties and the more unstable the total deterrence system.

1.5 The logic of deterrence

Thomas Schelling has given a description of the absurdities introduced by the logic of the system of deterrence, a system of weapons that must not be used, yet should be credible (Tunander, in Wiberg (ed.), 1989). He describes the system as 'a hierarchy of frontiers,' constituting a ladder of escalation. Each type of weapon from conventional weapons to tactical nuclear weapons, middle-range missiles and strategic weapons has its own geographical zone and a certain technical capability. Weapons with low range and small capabilities are based on the first step of the ladder closest to the frontier between the two opponents, the strongest weapons far away from the common frontier at the very top of the ladder of escalation. The use of each type of weapon in its geotechnical zone must be credible within the existing strategy in order to deter the opponent. The credibility of a threat according to the theory would make the enemy think twice and eventually back down. In game-theoretical terms this means becoming the chicken in 'the chicken game.'

However, these zones according to the logic must also be a gray zones as the opponent should fear an escalation to the next step on the ladder. Through a continous arms race the opponents compete for 'escalation dominance,' that is to have the best military capabilities at the end of the ladder of escalation or at each level. The 'gray zone' means that the opponent should never be sure that a conflict could not move up the ladder and thus bring the very existence of both Superpowers in jeopardy.

This part of the deterrence is called 'the slippery slope' where both parties tied to one another by a rope would slide into the abyss. The closer you move to the slippery slope the greater the danger. This makes it possible at each step on the geotechnical ladder to force the opponent to hesitate and thus open up the possibility for bargaining and negotiation, in reality to cede ground or give in. This is the whole idea of the game, even if none of the parties presumably would dream of starting a nuclear war. That is why the game has taken the form of a complicated (semiotic) set of signs and signals, rather than the actual use of military capabilities.

This hierarchy of frontiers is further complicated as the weapons are incorporated in various strategies. The power game becomes a game in which the two opponents try to render the strategies of the adversary less credible. The war of strategies makes no difference between defensive deterrence and an offensive power game. Both types of strategies presuppose *escalation dominance*, in the last instance at the strategic level. Only this way can a threat of escalation become credible and thus useful in a particular conflict. The nuclear weapon system then is a 'floating system of balances' *implicating a continous arms race* in order to get the upper hand (Tunander, in Wiberg (ed.), 1989: p. 68).

It is also useful to consider in this regard the concept of 'coercive bargaining' and 'deterrence as a theory of bargaining' (Allison & Ury, 1989: p. 206). In addition it should be noted that the nuclear game does not preclude the actual use of force at lower levels as demonstrated by the wars in Vietnam and Afghanistan and the 'low intensity conflicts' in the Third World in the 1970s and 1980s.

The 'semiotic' aspect of nuclear strategy is rather fascinating as it balances on the edge of the use of enormously destructive weapons not meant to be used but yet meant to be credible in order to deter. According to the theory, the more credible the use of nuclear weapons the more credible the deterrent and the less probable the use of nuclear weapons. In other words if the enemy advances, you could deter them by making a credible nuclear threat. They would conceivably stop their advance not wishing to engage in a nuclear exchange. However, the very threat which helped stop them now becomes a problem for the enemy, who might consequently overreact.

Thus it could also be argued that the more credible the threat from the defendant the more probable the risk of preemption by the enemy and the more probable the risk of inadvertent nuclear war (Tunander, in Wiberg (ed.), 1989: pp. 58-60).

1.6 'New Thinking'
Adopting 'new thinking' in international politics means perforce a new means to national security to be found within the notion of an international security community. Karl Deutsch developed this concept in his study of integration in the North Atlantic area

(Deutsch, 1957). Gorbachev was the first to adopt such a stance among the leading heads of state since World War II (Allison & Ury, 1989: p. 265 ff).

The burden of international commitments, the arms race and the necessity to reform the Soviet economy may have been the causes, but 'new thinking' about interdependence and hence the need for an international order to replace the anarchic world of power politics is a logical conclusion to be drawn from the security paradox (Halliday, 1989).

A very interesting aspect of international politics emerges from a change from a conception of independence to a conception of interdependence in world affairs. The dimensionality of international politics changes from being mainly territorial and security-related to mainly non-territorial and welfare-oriented. The possession of land has been of supreme importance in history up to the middle of this century. Agriculture or extraction industries were the main sources of income despite the importance of commerce and manufacture. It was not until the second half of this century that industry became the main source of income. Today the development of industry and the welfare of peoples are dependent on the availability of information and 'know-how' in the widest sense plus an international free market, providing access to raw materials at international market prices. This means that national prosperity is much less dependent on defense of the territory than on dimensions of international politics like free communication channels, freedom of transaction in international trade, international finance, open markets and above all international order to provide for non-discriminate and secure access to resources and transportation (Bialer, in Allison & Ury (eds.), 1989: p. 272).

It is precisely this change of the international agenda, which may in the long run make military investment more of a liability than an asset. This would in the long run provide the background for the abolition of nuclear, biological and chemical weapons, even if this open world will not be without conflict. These conflicts, however, will not be territorial in the conventional sense. [30] Some progress, has been made towards a new international order, but more is needed.

---

[30] In our interpretation of interdependence theory we rely more on Norman Angell's modernization theory and Karl Deutsch's transnationalism than on authors like Nye and Keohane, who scorn modernists and thus the potential of industrialization to create a more peaceful and positively interdependent world.

The break-down of collective security in the former Yugoslavia has demonstrated the frailty of the present security regime in Europe and has questioned the viability of what has been termed 'a new world order'. Scenarios could still be imagined that would pit new or old nuclear powers against one another in a dangerous game of threat and counterthreat. Today a nuclear crisis most likely cannot be controlled, it must be avoided.

Either nuclear weapons must be totally abolished, which is but a dim project, or an alternative security system must gradually displace the old one. A change of paradigms, 'new thinking' about national security is a prerequisite to forestall a future nuclear crisis.

Until a security community has been created and firmly rooted in the global political system the build-up of suitable political and technical institutions both in Europe and globally is a necessity to help avoid an international crisis that may develop into a nuclear crisis.

This should not close our eyes to the threat of accidental nuclear war emerging in the future from Third World countries.[31] Iraq is said to be close to the manufacture of nuclear weapons in an arms race with Israel. Similarly, nuclear arms races presumably take place in Korea (North-South), in Latin America (Brazil and Argentina), in South Asia (India-Pakistan), and between the People's Republic of China and Taiwan.

In the following section we shall demonstrate the dangers inherent in nuclear deterrence and in the final section argue that a largely unnoticed but, in our opinion, narrow escape from global destruction took place a few years ago.

2. The fear trap

2.1 Introduction
While a number of earlier studies of accidental nuclear war have concentrated on technological and psychological sources of potentially catastrophic failures in the nuclear deterrence system, less emphasis has been placed on political and organizational problems and how political doctrines or policies might influence the reliability of the control system. A number of researchers argue that the probability of nuclear war by accident is significant under conditions of extreme

---

[31] Cf. Leavitt and Bracken (Ch. 12) this volume.

stress or crisis but they do not attempt to describe the dynamics of the system under various levels of international tension. It is possible that even at lower levels of tension a dangerous situation could be triggered under certain conditions in the interacting political, organizational and technological systems.

2.2 A substantial rise in the number of false alarms in the early 1980s
In 1984 the North American Aerospace Command following a Freedom of Information Act request gave figures for various types of conferences in the Early Warning System for the years 1977-84. One type of conference (the Routine Missile Display Conference) has to do with the performance of the system as new sensors or computer systems are introduced and tested. Another type of conference is the Threat Evaluation Conference, which is called whenever the operators perceive a nuclear threat against North America. A Threat Assessment Conference is called if a Threat Evaluation Conference cannot discard a perceived nuclear threat. At the Threat Assessment Conference the magnitude and type of the perceived nuclear threat is assessed. It should be noted that whereas NORAD only acknowledges steps where the alert status has been heightened as the equivalent of a false alarm we take the view that Threat Evaluation conferences and Threat Assessment conferences that have subsequently proved to be incorrectly assuming the possibility of an attack indicate false alarms, as they indicate that a signature of a possible threat has emerged from the Early Warning System.

An inspection of the figures given in the table below shows a substantial increase in the number of false alarms in the 1980s.

Table 1
NORAD Figures for Threat Assessment (TAC), Threat Evaluation (TEC), and Routine Missile Display Conferences (RMDC)

	TAC	TEC	RMDC
1977	0	43	1567
1978	2	40	1009
1979	2	78	1544
1980	2	149	3815
1981	0	186	2851
1982	0	218	3716
1983	0	255	3294
1984	0	153	2988

2.3 Explanations given by various authors for the rising number of false alarms in the period 1979-84

In a study by Smoker and Grinyer (1986) great emphasis was put on the possibility that misinterpretations associated with electronic systems were a cause of the strong upward trend in Emergency Action Conferences in 1977-84. At the time there was widespread concern over the reliability of the computer systems associated with the Early Warning System caused by incidents in 1979 and 1980. On 9 November 1979, for instance, a 'war game' scenario was accidentally fed into the US Early Warning System. The simulated missile attack was read by operators as being a 'live launch.' During the six minutes it took to discover the attack was not for real, fighters from bases in the United States and Canada had taken off and missile and submarine installations worldwide had been placed on alert.

On 3 June 1980, a computer chip failed and reported an attack was coming from two Soviet submarines, then that more submarines had joined in, and finally, after the B52 pilots had scrambled, that a full-scale Soviet ICBM launch had begun. In this incident 100 B52s were readied for take off and, thousands of miles away, the US commander in the Pacific took off in his flying command post (the 'looking glass') in order to ensure an American retaliation to a possible Soviet decapitating attack.

The Australian strategic studies expert, Desmond Ball, has suggested another possibility to the authors: that the frequency of these conferences is dependent on Soviet ICBM on-site test launches. This hypothesis has been researched by the authors and it could not be confirmed by a study of the actual history of development and testing of Soviet ICBMs in 1977-84. In fact we disclosed an inverse relationship between numbers of Threat Evaluation conferences and estimated numbers of Soviet on-site ICBM test launches. We also found that there was no relationship between TECs and numbers of Soviet space shots (which are fairly stable over the years) (Petersen & Smoker, 1989: pp. 68-78).

In a personal communication to the authors, Desmond Ball has recently suggested another hypothesis: that SLBM on-site launches may be the cause of the upward trend, eventually together with ICBM on-site launches. We are presently exploring this other hypothesis, which may be of interest, as SLBM launches are likely in an initial phase of a decapitating attack. They would create an EMP pulse and destroy US command posts before the highly accurate ICBMs necessary for the destruction of US missile silos were launched. At the present stage of analysis we have not been able to confirm this other hypothesis either. Most SLBM tests seem to have been carried out at recognized test ranges without threatening fans. Only about 5-15 tests per year have been carried out in the Pacific (Petersen & Smoker, 1989: pp. 70-71).

Without discarding the possibility that a number of the Emergency Action conferences have actually been triggered by computer malfunctions or ICBM on-site tests, the present chapter explores the hypothesis *that the upward trend in Emergency Action conferences might best be explained by political factors interacting with technical and organizational systems.*

3. Examples

3.1 Polish crisis 1, 1980-81
One example of this type of interaction may be found in the announcement of an imminent Soviet invasion of Poland in December 1980. The situation in Poland deteriorated in the winter of 1980. On 3 December the White House began to express alarm about the possibility of a Soviet invasion. On the 7 December it announced that the Soviets had in fact completed preparations for an invasion. However, early in 1981 it became clear that the Carter Administration had grossly exaggerated the state of readiness of the Red Army.

The fear of Soviet intervention in Poland pronounced in Washington that winter, it can be argued, created an atmosphere that made the intelligence community particularly receptive to information which pointed to an invasion. It is possible to argue that this phenomenon - seeing what you expect to see - could interfere with intelligence assessments between the Superpowers. If a crisis were preceded by a period of rising tensions and fears or, worse still, expectations that the other side was preparing to resort to force, analysts would search for, and probably find, evidence that confirmed these expectations.

This last example is cited from Lebow's *Nuclear Crisis Management* (1987: pp. 69-70). Lebow's presentation of this phenomenon is based on the theory of *cognitive consistency, seeing what one expects to see.* This should not rule out the possibility that such a phenomenon could also be caused by motivational factors, *seeing what one wants to see*, especially in a period of acute ideological conflict such as in the early 1980s.

3.2 The Suez crisis, 1956

Paul Bracken describes the 1956 Suez crisis which took place against the background of Soviet communiques concerning the consequences of worldwide nuclear war. Unidentified jet aircraft were reported flying over Turkey, the Turkish air force went on alert; 100 Soviet MIGs were reported over Syria; a British Canberra bomber was reported shot down over Syria; and the Soviet fleet began moving through the Dardanelles out of the Black Sea, an event associated with the start of Soviet hostilities. The US general Andrew Goodpaster feared that these events could trigger the NATO operations plan, at that time all out nuclear strikes on the Soviet Union.

In fact the jets over Turkey were a flock of geese, the '100 Soviet MIGs' were a smaller routine escort returning the President of Syria from a state visit to Moscow, the Canberra crashed through mechanical failure, and the Soviet fleet were engaged in a long scheduled exercise. Gross misinterpretations and a tendency to view unrelated and even unconfirmed events as part of a pattern of enemy action may have been related to the anxiety created by a high level of international tension. Bracken (1983) argues that:

> The detection and misinterpretation of these events, against the context of world events from Hungary to Suez, was the first major example of how the size and complexity of worldwide electronic warning systems could, at certain times, create a crisis momentum of its own.

3.3 The KAL 007 incident, 1983

Still another example of this may be the shooting down of a Korean airliner in the Pacific coast area near a Soviet base in August 1983. The airliner was reportedly mistaken for an American RC 135 reconnaissance plane (Hersh, 1986). Tests of a new Soviet missile were carried out in the area at the time (Ball, 1988: p. 41). The United States charged that the new missile was a violation of the SALT II agreements, but had not been able to provide clear photographs of the launcher system from satellites as tests were carried out by night. Important elements of the US National Means of Verification (NTMV) capability had not been functioning at previous tests and finally the telemetry of the missile had been 100 percent encrypted and sent on frequencies difficult to pick up.

In fact the missile was the SS-25, considered by the US to be a new missile and thus a violation of the SALT II agreement. The agreement only allowed the parties to develop one new light ICBM missile. The Soviets had already tested the SS-24 missile, but held that the SS-25 was a modified version of an older missile, the SS-13. The tests of the SS-25 were deliberately concealed by the Soviet Union (Ball, 1988: pp. 41-42).

On the night of the shooting down of the airliner a new test was scheduled, but never took place presumably because of the intruding airliner.[32] The Soviets would *expect* the Americans to use all available means including RC 135 reconnaissance planes to obtain information on the new missile. It is clear from Seymour Hersh's analysis of the incident, that the Soviet air defenses continued to believe all the way through that the airliner was an American RC 135 reconnaissance plane, *the type of aeroplane that could be expected to carry out a spy mission. They saw what they expected to see.* During the operation they never recognized KAL 007 as a civilian airliner.

3.4 The Iranian airbus incident, 1988

The importance of an early detection of possible enemy actions can cause decision-makers in charge of C[3]I systems to search very energetically for information patterns that confirm such actions. There is a tendency to interpret coincidences of events conforming to a pattern of enemy action as threatening even if these events are unconfirmed or normally would not have been interpreted as belonging to such a pattern. Under conditions of stress these coincidences are more likely to be interpreted as a pattern of enemy action as the following incident illustrates.

On Sunday, 3 July 1988 the Aegis cruiser *USS Vincennes* and the frigate *USS Elmer Montgomery* were on patrol in the western curve of the Gulf near the Strait of Hormuz. Tension had been high in the area for some time and spectacular enemy action was expected on the following day, July 4. Early in the morning the *Vincennes* became

---

[32] Desmond Ball, personal information. Desmond Ball was part of the team trying to monitor the event through electronic means.

engaged in a fight with Iranian gunboats of which two were later claimed to be destroyed.

At 6.47 GMT the Aegis surface-to-air missile system on the *Vincennes* detected an aircraft over Iran heading out over the water. At 6.49 GMT the *Vincennes* sent the first of at least six radio warnings to the aircraft on civilian and military frequencies. The aircraft appeared to be heading towards the *Vincennes* at about 800 kilometers per hour. At 6.51 GMT the *Vincennes* declared the plane hostile, believing it to be a US built Iranian F-14 and shot it down at a distance of 10 kilometers from the ship. All 290 people on the airbus died.

In the airbus incident the Iranians claimed that the plane had been flying 'precisely in the international corridor' and that:

> Considering the regular and repeated flight of passenger planes through this international corridor, the American fleet should have been quite familiar with this route. (*Japan Times*, 5 July 1988)

A similar but less well known incident took place during the Cuban missile crisis. During the crisis an American U-2 was shot down over Cuba. The downing of the U-2 was a mistake: it was the spontaneous, automatic decision of a Soviet commander in intense circumstances, when the plane passed through the zone of fire for two minutes, leaving no time to obtain approval. Fyodor Burlatsky, former speech-writer and adviser to Krushchev, now states that: 'Krushchev was shocked to learn that the plane had been shot down; the incident made it painfully clear that his control over developments in Cuba had evaporated' (Allison & Ury, 1989: p. 115).

3.5 A hypothesis of a direct link between levels of international tension and levels of false alarms in the Early Warning System
The apparently emerging patterns of enemy action can be a consequence of expectations generated by the situation and thus a self-reinforcing process. The normal perception of events can change as a consequence of the logic of a situation where decision-makers have worst case expectations and there is insufficient mutual trust. Our essential argument is that the way people interpret a situation may change radically as a result of the anxiety caused by high or increasing levels of international tension. Events that would under

normal conditions be viewed as sheer coincidences or innocent
failures in the systems can become the cause for a 'false alarm.'
Furthermore, as the amount of information increases in a situation
of increasing tension because more C^3I systems are activated, so does
the probability of perceiving a pattern of enemy action where no
pattern would normally be seen.

Our working hypothesis resulting from such considerations is that
increasing levels of international tension would cause increasing levels
of false alarms in the Early Warning Systems of the Superpowers.

3.6 A short description of the way the US Early Warning System is
working
On a day-to-day basis NORAD tracks anything from missiles and the
4,600 human-made satellites and pieces of 'space junk' from old
broken-up satellites, to physical phenomena such as sun spots, meteo-
rites and even moon beams. The trick is to weed out the 'signatures'
made by these natural and known events and to distinguish them
from any new and unusual activity that might pose a threat to the
United States (Pringle & Arkin, 1983: p. 97).

Early warning satellites would provide the earliest indication of
a missile attack. Their infrared sensors would detect the fiery plumes
of ICBM and SLBM boosters during their first few minutes of
powered flight into space. Reports on the size of the attack would be
received immediately at the Pentagon, Fort Richie, SAC headquarters
and North American Air Defense Command (NORAD) headquarters
in Colorado. Rearward communications from the satellite ground
stations to these major facilities are routed over satellites, undersea
cable and terrestrial communications within the United States.
Radars scanning toward all potential launch sites in the Soviet Union
would confirm an ICBM attack within about 10 minutes after launch
and report to NORAD. Other radars on the perimeter of the
continental United States would confirm SLBM launches, and report
to all four major command posts. Several minutes after launch of the
attack, tactical warning would be flashed from the major command
centers to all nuclear units; this would trigger extensive precautionary
reactions at hundreds of locations. Bomber and command aircraft
crews would scramble to their planes and standby for take-off orders
to avoid destruction on the ground. Command aircraft on ground
alert, would probably be sent aloft immediately. Minuteman launch
crews would unlock their safes containing launch codes and keys,

insert the keys into launch switches and strap themselves into their chairs to brace for the expected shock waves.

3.7 False alarm or confirmed attack?
The NORAD commander is responsible for inhibiting the alert momentum if it is a false alarm, and for accelerating it if it is a confirmed attack. He is expected to reach a definitive judgment in a matter of a few minutes. If *possible* this judgment would be based on a combination of various preexisting strategic warning indicators, tactical warning of the attack from at least two distinct and independent sensors such as detectors on infrared satellites and ground-based radars, and confirming reports from human operators of the sensors.

3.8 Retaliation
The timing of retaliation would also be an essential consideration. A prompt launch of the Minutemen force to prevent its destruction by incoming ICBM warheads would require an almost instantaneous decision by the president. A quick decision would also facilitate delivery of the launch order to the other legs of the triad, sea-based and air-based missiles. The earlier approval is granted, the better are the chances of finding the command system still intact to transmit the order. Even under the best of circumstances, however, launch-on-warning or launch-under-attack would permit the president only a few minutes for deliberation, and the information available would not provide a clear picture of the attack.

3.9 Decapitating attack
Furthermore, the attack might be specifically designed to prevent prompt launch. To that end the Soviets could attempt to disrupt communications at the very outset by jamming and perhaps sabotage, followed a scant few minutes later by an environmental disturbance (a so-called electromagnetic pulse) by exploding a nuclear device in the atmosphere over the US mainland and some minutes thereafter by physical destruction of vital command elements.

4. Analysis of hypothesis

The project on which this chapter is based has attempted to analyze international tension during the period 1977-84 in both qualitative and quantitative terms. The full description of the project draws upon available historical treatments and time-series data (Petersen & Smoker, 1989). The present essay reports primarily on some of the quantitative analyses of the relationship between international tension and Threat Evaluation conferences in the NORAD.

Were true time-series data available in the unclassified literature on the occurrence of TECs then it would be possible to undertake a relatively reliable time-series analysis of the relationship between all indicators with the exception of the defense ratio, using disaggregated events data.

Here we are limited to the use of a correlational analysis as far as the quantitative indicators are concerned. Consequently the inference drawn in the following section must be drawn with considerable caution since the potential for error in such a small sample is considerable.

4.1 The dependent variables
Emergency Action conferences at NORAD headquarters 1977-84. Statistics for the various types of Emergency Action conferences at NORAD headquarters have been made public by NORAD for the period 1977-84 (displayed above).

The independent variables
Indicators of tension: (see tables 2-4 below).

Table 2
Statistics of US Accusations of the Soviet Union in the Department of State Bulletin 1977-84

6 AND 12 MONTHLY AGGREGATES

6 MONTHS AGGREGATES			YEARLY AGGREGATES	
1977	7	5	1977	12
1978	42	5	1978	47
1979	2	32	1979	34
1980	226	103	1980	329
1981	178	276	1981	454
1982	309	176	1982	485
1983	330	268	1983	598
1984	292	109	1984	401

Table 3
US Defense Ratio 1977-84

MILITARY EXPENDITURE AS A PERCENTAGE OF GDP	
1977	5.3
1978	5.1
1979	5.1
1980	5.6
1981	5.8
1982	6.5
1983	6.7
1984	6.5

Source: *SIPRI Yearbook*, 1986.

Table 4
Correlational Analysis - Correlations of Main Variables

VARIABLE	TIME	TEC	DR	DSB
TIME	---	.83	.91	.87
TEC	.83	---	.88	.97
DR	.91	.88	---	.90
DSB	.87	.97	.90	---

The probability of obtaining a correlation of .83 or above in an uncorrelated population of statistics is less than .01. The three central variables in this study all intercorrelate at .83 or above. These three variables are the frequency of Threat Evaluation Conference (TEC), the Defense Ratio (DR), and the number of verbal accusations by the US president, vice president, secretaries of state and other high ranking officials reported in the Department of State Bulletin (DSB). The three central variables also have correlations of .83 or above with time.

These results are consistent with the assumption that during the period 1977 to 1984 there is a direct correlation between the level of alleged international tension, as inferred from the verbal accusations of leading US decision-makers, and the level of false alarms in the North American Air Defense (NORAD) system.

In order to explore the relationship between these variables further, partial correlations were used to remove the correlation with time. When this was done the linkage between Threat Evaluation Conference (TEC) and accusations in the Department of State

Bulletin (DSB) remains at a level that would be significant at the .01 level in an uncorrelated population of statistics, the partial correlation being .90. The Defense Ratio (DR) gives partial correlations of .53 with DSB and .54 with TEC, figures that are beneath the .05 level of .71 for an uncorrelated population of statistics.

Thus, while all three central variables are probably correlated in time and are almost certainly related indicators of the psycho-political dynamics of the period, the frequency of Threat Evaluation conferences and of official US anti-Soviet accusations are also linked independent of time. This is consistent with the hypothesis that subjective perceptions of international relations, as indexed by DSB, are an important source of errors in the command and control systems, as indexed by TEC, independent of genuine computer generated incidents.

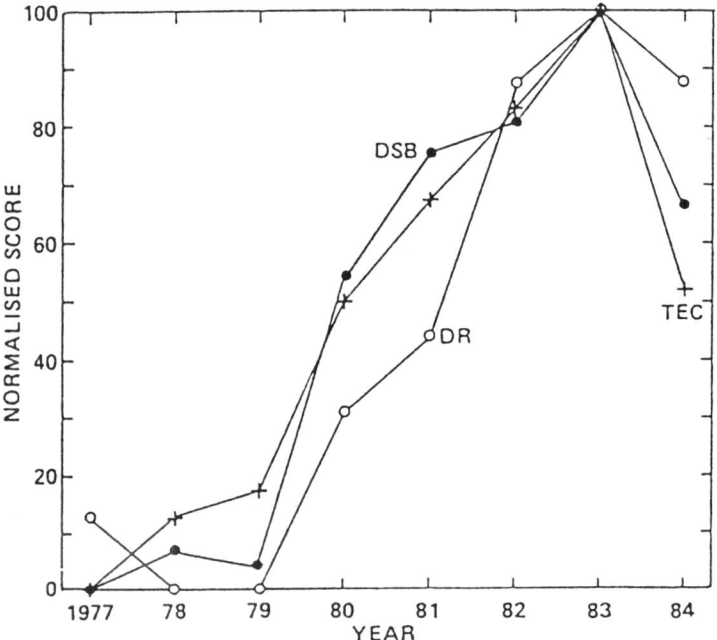

Figure 1
This diagram shows the covariation of the Defense Ratio (DR), US governmental verbal aggression (DSB) and frequencies of Threat

Evaluation Conference (TEC). They are all very closely related despite the fact that the indicators were drawn from very different sources by three different people without any prior connection and brought together in this study.

5. Four phases of US attitudes towards the Soviet Union, 1977-84 [33]

5.1 Phase 1: 1977-79. Conciliatory/provocative
In the period 1977-1979 the level of US accusations in the Department of State Bulletin was very low. The level of Soviet aggressiveness in Africa and elsewhere, however, according to the historical analysis seemed to have been most disturbing to the US government. In this period then it can be argued that there was a deliberate policy by the Carter Administration to play down the real level of international tension in order to preserve détente, except for the year 1979 when both sides showed restraint in order to secure the conclusion of the SALT II agreement. Four TACs took place in this period.

5.2 Phase 2: (1979)-80. 'Realistic'/provocative
In 1980, the Carter Administration changed its conciliatory approach and demonstrated a fast rising aggressiveness both in the defense ratio and in the Department of State Bulletin as a reaction to Soviet intervention in Afghanistan, which was seen as crowning a series of interventions throughout the 1970s which had been a cause of concern to the administration. Two TACs took place within this period.

5.3 Phase 3: 1981-83. Provocative/conciliatory
In the next three years during President Ronald Reagan's first term in office, US governmental aggressiveness towards the USSR continued to rise together with the defense ratio and the number of Threat Evaluation conferences. All three indicators peaked in 1983.

An aggressive American policy in this period was not founded on any particularly aggressive behavior of the Soviet Union towards the United States. In fact the Soviet Union proceeded with the utmost caution during this whole period. No less than three wars (Falkland,

---

[33] Petersen and Smoker, 1989

Lebanon and Iran-Iraq) were fought in these years, but there was never any indication of Soviet military intervention even if the Soviet ally Syria was utterly defeated by Israel in a large air battle. The Soviet Union also restrained its allies Cuba and Vietnam and showed restraint in Africa. *The only possible military confrontation in the period was linked to the Polish crisis which might have prompted an escalatory process in Europe if Soviet military intervention had materialized.*

Rather, American foreign policy towards the Soviet Union was an 'autistic' behavior, rooted in the American political system itself. It was, however, partly a reaction to Soviet foreign policy in the 1970s, which had been a cause of concern in the United States.

It can be argued that during these years there was a deliberate US policy to whip up tension through an ideological crusade and large-scale rearmament in order to create the background for a new role for the USA in the world and an attempt to roll back Soviet influence in the Third World by means of not only counter-insurgency, but also pro-insurgency strategies and occasionally direct intervention (Halliday, 1989).

This happened, however, in a period with only few 'objective' indications of possible direct military clashes between the Superpowers. The high level of tension was testimony to the essentially politico-ideological conflict between the Superpowers during Ronald Reagan's first term, not to any immediate military threat caused by territorial disputes in which both Superpowers were directly and openly involved.

There is thus in this period strong evidence of a self-reinforcing feedback loop within the American political and military est-ablishment, creating ever mounting tension.

One unanticipated consequence of this political development was a more than sixfold rise in the number of 'false alarms' in the US Early Warning System between 1978 and 1983, from a level of 40 in 1978 to a level of 255 a year in 1983, almost one every day, closely linked to the number of US accusations towards the Soviet Union and the rising level of military expenditure. No TACs have been reported in the Early Warning System in the period 1981-83.

5.4 Phase 4: Relaxation of tension, September 1984. Conciliatory/ conciliatory
This situation changed in the last phase, the fall of 1984, where all indicators point towards a relaxation of tension.The causes of this

change in the attitude of the US government cannot be fully explored here, but a significant drop in aggressiveness as measured by the Department of State Bulletin and the Defense Ratio is in this period closely correlated with a drop in the number of false alarms. No TACs have been reported in this period.

5.5 Hypothetical patterns that might lead to unintended nuclear war
Lacking as we do good indicators for Soviet equivalents of DSB, TECs and TACs, any hypothesis concerning the relationship between TACs, TECs and the probability of nuclear war is at the present time purely speculative. The evidence presented in this chapter certainly suggests that, contrary to the opinion of Desmond Ball, the frequency of TECs may be related to the state of verbal tension. The following hypothesis is presented to illustrate one possible pattern that can be explored further by future research.

Phases 1 and 3, it can be argued, may be in a psychological sense mirror images of each other, During such periods one of the actors pursues a confrontational policy, with an associated increase in TECs since important but lower level decision-makers are involved in the TECs and the tension associated with such a phase is a factor that can, as in the case of the *Vincennes* incident, cause such decision-makers to interpret patterns of events, including technical malfunctions, unusual information, or operational missile tests as potentially hostile. The correlational evidence, it should be remembered, suggested such a possibility.

The other actor will be more likely to generate the more serious TAC type errors because of the aggressiveness and hostility of the potential adversary and the apparently real threat this poses. In phase 3, from 1981 to 1983, we would therefore anticipate a higher probability of TAC type errors in the Soviet system, as was the case in the NORAD system during phase 1.

Similarly during a period such as phase 2, where all indicators move up together, we would expect an increase in TECs in the command and control systems of both actors, as well as a higher probability of TAC type errors in both command and control systems if the Soviet equivalent of DSB also moved up. Two TACs occurred in the NORAD system during this phase as did a close to doubling of the frequency of TECs in the NORAD system. In phase 4 as defined above we would expect a reduction in TECs and a lower probability of TAC type errors in both C^3I systems since all indicators of verbal aggression moved downwards.

This hypothesis would argue that, all other things being equal, the probability of a nuclear war will be higher in a phase 2 type situation since TAC type errors are more likely to occur on both sides, and TEC type errors associated with perceived increased hostility of the other actor are likely to increase. This argument conforms to the view that the probability of nuclear war increases substantially during a crisis where the interaction between the C^3I systems can under worst case analysis generate a self-exciting situation.

In addition, it suggests an increase in the probability of nuclear war during situations such as phases 1 or 3 where the aggressiveness of the first actor is associated with an increase in first actor TECs and the probability of second actor TACs.

5.6 The generation of expectations of enemy action by the political leadership

The important thing emerging from the above analysis is that an ideological confrontation occurring on the background of an arms race can create the expectation of possible enemy action in the Early Warning System even if there are only a few 'objective' indications of possible military disputes between the Superpowers. These expectations generated by the political system would directly affect the number of false alarms occurring in the system. The larger the number of false alarms the greater in our view the probability of some situation where a false alarm may be acted upon with consequences beyond imagination.

Threat Evaluation conferences (TECs) are strongly associated with US accusations as found in the official Department of State Bulletin (DSB). This is consistent with the assumption that the attitudes and perceptions of decision-makers within the system itself are of central importance in calling TECs and that the operators of the NORAD command and control system take their cues from the leaders of the country. The probability of an unintended nuclear war appears to be closely related to the attitudes and perceptions of leading decision-makers.

The authors of this chapter take the view that the psychological mechanisms discussed in the chapter's introduction lie behind this close relationship. This is not to deny the fact that technical problems play a large role in the huge complex C^3I systems and may have contributed to many of the false alarms reported by NORAD. On the other hand, a very strong relationship has been shown to be present in the linkage between an entirely subjective concept of international tension, as perceived by high-ranking US decision-makers, and frequencies of what can be thought of as false alarms.

It is our opinion that high-ranking political decision-makers should be aware that their behavior and perceptions can affect the nuclear deterrence system. The command and control of nuclear weapons must be seen within the psychological and political climate cultivated by leading decision-makers. While technological and administrative factors are of the greatest importance, the 'political factor' is central in the avoidance of accidental nuclear war.

6. Close to catastrophe

6.1 The spectre of a limited nuclear war
Tension as seen from the Soviet side was linked to the possibility that a US ideological crusade might spill over into a military conflict with the Soviet Union if the US government decided to challenge the Soviet Union within its own territory and sphere of influence in Eastern Europe. There are strong indications in the historical analysis that the Soviet Union in 1981-84 feared a decapitating US nuclear attack within the planned framework of a limited nuclear war, as disclosed by the *New York Times* in May 1982 but foreboded by President Carter's famous *Presidential Directive PD 59* in 1980.

We are arguing (Petersen & Smoker, 1989) that the Soviet Union at the end of the period 1981-83 became convinced that the ultimate goal of US foreign policy was the destruction of Soviet power in a decapitating nuclear attack in a limited nuclear war. This *political* warning would be reinforced by *strategic* warnings such as the development of the neutron bomb, large scale worldwide exercises in 1983 termed by the Soviets a 'rehearsal of the Third World War,' and the deployment of Pershing IIs and cruise missiles in Europe. Ola Tunander has compared the deployment of Pershing II and the cruise missile Tomahawk beginning in 1983 with the Soviet deployment of missiles in Cuba in 1962 (Wiberg (ed.), 1989: p. 72).

It should be recognized that the present Early Warning Systems of both Superpowers have a poor capability to detect low-flying cruise missiles that could be aimed at command centers as the precursor to a large scale attack (Gottfried & Blair, op. cit.: p. 86), but considering the defects of the Soviet Early Warning System in particular the limited cover of possible American SLBM launches and limited radar capabilities at the time, a *tactical* warning coming on top of a political and strategic warning could have unleashed *a prompt launch* during the height of tension in 1983-84. Such a tactical warning might well have been caused by *a false alarm* generated in the Soviet Early Warning System by the very tense situation, emulating what we have seen on the American side, despite the absence of any real situation of crisis involving the possible use of military action. In this regard it should be pointed out that the September 1983 crisis over the downing of the Korean airliner contained no military threat for either side.

The Soviet Marshal Kulikov in an interview with the *New York Times* on 14 October 1983, warned that the deployment of American Euro-missiles *'would make it practically impossible to prevent a conflict resulting from an error or technical fault'* (Allison & Ury, 1989: p. 216).

In the years 1983-84 we might have been closer to an all out nuclear war than at any time since the Cold War in the 1950s, with the possible exception of the Cuban missile crisis. The use of nuclear weapons in the early 1950s, however, would have been on purpose.[34] A nuclear war in 1983-84 would not have been on purpose, but inadvertent - i.e. an *unintended* nuclear war.

This opinion is corroborated by several interviews with the former Soviet KGB officer Oleg Gordievsky who defected in 1985 (*The Times*, 27 February, 28 February, 1 March 1990; *Time International* 5 March, 1990; also British TV interview, Spring 1990). He maintains that during the whole period 1980-85 the Soviet leadership believed that the West might commit aggression and launch a nuclear war. The years from 1982 to 1985 were a period of particular high tension during which the Soviet government had ordered reports every two weeks about a possible US strike against the Soviet Union.

This period of high tension fits in well with events. On 31 May 1982 the *New York Times* revealed that:

US Defense Department was drawing up a plan for fighting a 'protracted' nuclear conflict with the USSR on the basis that American forces must prevail and be able to force the Soviet

---

[34] Gottfried and Blair, 1989: p. 48, on Eisenhower's view of nuclear weapons and the doctrine of 'massive retaliation'.

Union to the earliest termination of hostilities on terms favorable to the United States.

A few weeks later on 18 June came a largely unnoticed but remarkable and unique Soviet answer to this: an *integrated* test of all Soviet nuclear capabilities, including ASAT, ABM and C³I. This was followed by a number of speeches warning the US that redundance was so great that no nuclear attack could escape retaliation. Just before his death in October 1982, Brezhnev accused the American president of 'pushing the world into the flames of a nuclear war' (Petersen & Smoker, 1989: p. 34).

In an interview Gordievsky asked rhetorically:

Is it possible that anyone in Moscow seriously believed that the West could commit aggression and launch a nuclear war? The answer is, unfortunately, yes, there were such people and evidently from 1980 to 1985 they were in the majority in the political and military leadership of the USSR.

It is interesting to see that the Soviet leadership according to Gordievsky was thus captured in the realist power-maximizing paradigm and of course in Marxist-Leninist thinking about antagonistic interests as it judged that if the US possessed the means for a decapitating surprise attack it would certainly use it. Not until the advent of Gorbachev, who in his thinking seemed to reflect the paradigm of interdependence, was this dogmatic stand challenged and cautiously replaced by a notion of the possibility of compromises between socialist and capitalist states (Halliday, 1989; Gorbachev 1986 & 1987).

In his first interview with a British journalist in 1988, Gordievsky held that on 9 November 1983 the Soviet leaders panicked, fearing that a secret NATO exercise 'Able Archer' was the precursor of a decapitating attack on the Soviet Union.

From 2 to 11 November 1983, NATO staged a command-post exercise code-named 'Able Archer', to practise its own nuclear release procedures. As a matter of routine, Warsaw Pact intelligence began to monitor the exercise. In equally routine fashion, Western intelligence began to monitor the monitors.

It soon became clear to both the British and American listening centres that something was going badly wrong. Instead of the monitoring normally to be expected from across the Iron Curtain, a sharp increase was registered in both the volume and the intensity of the East-bloc traffic. On 8-9 November, the Kremlin pressed what came close to a panic button. Having noted what appeared to be significant changes in Able Archer's message formats, Moscow Centre sent an urgent Ryan information request to all its Residencies. The incredible seemed to be happening, namely that the Warsaw Pact suspected it might really be facing nuclear attack at any moment.

Gordievsky was to explain that this was, in fact, far from incredible. The classic Soviet plan for an offensive against the West envisages that manoeuvres will be used as a combined camouflage screen and springboard for the real attack. The Russians naturally assume that their adversaries would do the same. Moscow Centre therefore, Gordievsky explained, had always given highest priority to intelligence on NATO exercises and alert procedures. It was vital for the West not to make these appear misleading. As a result of his warnings, certain adjustments to Western practices were made, all designed to avoid needless provocation in the future. So far as is known the ill-founded panic of November 1983 has never been repeated.

On the broader political front, Gordievsky's message led to even greater changes. In September and October 1985, British officials passed Gordievsky's information on the Ryan exercise to the Americans, including his detailed analysis not merely of the Kremlin's strategy but of the Kremlin's psychology as it affected that strategy. The paper, entitled 'Soviet Perceptions of Nuclear Warfare', was fifty pages long. . . . President Reagan is said to have read these Gordievsky reports from beginning to end, which was far from being his standard practice. The cautionary tale they contained sank in. [35]

In a later interview with *The Times* (27 February 1990), Gordievsky maintained that the Soviet leadership in November 1983 was fearing a new weapon connected with the American plan for an SDI system

[35] Brook-Shepherd 1988: pp. 269-70.

(announced by President Reagan in April 1983). Two reports on the SDI were presented in October 1983 and part of them was published. However, at this juncture most of the ideas could only be realized in the far future, if ever. What weapon could have given the Soviets a scare like the one mentioned by Gordievsky? A possible weapon might have been the ASAT weapon MHV, which had been initiated under Ford and developed under Carter. This weapon later played a central part in the SDI system as a weapon to intercept incoming missiles in the final phase. This weapon was able to destroy enemy satellites without an explosion.[36] We can see no other likely candidate. The Soviet leadership, however, could also have seen Able Archer in combination with the deployment of Pershing II and Tomahawk missiles. (The first Pershings were deployed in UK, Italy and West Germany between 14 and 27 November.) Tomahawk missiles would be capable of destroying Soviet radar installations and command posts in a sneak attack and Pershing IIs would be able to knock out Soviet hardened command posts within 8-12 minutes. Many ingredients of a decapitating attack were there and this was coming on top of the most intense (pseudo) US-Soviet crisis in the 1980s, following the downing of the Korean airliner a few weeks before, which led to a universal condemnation of the Soviet Union.

The most convincing indication of a Soviet panic, that might have resulted in an accidental nuclear war, however, is not Gordievsky's interviews, but information from American participants in a symposium on accidental nuclear war which took place in Copenhagen (June 29-July 1, 1990). From interviews with high ranking American officials active in the Reagan Administration in 1983, they were able to confirm that Able Archer gave rise to great anxiety in the Soviet leadership and that the American government took extraordinary steps to demonstrate to the Soviet leadership that its fears were unfounded. [37]

One of the reasons why the Soviet Union was on the verge of a nuclear panic over Able Archer was its particular character. It was an

---

[36] The MHV system, however, may not have been tested for several years. In Håkan Wiberg ((ed.) 1989: pp. 92-94), it is said that the weapon was first tested in 1985. See also the Soviet general Vladimir Belous (1988) for a description of the capabilities of the weapon.
In a recent book (Beukel 1989) a number of Soviet speeches from the period have been analyzed. The results clearly reveal the Soviet fear of a nuclear attack.

[37] Paul Bracken personal information.

exercise in delegation (devolution) of authority to use nuclear weapons. [38] Whereas former such exercises had been carried out by high ranking officials in the role as key decision-makers, in November 1983 those taking part were the actual decision-makers that in time of war would have the authority to authorize the use of nuclear weapons.

That means that not only did the Soviet leaders believe that a decapitating nuclear strike against the Soviet Union was being planned by the West, not only did they believe that the capabilities of such a strike were present in November 1983, but *they also saw the actual decision-making capability to launch such a nuclear attack take shape in NATO headquarters in November 1983.*

All these perceptions nearly caught the Soviet leaders in the 'Fear Trap.'

Beukel (1989) maintains that the Soviet Union in the 1970s had abandoned former doctrines of nuclear war, according to which the Soviet Union should launch a preemptive nuclear attack if it was certain that the US was preparing such an attack against the Soviet Union. Whether this was true or not in 1983 we do not know. In 1983, however, the Soviet leaders thought that they had both a political and a strategic warning. A tactical warning (which means the actual observation of an enemy attack) *might have been caused by a failure in the Soviet Early Warning System.* Fearing a surprise attack the Soviet leaders would not have waited for impact but launched on warning in 1983.

According to the information conveyed to the authors by members of the US delegation to the Copenhagen symposium, the US through signals intelligence became aware of the threat of an inadvertent nuclear war and took a series of measures to reassure the Soviets, but to no avail. New measures of quite extraordinary character finally succeeded in convincing the Soviet government that it was not about to become the victim of a nuclear surprise attack.

Gordievsky reported his observations to the British Intelligence Service and they were conveyed to Ronald Reagan (who later used Gordievsky as an adviser on Gorbachev's policies before his first summit with Gorbachev). Taken together with US signals intelligence

---

[38] On delegation (devolution) cf. Ned Lebow: *Nuclear Crisis Management.* Cornell University Press, 1987: p. 86.

information this must have served as a severe reminder of the dangers of accidental nuclear war for President Ronald Reagan.

It was, however, not the only warning that reached him. The American historian Susanne Massey, who has spent years in the Soviet Union studying ancient Russian history, after the KAL 007 incident (possibly in October or November 1983) was approached by a Soviet official (presumably from the KGB) who sought her help to convey a message about the possible imminence of war to President Ronald Reagan. She went back to the United States and through a congressman got access to Ronald Reagan and his chief advisers. She carried a message back to the Soviet Union from this meeting. She since had no less than 14 meetings with Ronald Reagan, during which he informed himself about the Soviet Union from other perspectives than those presented by his ordinary advisers (Petersen & Smoker, 1989: p. 39-40). These events have been confirmed by the director of the Hudson Institute, Mitchell E. Daniels, who worked in the Reagan Administration, as he gave a lecture at the Institute of Political Studies at the University of Copenhagen in Spring 1990. He also confirmed the importance of these meetings for the president.

On this background it is remarkable then, that from December 1983 there seems to be a change in attitude to the Soviet Union in the speeches of the American president, which continued all through 1984 and culminated in a speech at the United Nations in September 1984, where he proposed regular meetings at cabinet level between Soviet and US officials and periodic political meetings to reduce the risk of a confrontation between the US and the USSR and to deal with regional conflicts which might escalate to nuclear world war. Also in September, he held his first meeting with a high ranking Soviet politician (foreign minister Gromyko) since his inauguration. Such regular meetings were institutionalized in 1985 when Gorbachev came to power and they were later instrumental in many of the agreements on regional conflicts in later years.

On the Soviet side, the new general secretary Konstantin Chernenko followed up in a speech in February 1984 proposing:

To consider the prevention of nuclear war to be the principal goal of any power's foreign policy, not to allow situations fraught with the danger of nuclear conflict and if such danger arises to hold urgent consultations to prevent a nuclear conflagration.

In our view there is a direct connection between the nuclear scare in 1983 and the later détente following the advent of Gorbachev to power in 1985.

It is only possible to reduce the threat from nuclear weapons if an alternative security community is created. Until a security community has been created and firmly rooted in the global political system the creation of suitable political and technical institutions both in Europe and globally is still needed to help avoid an international crisis that may develop into a nuclear crisis.

7. The international tension monitor and the World Forum

7.1 The international tension monitor
This is the background for a proposal set forth by the authors in 1988 for an international network that could on a continuous basis monitor levels of international tension both globally and regionally (Petersen & Smoker, 1989b; Rodley (ed.), 1989: pp. 281-93).

We think that an independent international network, linked up via electronic media and with direct access to governments and international institutions like the Risk-Reduction Centers and the United Nations is needed. We think of a model like the international network of 60 seismic stations monitoring nuclear tests that was created following a diplomatic initiative by Australia. We also think of this initiative as designed to sustain the present process of disarmament and détente.

Projects of a similar nature have been proposed by various authors and institutions, inter alia William L. Ury in his book *Beyond the Hot-line* and by Tapio Kanninen of the United Nations (ORCI) in his proposal for *Frameworks for the Monitoring of Emergent and Ongoing Conflicts* (ISA paper, April 1989).

7.2 The World Forum
As part of this system we imagine a supplementary system of videoscreen-conferences created by the technical means at the disposal of international TV networks and planned by a secretariat close to the United Nations. These conferences would be termed 'The World Forum.' The World Forum would bring together with short notice presidents or foreign ministers involved in an emerging crisis. At such conferences organized by The World Forum they would in front of the world public deliberate warnings issued by the tension monitoring network. The World Forum would be presided over by the

General Secretary of the United Nations. Such a system would make the United Nations visible worldwide and focus public attention on problems of peace and war. This would in turn generate pressures for an ordered and peaceful world among the general public. Transmitted worldwide such conferences could have a tremendous effect on world opinion. The idea of The World Forum is simply the realization of the potential of the electronic age for the creation of peace instead of destruction as exemplified here by the Superpower nuclear deterrence systems.

Chapter 12

Nuclear Proliferation: Neither Safe nor Stable

Lloyd R. Leavitt

Paul Bracken

1. The evolving crisis

Several nations today have the technology to develop nuclear weapons, and are considering either the overt or covert acquisition of a nuclear capability. Usually, these nations are nonaligned and are not protected by either the Russian or the United States nuclear umbrellas. In any case, with the decline of the Cold War the inclusion of their forces within any bloc loses much of its meaning. Most of these same nations already have aircraft and missiles that are quite capable of delivering a nuclear attack, if the nuclear components were available. Typically, they have longstanding disputes with their neighbors that defy rational adjudication.

Under such circumstances, the political and military leaders of these nations are too frequently tempted to strengthen their nation's status and position in these disputes by developing a nuclear arsenal. Self-serving arguments have been voiced as to why the acquisition of nuclear weapons is both ethically and militarily correct for their purposes. 'The United States, Russia, France, United Kingdom, and China have nuclear weapons, why shouldn't we?' 'Country X threatens our security with overwhelming numbers of soldiers (or tanks, or guns, or chemical weapons, or airplanes, or missiles). We need nuclear weapons to offset their advantages.' 'Nuclear deterrence has prevented war between the US and USSR/Russia. If we had nuclear weapons, our enemies would be deterred and the entire region would be peaceful.' 'We are a peaceful nation and will not use nuclear weapons unless all else fails.'

For years, world opinion has discouraged both the 'vertical' and 'horizontal' proliferation of nuclear weapons. The consensus is that proliferation of weapons will inevitably lead to their use, and their use will lead to disastrous consequences - well beyond our intentions and nearly to the limits of our imaginations. The US and CIS are attacking the vertical proliferation problem through mutual reductions. But despite world opinion, some other nations apparently are convinced that acquiring a nuclear capability would be in their best interests. This horizontal proliferation threatens international stability, and needs to be stopped.

The purpose of this chapter is to cite the complexities and ramifications that are associated with the acquisition of weapons of mass destruction. We offer a different emphasis than most others in thinking about the proliferation of such weapons. Instead of focusing exclusively on political aspects of the problem, we take an institutional view based upon the experiences of the United States and the Soviet Union/Russia. This reinforces the wisdom of nonproliferation for the preservation of world order. But it also emphasizes some of the difficulties that have not adequately been considered, or in some cases that have even been denied.

Forty-five years ago, two nuclear weapons were exploded in Japan by the United States. World War II ended a few days later. Whether the weapons should have been used, or were necessary to end the war, has been the subject of debate since that momentous August. The entire world instantly became aware of the awesome, devastating power of nuclear weapons as a by-product of the attacks on Hiroshima and Nagasaki. The Soviet Union, France and the United Kingdom soon tested and built nuclear weapons of their own, followed thereafter by China. The nuclear arms race was off and running.

As nuclear inventories began to grow, so did our realization of the consequences of becoming a 'nuclear power'. Two different tracks were followed by both the United States and the Soviet Union. First, both Washington and Moscow moved against increased spread of these weapons. At one level, NATO and the WTO served as one way to check the spread of national European nuclear forces. In this regard, the US shift towards a flexible response strategy in Europe in the early 1960s was undertaken in part to block French acquisition of an independent nuclear force. Second, national policies and doctrines in both countries concerning the possible wartime use of nuclear weapons were significantly modified, tighter procedural controls were established, weapons security was enhanced, and weapons safety was greatly improved.

For example, atmospheric testing was a relatively cheap and easy way to test new weapons. It also was a useful way to measure weapon effects and demonstrate to all the world that nuclear weapons could destroy any conceivable array of targets. But atmospheric testing threatened the health of millions and was eventually discontinued through mutual agreement.

There were other prominent examples of the maturing national sense of responsibility towards nuclear weapons. Elaborate command and control procedures were developed to preclude the unintended release or firing of nuclear weapons. Human reliability programs were established to eliminate personnel from nuclear operations who had tendencies, traits, personal problems, or weaknesses that could compromise nuclear weapon safety or reliability. The United States stopped flying bombers with nuclear weapons on board in peacetime because of a dangerous series of aircraft accidents and mishaps. As terrorism spread in the 1960s and 1970s, weapons were modified with Permissive Action Links (PALs) to eliminate the possibility that a psychopathic crew could make an unauthorized attack or to deny weapon use if seized by terrorists. As a further precaution against terrorists, security around nuclear storage sites was significantly increased.

While all this was happening, new weapons were designed and old weapons retrofitted to improve safety, minimize fallout, reduce size, improve reliability, vary yield, etc. Warheads were designed that could not detonate accidentally because of fire, explosion or other forms of severe stress. The value of this program was clearly demonstrated when, in 1980, a Titan ICBM exploded in its silo causing immense damage, but leaving the warhead intact. Other accidents involving fires on parked, alert bombers have not caused any damage from the nuclear weapons on board.

Looking backwards often fails to provide adequate insight to the future. But in the case of acquiring a national nuclear capability, there are lessons worth learning. The most obvious lesson is that both the Soviet Union and the United States traveled a very hazardous path during the many years that passed from the acquisition of their first nuclear weapons until nuclear C^3 and weapon systems matured. Fortunately, the Cold War stayed cold during these many years and immense resources could be devoted to solving the problems of owning nuclear weapons.

2. Nuclear stability

A paradox exists today. On one hand, the United States and Russia have by far the largest arsenals of nuclear weapons. Because of the sheer size of these arsenals, both could virtually annihilate each other as well as cause immense collateral damage in many other nations if a nuclear war ever occurred between the Superpowers. The paradox is that despite the size of the arsenals, the probability of nuclear war occurring between these nations is extremely low and remains that way regardless of current relationships between the Superpowers.

The reason for this, of course, is that the nuclear relationship between the two countries is essentially stable, although current domestic developments in the CIS could cause that judgment to change. Both have adopted deterrence as a national strategy, and they effectively deter each other. Both nations have sufficiently large and survivable strategic forces that a first strike against either one would not prevent a devastating retaliatory attack -hence, both are in a 'no win' situation.

The question facing the Superpowers is how to maintain nuclear stability over the long term. Fundamental to long term stability are stable governments, adequate internal controls, reasonable modernization programs, arms control measures and non-provocative nuclear policies.

Stable governments are perhaps the most essential aspect of nuclear stability. Countries that are subject to revolution, terrorism or extremist politics are least able to achieve nuclear stability. Can a nation in revolt protect its nuclear assets from some disgruntled faction bent on nuclear suicide? How are strict controls over release authority maintained when subordinates are disloyal or unreliable? Can a fundamental religious extremist, viewed as psychotic by much of the world, be trusted with the stewardship of nuclear weapons? Will a future dictator, unable to solve internal problems, shift his attention to coercing neighbor states with nuclear blackmail? These questions are hypothetical, but they become reality if proliferation extends to unstable nations or nations equipped with nuclear weapons become unstable. To illustrate, Libyan leader Gadhaffi was reported by JANA to have said that he would have directed missiles at New York in 1986 when US planes bombed Tripoli.

In regard to internal controls, the CIS and the United States have extensive and redundant systems to preclude accidental, unintentional, inadvertent, or unauthorized release of nuclear weapons. While it should not be claimed that these internal controls are absolutely foolproof, they have served their purpose to date and are constantly subject to improvement through revision.

Reasonable modernization of nuclear weapon systems is probably necessary, but always controversial and expensive. In a rough way, US modernization efforts could be categorized with some examples as follows: 1) improvements in weapon effectiveness (larger/smaller yields, improved delivery accuracy, MIRVs, D-5, MX, etc.); 2) improvements in survivability (hardened silos, mobile ICBMs, quieter submarines, etc.); 3) improvements in command and control (better satellites, redundant communications, improved radar coverage, ELF communications, airborne command posts, EMP hardening, PAL systems, etc.); 4) improvements in penetrability (ICBM decoys, cruise missiles, low observable bombers and missiles, etc.); and 5) replacement of obsolete systems (solid fuels replacing liquid fueled ICBMs, MX replacing Titan, Poseidon submarines replacing Polaris, B1 replacing B52, etc.). At the present time, neither nation seems to have gained a clear edge through modernization. The trick is keeping it that way.

Arms control has proven to be the only mutually acceptable way to cap weapon production and modernization efforts. The CIS and United States now acknowledge that ceilings at lower levels of parity would not destroy their deterrent capability and would reduce both risks and costs. Since the two opposing forces are dissimilar (Russian emphasis is on the ICBM, US is on the Triad), achieving a new parity involves a great deal of subjective analysis. The START Treaty, signed in July 1991, was a major step forward in comparison with the de facto arrangements of SALT II, to which both sides had adhered until then. It provides for deep cuts; while it gives both sides some freedom how to rearrange their force structures, it encourages them to move away from attractive targets and potential first strike weapons.

Another important aspect of arms control agreements is the establishing of verification systems and practices that confirm the agreement and allay concerns about cheating, breakout and surprise attack. Russia and United States have fielded expensive, sophisticated satellites and other technical means to verify compliance. They have also established a standing consultation committee at Geneva to discuss alleged violations to arms control agreements. Because these verification and challenge systems exist, both sides are comfortable with negotiated agreements. Assuming for a moment that nuclear proliferation continues unabated, can one imagine Israel and Iraq, or Pakistan and India functioning in this cooperative manner?

The final point concerning stability has to do with peacetime policies and deployment practices. These must be sufficiently non-provocative that neither nation finds them intolerable. Examples come to mind. When testing ICBMs, missile trajectories do not point towards the United States or the CIS. Russian SSBN submarines are no longer in close proximity to Washington. The US does not fly airborne alert with its bomber force. The Rules of Engagement for naval vessels are more restrictive than previously. The 'Hot Line' capability between the two capitals has been enhanced. On a broader scale, the United States and Soviet Union have made concerted efforts through the years to settle their differences through negotiation, rather than military confrontation. In 45 years of Cold War, no American soldiers have died in combat fighting Russian armies, and vice versa. Since the 1962 Cuban missile crisis, both sides have avoided using their nuclear capability in a threatening way and are particularly sensitive to actions that might be interpreted by the other side as 'nuke-rattling'. One must question whether other historic adversaries equipped with nuclear weapons would show similar restraint, thus avoiding military confrontations that might lead inexorably to nuclear war.

3. Interacting nuclear capabilities

As mentioned above, there are politically opposed nations who are not presently equipped with nuclear weapons but show signs of developing a nuclear capability. Because of the increased military capabilities of these nations, regional conflicts on a fairly large scale seem more rather than less likely. Countries outside of NATO and the former WTO accounted for over 20 percent of the 1990 worldwide defense expenditure of .75 trillion dollars. Equipment purchased will include tanks and other armored vehicles, artillery, supersonic aircraft, surface-to-surface and surface-to-air missiles, major combatant ships and submarines.

These countries possess substantial land and air forces. The ultimate disposition of equipment reduced through the CFE negotiations is a source of added concern in regions like the Middle East and South Asia where history records a tendency towards continuous hostility.

The spread to the Third World of chemical, biological and nuclear weapons, delivered by ballistic missiles, emerges as a great danger to worldwide stability. A disturbing summary of countries confirmed or suspected of possessing chemical and nuclear weapons and potential missile delivery systems follows:

Table 1

Countries which are confirmed or suspected of possessing chemical weapons

POSITIVE OR STRONG POSSIBILITY

Afganistan	Ethiopia	Israel	Syria
Burma	Iran	Libya	Taiwan
China	Iraq	North Korea	Vietnam
Egypt			

SUSPECTED

Brazil	India	South Korea	South Africa
Chile	Pakistan	South Yemen	Thailand
Cuba	Somalia		

Table 2

Countries that now have or are capable of having nuclear weapons by the year 2000 and beyond

HAVE OR ARE SUSPECTED

China	Israel	India	South Africa

POSSIBLE BY YEAR 2000

Argentina	Brazil	Pakistan

POSSIBLE BEYOND YEAR 2000

Egypt	Libya	Saudi Arabia	Syria
Iran	North Korea	South Korea	Taiwan
Iraq			

Table 3

Countries with significant ballistic missile arsenals in 1991

COUNTRY	MISSILE	RANGE (MILES)	PRODUCER
Egypt	Frog 7	40	USSR
	Scud B	190	USSR
	Badr-2000 *	500-600	Egypt/Argentina
	Sakr-80	50	Egypt
Iran	Scud B	190	USSR
	Oghab	25	Iran
	Iran-130	80	Iran/China
Iraq	Frog 7	40	USSR
	Scud B	190	USSR
	Scud B	375	USSR-modified
	Scud B	560	USSR-modified
	Badr-2000 *	500-600	Egypt/Argentina
Israel	Jericho 2 *	900	Israel
Kuwait	Frog 7	40	USSR
Libya	Frog 7	40	USSR
	Scud B	190	USSR
	SS-21	75	USSR
North Yemen	SS-21	75	USSR
Saudi Arabia	CSS-2	1600	China
South Yemen	Scud B	190	USSR
Syria	Frog 7	40	USSR
	Scud B	190	USSR
	SS-21	75	USSR
China	CSS (various)	700-6000	China
India	Frog 7	40	USSR
	Prithvi	150	India
	Agni	1500	India
Pakistan	King Hawk *	180	Pakistan/China
North Korea	Frog 7	40	USSR
	Scud B	190	USSR
South Korea	Frog 7	40	USSR
	Scud B	190	USSR
Argentina	Candor	60	Argentina
	Candor II *	500-600	Argentina
Brazil	6 Missiles *	90-620	Brazil
Cuba	Frog 7	40	USSR

* = Development

Nuclear capabilities should be overt if deterrence is to be effective. Not knowing whether an enemy possesses nuclear weapons greatly increases the danger of uncontrolled escalation through miscalculation. Regardless of pronouncements, an unresolved question is whether nuclear weapons would actually be used by any nation involved in regional conflict. One can hardly visualize a higher degree of instability at the international level if regional conflicts are resolved by the use, or threatened use, of nuclear weapons.

Assuming that two politically opposed societies were to develop nuclear capabilities, what would be required for their relationship to become stable? The closest approach to nuclear stability between opposing societies is the traditional US-Soviet model. This model is sketched on the following page and has several essential characteristics.

- Each government is stable.
- Command and control procedures are reliable.
- Nuclear policies are non-provocative.
- Nuclear systems can survive a surprise attack.
- Personnel are reliable and highly trained.
- Weapon security is comprehensive.
- Weapon design emphasizes safety.
- CSBMs are installed and accepted.

The model emphasizes the linking of nuclear system components (portrayed vertically) with Confidence and Security Building Measures (CSBMs - portrayed horizontally) to which the two governments agree. CSBMs in the model also include all other nuclear arms control agreements. Since CSBMs are essential to the security process, a brief explanation is offered.

Both formal and informal arrangements link the two Super-powers, and these arrangements constitute a panoply of CSBMs. For example, summit conferences between the two leaders have become the usual platform for announcing major policy changes. World opinion, as well as domestic opinion, has come to expect positive developments from these periodic meetings and the pressure for success flows down throughout both bureaucracies, dampening whatever enthusiasm exists for hard line policies. The candid talks

Table 4

A stable system involving politically opposed nations having approximate parity in nuclear weapons

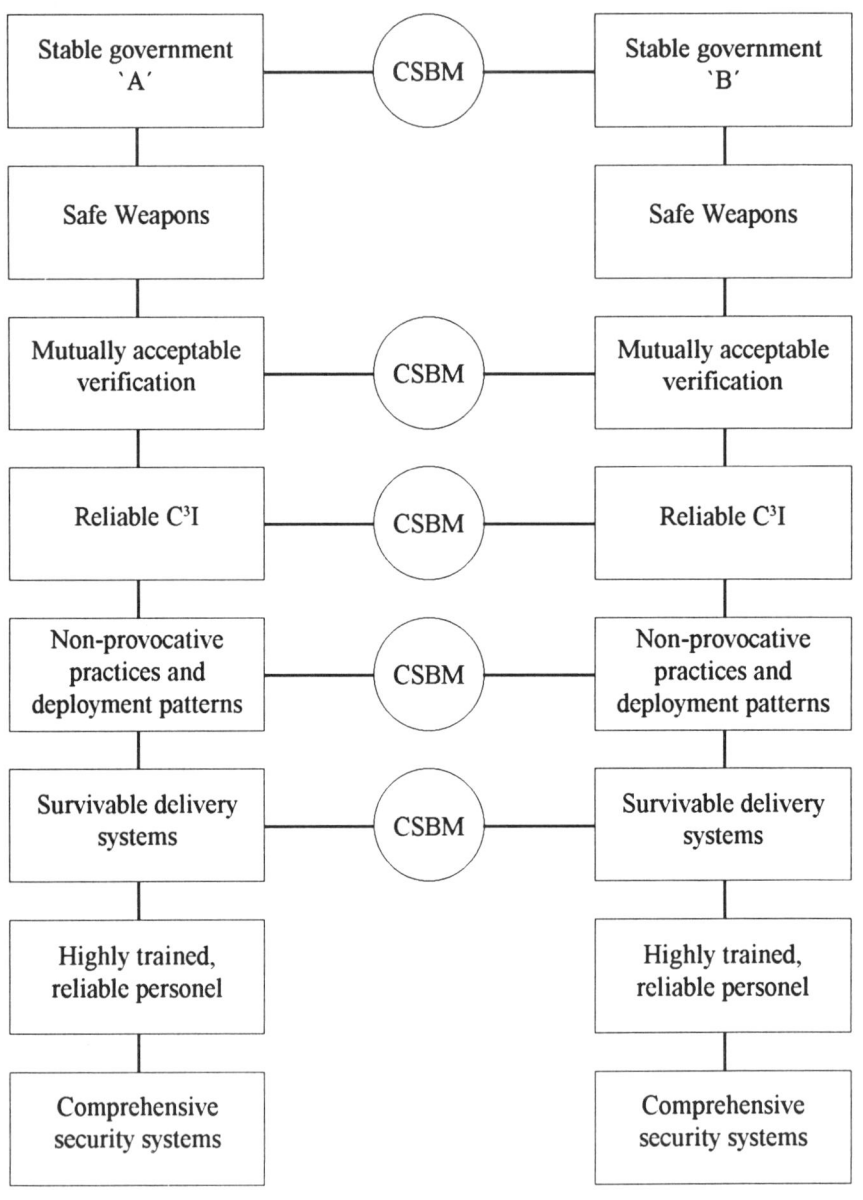

that typify more recent summit conferences also build confidence and cut through the wall of rhetoric built by bureaucratic pronouncements.

The 'Hot Line' between Moscow and Washington is an interesting formal CSBM between governments. Direct, timely contact during crisis is now possible and may be necessary if an inadvertent, accidental or unintentional act should threaten world peace.

National Technical Means (NTM), primarily satellites, have been the normal method for verifying nuclear arms control agreements. Both sides have cooperated with this method of verification and adopted various rules that enhance the process. Sometimes the rules have been negotiated, sometimes they are de facto, but they benefit both sides by providing continual assurance about the size and disposition of opposing nuclear forces.

The command and control of nuclear forces is both expensive and a daunting technical challenge. The stress imposed upon communications by nuclear explosions is so severe that various communication techniques are required to insure connectivity to strategic forces when under attack. Much of the C^3 architecture is dependent upon satellites functioning properly for both warning and communication purposes. The ABM Treaty, decisions not to develop anti-satellite weapons, discontinuance of atmospheric testing, and mutual avoidance of depressed trajectory ballistic missiles are formal and informal examples of CSBMs that protect C^3I.

Just as Washington was once threatened by minimum warning attacks from Soviet submarines too close to our coast line, so the FRG-based, Pershing II apparently threatened Soviet leadership. The Soviet decision to move its submarine patrols back from our coast lines reduced somewhat the need for a launch-on-warning (LOW) American response. Similarly, the INF agreement removed Pershing II as a minimum warning threat to Soviet leadership.

Both sides now recognize that survivable strategic nuclear delivery systems are essential. Against survivable weapon systems, a counterforce first strike attack will not disarm the defender and will not prevent an unacceptably severe retaliation. Survivable weapon systems are therefore a stabilizing factor. Both SALT II and START recognize this important point and strive to find a mutually acceptable formula that enhances force survivability without increasing the overall threat. The current development of mobile, single warhead ICBMs is an example. Unfortunately, survivability carries a very large price tag - one that Third World nations who want to join the nuclear club should carefully consider.

The last two components of the model are 'Highly Trained, Reliable Personnel' and 'Comprehensive Security System.' They are closely linked. The United States military uses a comprehensive screening system to select personnel for nuclear operations. Millions are spent annually on background investigations, physical and mental examinations, specialized training, surveillance programs, counseling and other forms of personnel development. The Soviet Union has comparable programs. This emphasis on human reliability is mandatory for any nation acquiring nuclear weapons. Millions more are spent on security. The Strategic Air Command, for example, has 14,000 airmen devoted to protecting nuclear assets.

4. Related institutional issues

Most of the problems we have raised exist because states will place 'new weapons in old bottles.' That is, however modern nuclear and chemical weapons may appear to be, and however sophisticated ballistic missiles may seem, these technologies will be imbedded in old military organizations that have their own norms, structures, and behavior patterns. These have developed over decades, or even centuries, for their own unique reasons for the state in question. But they have not been much influenced by the responsibility or problems arising from ownership of weapons of mass destruction. The United States and the USSR/CIS, in contrast, have a forty-year record of having their military and political institutions shaped by the responsibilities for such weapons. While we feel that both Superpowers have behaved responsibly in this regard, even if one does not believe this it should be a source of concern that there is no comparable institutional pattern in many states who are today seeking to acquire these systems. (Some of this discussion is based upon Bracken, 1990.)

Several of these institutional differences deserve greater attention. (Here we use the term institutional to mean organizations and associated laws and norms that govern its behavior.) The indications and warning (I&W, for short) systems of the two Superpowers relied on for determination of when an attack is being launched, or will soon be launched, consist of interrelated and highly redundant intelligence information.

In developing states this will not be the case. Their I&W system consists overwhelmingly of human intelligence (or 'HUMINT') networks. These are spies placed inside another nation. Superpower experience, and organization theory, both point to the very low reliability of human beings to process subtle and complicated information for this purpose. During the 1962 Cuban missile crisis, for example, the United States ignored reports even from highly placed agents inside the Soviet government because we did not believe the reliability of such information could justify linking it to critical war and peace decisions. In this instance, KGB Colonel Oleg Penkovsky erroneously sent a message during the height of the crisis that the Soviet Union was about to attack the United States, a report that was in fact incorrect. The point to emphasize is that the United States absorbed this false report without it triggering a response because of institutional checks and balances including an extensive I&W system.

In many developing nuclear states deadly arsenals will be essentially attached to a disparate collection of low reliability human agents reporting on enemy actions. This could produce a very unstable situation in a crisis if competing reports arrive at headquarters indicating that country A is about to attack country B. Both authors have participated in a Middle East crisis game in which erroneous reports of Israeli preparation for a nuclear weapon attack triggered a major response by opponents. In the tension surrounding a crisis these reports were readily believed, despite the absence of a redundant system to check their authenticity.

Another institutional consideration is government structure and its influence on national administrative capacity. Some states developing weapons of mass destruction have an authoritarian organization in which military and 'stasi' type police and paramilitary forces are headed by a supreme leader. In such a structure decision-making rests with this supreme leader and nowhere else. What characterizes this structure is a relatively undeveloped military high command. There is no general staff system or its equivalent, there is little or no fusion of intelligence information with military and political context, and the orders of the supreme leader are followed without question.

The high commands of the United States and the CIS serve a very important role in creating checks and balances to the perceptions of political leaders. Indeed, they go beyond this because these institutions shape the reality that political leaders see in the world. At the other extreme are the security institutions of states like North

Korea, Romania before 1990, Iraq, Iran, Libya, and others where there are fewer institutional checks on the political leadership. Fewer checks exist to stop them from taking action, and fewer balances exist to ensure that a multitude of important factors are considered. In the United States and the CIS general staff organizations, national security councils, and intelligence councils perform this important role.

In some versions, authoritarian governments can develop particularly dangerous institutional forms. Most military organizations develop a 'fact seeking' character, in which they try to determine the state of affairs in the world so that rational decision-making is possible. But in a state like North Korea, a 'belief seeking' system appears, in which there is an attempt to impose a particular political interpretation of events onto the situation. This arises because of the inverse relationship that exists between authoritarian government and information flow. The more authoritarian the government, the less information flows from the bottom to the top of the organization. 'Bottom up' information flow is reduced because of the fear of contradicting the views of the leadership, and is a widely observed phenomena in political modernization theory (see, for example, Apter, 1967). In this case, not only does the security organization not check or balance the leader, it reinforces the distortion of reality, adding organizational to already existing psychological dislocations.

The implications of this for crisis stability in the face of weapons of mass destruction are fairly clear, but have not been adequately understood. The forms of government in many states may make any evolution toward responsible behavior accompanying acquisition of weapons of mass destruction much harder than originally foreseen.

In summary, we note that institutions can seriously distort the utilitarian calculations of strategy that dominate most of the research and analysis on proliferation of weapons of mass destruction. It is most often argued that states acquiring these weapons may have problems, but in the final analysis, they will still follow a rational logic and pattern of behavior, even if it is a logic that fits their own situation. This perspective neglects the confounding effects of placing deadly weapons in security institutions that have their own impact on logic and behavior patterns.

5. Conclusion: avoid further nuclear proliferation

This chapter has only touched on the many factors that must be considered by any nation that considers the acquisition of nuclear weapons. No Third World nation can reasonably afford building a nuclear capability that would have the essential safety and institutional features that are inherent to the US and Russian systems. Unless all these factors are incorporated into their system, their nuclear arsenal will be unstable and threatening to all other nations. There are no acceptable short cuts.

PART V

What Can Be Done - and by Whom?

Chapter 13

Minimizing the Risks for Accidental Nuclear War: An Agenda For Action

Michael D. Intriligator

Dagobert L. Brito

1. Introduction

This chapter develops an agenda for minimizing the risk of accidental nuclear war.[39] The problem of accidental nuclear war looms as a more and more serious one as its risk of occurring has probably risen relative to the risk of a deliberate nuclear war, particularly given the dramatic changes that have occurred in Eastern Europe, the end of the Cold War, and the collapse of the Warsaw Pact, and the dissolution of the Soviet Union. The risk of accidental nuclear war may have increased absolutely as well, due to the nature of new weapons and command and control systems. As a result, military and political leaders, including defense policy makers and analysts, who in the past had tended to dismiss the problem of accidental nuclear war as unimportant, both relatively and absolutely, have begun finally to consider this problem to be a very serious one, as seen both in statements of leaders and in the establishment of crisis control centers in the United States and Russia. Nevertheless, the general public has not yet shown an adequate appreciation for the importance of this issue. Nor have formal arms control agendas, whether in bilateral or multilateral negotiations or through unilateral action, yet begun to take into consideration the problems of accidental nuclear war. The issue should, in the future, be taken much more seriously once leaders and the general public begin to appreciate that the probability of such an event, while small, is not zero and may in fact be rising and that the consequences of such an event are catastrophic.

---

[39] This chapter builds on our earlier papers on accidental nuclear war, in Intriligator & Brito (1988 & 1990a).

The agenda to be developed in this chapter to minimize the risk of accidental nuclear war is proposed as a set of new initiatives for bilateral, multilateral, and unilateral arms control to deal with a problem of growing significance. Before developing an agenda for action, however, this chapter first defines accidental nuclear war and gives examples of initiating accidents that could lead to an accidental nuclear war. It then explains why the probability of accidental nuclear war has risen relatively and perhaps absolutely as well.

A significant point, which has not yet been fully appreciated by either military or political leaders or by the general public, is that the problem of accidental nuclear war is not one confined to the mature nuclear weapons states of the United States and Russia. It is also a problem applicable to the newer nuclear weapons states, including the other successor states of the USSR with nuclear weapons, especially Ukraine and Kazakhstan (each of which has more nuclear warheads than the United Kingdom and France combined); the smaller nuclear powers of the United Kingdom, France, and China; and the covert nuclear weapons states of Israel, India, Pakistan, and perhaps others. Accidents of various types could occur in any of these states. In fact, the newer, smaller, and covert nuclear nations may face even more severe problems in controlling potential accidents, given their less developed safety systems and command and control systems. For example, an accidental nuclear war might possibly occur in connection with an escalating crisis involving India and Pakistan, one involving Israel and Iraq, or one involving Iran and Iraq. Iraq has already having used missiles against both Israel and Iran, it has chemical weapons, and it has repeatedly tried to develop nuclear capabilities. Iran also appears to be trying to develop nuclear capabilities. An accidental nuclear war might also occur in connection with hostilities between various domestic factions within a current nuclear weapons state, possibly in Russia or China, where various military or civilian factions may have access to nuclear weapons in a possible local conflict, insurrection, or even civil war situation. In any of these cases an accidental nuclear war would have repercussions on all nuclear weapons states and indirect effects on all states. Thus all states, especially all nuclear weapons states, have a common interest and concern in avoiding accidental nuclear war, which should be seen as a common global problem.

2. Accidental nuclear war: definition and examples

An 'accidental nuclear war' will be assumed here, by definition, to be any nuclear war without a deliberate and properly informed decision to use nuclear weapons on the part of the national command authorities of the nuclear weapons state(s) involved. [40] An accidental nuclear war could be initiated by a variety of possible accidents, all of which involve some mixture of failures involving people (human factors), equipment (hardware), and procedures (software). Some possible initiation scenarios, illustrated from the Soviet and US experience with nuclear weapons (in the absence of information about the experiences of the newer nuclear weapons states) include:

1. *Accidents in warning sensors.* A most important type of accident that could lead to an accidental nuclear war is that involving a false warning of an enemy attack. An example of such a false warning, which fortunately did not involve the use of nuclear weapons but did involve major loss of life, was the July 1988 attack by the US Navy ship *USS Vincennes* on an Iranian A300 civilian airliner in the Persian Gulf. [41] Another example of such an accident, which also did not involve the use of nuclear weapons, was the Soviet shooting down in September 1983 of the Korean airliner KAL007 that had entered Soviet airspace, in the mistaken belief that it was a US military aircraft. Other examples of false warnings, which *did* involve nuclear weapons but fortunately did not lead to war, were the 1980 incidents at NORAD. These incidents involved two different false warnings of a massive Soviet attack, one involving a faulty computer chip and the other involving the reading of a computer tape prepared for training

---

[40] Some authors distinguish an 'accidental nuclear war' from an 'unintended nuclear war' or an 'inadvertent nuclear war' based on whether the war stemmed from a technical or a human failure. Here no distinction is drawn among these alternatives, but it should be understood that concern is broader than just accidents per se. Perhaps a better descriptor would be 'unsanctioned nuclear war,' but the term 'accidental nuclear war' has become the standard one for describing the problem in various conferences and publications over recent years, e.g. the 1990a book *Accidental Nuclear War*, edited by Paul, Intriligator, and Smoker, based on the 1989 Pugwash conference on this topic.

[41] Using the language of statistical decision theory, the *USS Vincennes* incident involved a Type II error, where action was taken that was not warranted. See also footnotes 45 and 46.

purposes as if it involved events that were actually happening.[42]
A *Vincennes*-type error or KAL 007-type error at NORAD or
somewhere in the warning systems of any of the nuclear weapons
states could lead to an accidental nuclear war. Such accidents in
warning sensors are mitigated by the presence of requirements
like that of 'dual phenomenology,' which requires that a warning
from one type of sensor must be confirmed by another type of
sensor involving different physical principles.

2. *Accidents in C³I systems*. These are accidents involving command,
control, communication and intelligence, which link the warning
systems to the national command authority and the national
command authority to the operational units that would conduct
an attack or a retaliatory strike. Accidents in this area include
misread or misinterpreted signals, accidents with computers, and
losses of electrical power. An example is the Soviet intelligence
reaction to the secret NATO nuclear weapons exercise Able
Archer in November 1983, in which the KGB issued a nuclear
attack alert to its overseas agents.

3. *Accidents with actual or potential nuclear weapons carriers*. These
accidents involve a variety of possible carriers of nuclear
weapons, including planes, ships, submarines, and missiles.
Examples include the accidental dropping of a hydrogen bomb,
which did not explode, by a US bomber in Spain in 1956; the US
bomber carrying nuclear weapons that came apart above
Goldsboro, North Carolina in 1961; the explosion and fire on a
Soviet Yankee class submarine, which was carrying nuclear
weapons, in the Atlantic in October 1986; the April 1989 sinking
of a Soviet submarine off Norway; and various accidents that
have occurred on US and Soviet submarines carrying nuclear
weapons.

4. *Accidents with nuclear weapons*. These accidents include accidental launches or firings of warheads. Examples include the
explosion and fire of propellant fuel in a US Titan silo near Little
Rock, Arkansas in September 1980; the July 1984 explosion at a

---

[42] See Goldwater & Hart (1980) for the Senate Committee on Armed Services
report on false alarms in NORAD in 1980.

Soviet naval base on the Kola peninsula; and the cruise missile accident in West Germany in 1985. Such accidents are mitigated by the presence of Permissive Action Links (PALs), electronic locks that prevent a nuclear weapon from being armed without the explicit instruction of the national command authority. Such PALs are present on all US nuclear weapons other than submarine-launched ballistic missiles (SLBMs) and other nuclear weapons on naval ships and submarines.

5. *Accidents involving nuclear power plants.* An accident at a nuclear power plant could lead to reactions involving nuclear weapons in the mistaken belief that the plant was the target of another nation or that the accident involved the use of a nuclear weapon. Accidents involving such power plants, including those at Three Mile Island in the United States and at Chernobyl in the Soviet Union (in Ukraine) have, fortunately, not had secondary consequences. Future accidents in any nuclear power plant worldwide could, however, lead to reactions involving nuclear weapons, particularly if a regional rival, such as India or Pakistan, were suspected of involvement. An accident at a nuclear power plant in the Middle East might lead to a possible reaction against Israel in the mistaken belief that the accident was a strike by Israel, like its 1981 strike against Iraq's Osirak nuclear power plant near Baghdad.

6. *Accidents involving delegated or predelegated authority.* These accidents include accidents in communications links with US submarine commanders which could, particularly in a crisis situation, lead to accidental launch decisions in view of the lack of PALs on SLBMs.

7. *Accidents involving automated decision making.* Systems with automatic response, such as a computer-driven launch-on-warning system or a doomsday machine could, when coupled with false warning, lead to an accidental nuclear war.

8. *Accidents involving non-nation actors.* These accidents involve various national or subnational terrorist groups. Such groups may have access to nuclear capabilities, possibly through the interception of fissile material moving in international commerce, which

could be used to make nuclear weapons. In fact, international commerce involving fissile material has expanded enormously as a result of the implementation of the Japanese decision to reprocess their spent nuclear fuel rods in Europe. Terrorist groups may also have the capacity to threaten to destroy nuclear facilities, including not only nuclear weapons sites and depots, but also nuclear power facilities. An attack using conventional weapons against a nuclear power plant near a city could give rise to Chernobyl-type effects, with extremely serious consequences even if there were no retaliation. In fact, it is possible to have a nuclear war or an accidental nuclear war *without* nuclear weapons, using nuclear power plants as targets for conventional weapons by non-nation (or nation) actors.

9. *Accidents in a civil war in a nuclear weapons state.* Conflict or civil war in a nuclear weapons state, such as Russia or China, which have both experienced recent domestic instabilities, could lead to a variety of possible scenarios leading to an accidental nuclear war. These scenarios include, among others, disorder in situations involving nuclear weapons, as competing groups seek access to such weapons; the use of nuclear threats and counterthreats by domestic rivals; and the use of nuclear weapons against another nation as an alternative to defeat by a rival domestic group.

3. The increasing probability of accidental nuclear war relative to intentional nuclear war and perhaps absolutely as well

While the chance of an accidental nuclear war is generally considered 'low,' it has probably risen relative to the chance of a deliberate nuclear war, and it may have risen absolutely as well. In fact, accidents may be among the most likely current routes to nuclear war, as opposed to other routes, such as a preemptive or preventive bolt-out-of-the-blue type attack or escalation from a conventional war. Various types of accidents, such as the nine listed above, have to be coupled with an escalation process that leads from the initiating accident to an accidental nuclear war. There are, in fact, various mechanisms, human, mechanical, and procedural, to prevent such an escalation. The presence of PALs on nuclear weapons, for example, represents a mechanical device to prevent escalation, while dual phenomenology represents a procedural device to prevent escalation. Thus, the major challenge in minimizing the risk of accidental nuclear war is either to prevent the initiating accident or to reinforce existing mechanisms preventing its escalation to nuclear war. The chance of accidental nuclear war undoubtedly rises rapidly in a crisis situation or in a period of great international tension, both because there is a greater chance for accidents and because the mechanisms preventing escalation of accidents to nuclear war may be less effective in such a situation. There is also, however, a small but non-zero chance of an accidental nuclear war happening in a non-crisis situation, as accidents will happen and the mechanisms preventing escalation to nuclear war are not perfect.

There are several reasons for the increase in the relative and possibly also absolute probability of an accidental nuclear war, all of which suggest that there should be a relatively greater emphasis on preventing the accidents themselves and/or on reinforcing existing mechanisms that prevent their escalation to war as part of the arms control agenda. These reasons include:

1. *Changes in Eastern Europe and the former Soviet Union.* The 1989 sequence of 'falling dominoes' revolutions that occurred in Eastern Europe led to the demise of the Warsaw Pact and the end of the Cold War. The result is that there is now probably the lowest chance ever of a deliberate war involving the four Nuclear Powers in Europe. The declining chance of a deliberate nuclear war heightens concern about a possible accidental nuclear war. It also increases concern about the potential role played by other nuclear weapons states. At the same time, the dissolution of the Soviet Union has led to nuclear weapons being stationed in four nations, Russia, Ukraine, Kazakhstan, and Belarus, while the unstable political, social, and economic situation in these Soviet successor states raises serious concerns about the security, safety, and control of nuclear weapons in all four nations.

2. *Effects of mutual deterrence.* The presence of large stockpiles of nuclear weapons and means for their delivery and their control, even after a nuclear or conventional first strike attack, has created a situation of mutual deterrence between the United States and Russia and, earlier, between the United States and the Soviet Union, which has undoubtedly lowered the chance of a

deliberate nuclear war. Deterrence, based on an assured threat of a retaliatory second strike, is a psychological-political-technical reality which has worked to reduce the chance of a deliberate decision to use nuclear weapons. The same structures that have resulted in a mutual deterrence situation, involving strategic nuclear weapons, a variety of delivery systems, and sophisticated C^3I systems for their control, could, however, result in an accidental nuclear war.[43]

3. *Growing complexity of protecting and controlling nuclear weapons.* It becomes more and more difficult to protect and to control nuclear weapons in view of the variety of types and sophisticated nature of these weapons. Compounding this problem is the fact that the Soviet strategic nuclear weapons are now stationed on the territory of four independent states, but controlled by the Commonwealth of Independent States.

4. *Greater automation and technical sophistication of C^3I systems.* The highly sophisticated and state-of-the-art systems for command and control are vulnerable to human error, computer failure, and other technical malfunctions, especially at human-machine interfaces. For example, the *USS Vincennes* accident in 1988 involved the latest type of radars, electronics, computers, etc. in the billion-dollar Aegis system. The crew of the *Vincennes* was

---

[43] Nuclear weapons play two different roles with regard to reducing the chance of nuclear war. First, they have a positive role in establishing a mutual deterrence regime, which lowers the chance of a deliberate nuclear war. Second, however, they have a negative role in leading to the possibility of accidental nuclear war. An optimal level and structure of nuclear weapons would balance these two, allowing for the continuation of a deterrence regime but restructuring forces and their control systems so as to reduce the chance of accidental nuclear war. Very large-scale reductions in stockpiles of nuclear weapons would be counterproductive in eroding deterrence, and there is probably a greater risk involved in eliminating such weapons than in managing them properly. Furthermore, the problem of accidents is related more to the configuration and control of nuclear weapons than to the sheer number of such weapons. It is useful to think of the problem of the desired number of nuclear weapons (that is, the problem of 'how much is enough?') as one in inventory theory, where an optimal policy creates a balance that takes into account both holding costs and stockout costs. Here the 'holding costs' are those involving the risk of accidental nuclear war, while the 'stockout costs' are those involving the risk of deliberate nuclear war through an erosion of deterrence. According to inventory theory, there is an optimal level of stockpiles of nuclear weapons that takes account of both types of costs and minimizes total costs. On the requirements for deterrence see, Intriligator and Brito (1984, 1986 & 1987b) and Intriligator (1975 & 1989b). On their relation to nuclear proliferation see Brito and Intriligator (1993).

hypersensitive to an attack from the air due to the earlier incident in the Gulf, where Iraqi warplanes attacked another US ship, the *USS Stark*.[44] While the Aegis system was working properly, though human error possibly caused or amplified by the psychological effect on the captain and crew of the *Vincennes* of the *Stark* incident, the operators of the Aegis system believed that they thought the Iranian airbus was *descending* toward them when it was actually *ascending* on its normal course as a commercial airliner.[45] The result was an accidental shooting down of an innocent airplane.

5. *Complexity and mobility of weapons carriers*. There are significant difficulties in communicating with submarines and other mobile systems that create problems in their control. These systems are also themselves highly susceptible to accidents, particularly with submarines operating close to one another in an environment in which monitoring and control are difficult.

6. *A possible announced or de facto launch-on-warning policy*. The possibility of a launch-on-warning ('use them or lose them') policy, when coupled with a possible Type II error for warning systems, involving a false signal of an enemy attack, could lead to an accidental nuclear war, with the side initiating the war having the false belief that it was retaliating against the other side. This problem is compounded by the short warning times present in the system, particularly for nuclear weapons states in close proximity, such as India and Pakistan or, possibly in the future, Iran and Iraq.

7. *Critical relationships in a very complex system*. The command and control system for nuclear weapons is a very complex one, including warning systems, sensor system operators, national

---

[44] Using the language of statistical decision theory, as in footnote 42, the *USS Stark* incident involved a Type I error, where action was not taken that should have been taken, in that case, action against Iraqi planes that were attacking the US Navy ship in the Gulf.

[45] In terms of footnotes 42 and 45, it is possible that actions taken to avoid a Type I error, as in the *USS Stark*, resulted in an increase in the chance of the Type II error that occurred with the *USS Vincennes*.

command authority, weapons, and many other components. It involves people (including the national command authority, field commanders, and C³I personnel), equipment (including computers, sensors, communication equipment, satellites, radars, platforms, weapons), and procedures (including computer software and human decisions). There is the possibility of a cascading and escalating set of errors and instabilities among these components in view of the short decision times, speed, automation, and complex interdependencies of this system. Such a possibility becomes even more serious in the case of a multilateral alert during an international crisis. A small problem or malfunction in one system could lead to reactions in the system of a potential enemy state, with magnified feedback to the first state or other states, and so forth. Through such action-reaction interactions, a relatively minor problem, such as a component failure or a human error, could ultimately lead to an accidental nuclear war.[46] Thus, there is a problem in the coupling of rival nuclear weapons states systems, whether those of the United States and Russia, those of Russia and China, those of India and Pakistan, or those of Israel and Iraq (even without nuclear weapons in Iraq). The problem is exacerbated in a crisis situation when people suffer from stress, fatigue, and anxiety; when the procedures being used are facing situations not experienced before or ones with little prior experience; and equipment may be overloaded.

4. Arms control initiatives, unilateral, bilateral, and multilateral, to reduce the chance of accidental nuclear war

If 'arms control' is defined, as it should be, as actions taken to reduce the chance of war, especially nuclear war, then actions taken to reduce the chance of *accidental* nuclear war should be a significant part of the arms control agenda.[47] In fact, the problem of accidental

---

[46] Because of the coupling of systems it is impossible to calculate the probability of accidental nuclear war from simply the probability of component failure. Thus, one cannot analyze the robustness of the system as a whole from its component parts.

[47] For a discussion of the implications of this interpretation of arms control see Intriligator and Brito (1987a & 1989) and Intriligator (1992). Some people have interpreted or even defined arms control as negotiated limitations or reductions in nuclear stockpiles, which confuses ends with means.

nuclear war should be seen as a *shared* problem, leading to cooperative solutions by way of both agreements among two or more states and reinforcing unilateral initiatives. In particular, there can be cooperation among potentially antagonistic states, whether the United States and Russia or India and Pakistan, in recognition of their shared interests in preventing an accidental nuclear war. The problem of accidental nuclear war and attempts to reduce its chances are, in many respects like those of nuclear nonproliferation, where opposing states have cooperated in a variety of ways to deal jointly with a common threat to all.

Arms control initiatives to reduce the chance of accidental nuclear war must be taken in recognition that this is a *systems* problem, not a *numbers* problem. The various routes to accidental nuclear war, as outlined above, depend on the critical relationships in a very complex system, not on simply the numbers of weapons. In fact, increasing the numbers of weapons, along with the development of the triad of launching platforms and secure basing modes, has probably *reduced* the chance of nuclear war by reducing the chance of deliberate nuclear war. Conversely, weapons reductions, whether by negotiated agreements, as in the START treaties or by unilateral action, does little to treat the problem of accidental nuclear war. Given the immense damage that could be done by strategic nuclear weapons, as, for example, the damage that could be caused by one submarine carrying SLBMs, even huge reductions in inventories of strategic nuclear weapons will not solve the problem of accidental nuclear war. The lethality remains, and the problems of control, warning, etc. exist regardless of the numbers of nuclear weapons. Thus, simply reducing stockpiles does not address the problem of accidental nuclear war. There are other initiatives, however, which could play a major role in reducing the chance of accidental nuclear war. These initiatives include, roughly in order of importance:

1. *Actions and agreements to contain or deescalate any potential crisis situations.* It would be useful to establish *in advance* a set of procedures and code of behavior to follow in case of any potential crisis situations involving any of the nuclear powers. One such procedure might be a process of consultation or mediation using third parties. For example, the United States and Russia have established crisis control centers. As to the newer nuclear weapons states, concerns have been expressed about

another India-Pakistan war, which could involve nuclear threats or even the use of nuclear weapons or about another war involving Israel and Iraq. Similar concerns might be expressed about future relations between Ukraine and Russia and between Kazakhstan and Russia. Procedures should be agreed to ahead of time to deal with such a situation. In particular, the United States and Russia have a major responsibility in ensuring that nuclear weapons are not used in a regional crisis or conflict situation, as such use could lead, via a set of accidents, technical or human, to a global accidental nuclear war.

2. *Agreements in advance on how to deal with possible accidents.* Such agreements could build on the 1971 Accidents Measures Agreement between the United States and the USSR, an agreement of unlimited duration which calls for immediate notification of an accidental or other unexplained incident involving a possible detonation of a nuclear weapon that could create the risk of a possible nuclear war. For example, the Soviet Union notified the United States immediately about the 1986 explosion on its Yankee class submarine carrying nuclear weapons, in full compliance with this treaty (and in contrast to the Soviet delay in notifying affected nations about the Chernobyl accident, which was not, at that time, covered by such an agreement). All nuclear nations should be parties to such agreements, and these agreements should be strengthened to cover what should be done in various contingencies. Given the short times involved in warnings, flights of weapons, and consequent decision times, it is important to decide *in advance* of the event how to deal with a wide variety of possible contingencies involving accidents, crises, and threats, including threats from terrorist groups. International cooperation to develop such procedures would be valuable in itself in reducing the potential escalation from an accident to accidental nuclear war. It would also be a useful confidence building measure.

3. *Prenotification of any major military exercises or missile flight tests.* Advance notification of major military exercises in Europe (and the exchange of observers) was a result of the Conference on Security and Cooperation in Europe (CSCE) Stockholm multilateral negotiations. Such greater openness or transparency is useful

in reducing the chance of false warnings that could lead to accidental nuclear war, such as in the Soviet reaction to the NATO Able Archer exercise in 1983. It would be useful to build on the Stockholm agreement by extending it to missile flight tests, to major naval exercises, and to other contingencies that could be misinterpreted as an attack. It would also be useful to extend it to other parts of the world, including South Asia and the Middle East.

4. *Improvements in C^3I systems.* One of the most important unilateral actions that all nuclear weapons states could take would be improvements in their C^3I systems so as to avoid false commands or communications. Such improvements, which apply to the covert as well as the overt nuclear weapons states, should include hardened and secure command and control systems. They should also include defenses, both active and passive, of such systems in order to ensure their survivability and reliability, thereby reducing the danger of a decapitation strike and eliminating the need for a launch-on-warning system. There could also be bilateral and multilateral global and regional agreements on exchanging information on such systems and agreeing not to strike such systems. Such agreements are important for the United States and Russia, but are also important for India and Pakistan.

5. *Improved communications links.* While the 'hotline' provides an important communications link between the United States and Russia, there should be comparable communications channels connecting all nuclear nations, including covert nuclear nations.

6. *No ASAT deployments.* Deployments of anti-satellite (ASAT) systems would create incentives for a launch-on-warning system, which could trigger countermeasures, thereby increasing the chance of an accidental nuclear war. The ASAT systems themselves could involve accidents, further increasing the chance of accidental nuclear war. Thus, there should be agreements and unilateral actions on not deploying such systems.

7. *Command/destruct capability for all missiles.* A command/destruct capability for missiles, which would enable operators to

destroy the missile after launch, exists in the US for non-military missiles of NASA, but not for military missiles. Such a capability would be valuable in allowing accidentally launched missiles to be destroyed. Military commanders have traditionally argued against such a capability on the basis that if the enemy could obtain access to this capability then the missiles could be rendered useless, but the system could be protected against enemy use by the same coding devices as those currently used in PALs.[48]

8. *'Rules of the road' to cover incidents at sea.* Accidents at sea, particularly in the undersea environment, could lead to accidental nuclear war. A multilateral agreement on 'rules of the road' to cover incidents at sea, including submarines, would be useful in avoiding mishaps and containing the problems stemming from naval encounters or incidents.

9. *A strengthening of the nonproliferation regime.* The existing nonproliferation regime has been relatively successful, but not perfect, in curbing the numbers of nuclear weapons states and thus contributing to a reduction in the risk of accidental nuclear war by reducing the number of national command authorities controlling nuclear weapons. This regime would be enhanced by limiting nuclear exports of the second-tier nuclear supplier states, by enhanced safeguards against the diversion of nuclear materials to states or subnational groups, by avoiding international commerce in fissile material as has begun with the reprocessing of spent fuel rods by Japan in Europe, and by a major extension and strengthening of the Non Proliferation Treaty (NPT) in 1995, when the current treaty expires.

10. *A sharing of technology, including PALs, command/destruct capabilities, C^3I, etc.* These technologies are useful in avoiding irrevocable decisions, in controlling nuclear weapons, and in

---

[48] Some have argued for PALs on naval nuclear weapons, as a protection against accidental launches from submarines or ships. The result, however, of putting PALs on these weapons would mean that all nuclear weapons would have such locks, possibly inviting a decapitation strike in the knowledge that if the national command authority is destroyed then PALs could not be overcome, making nuclear retaliation impossible. As a result, it may be more important to have command/destruct capability for naval nuclear weapons than PALs on such weapons.

destroying accidentally fired missiles. It would be a valuable contribution if such technologies, or perhaps earlier generations of these technologies, were widely available to all states with nuclear weapons, overt or covert, and also to all states with access to missiles. Provision of these technologies could be done on a cooperative basis by the United States and Russia with newer and also potential nuclear weapons states.

11. *Adoption of military doctrines stressing defensive defense and reduced reliability on vulnerable and firststrike weapons.* A doctrinal change which could reduce the chance of accidental nuclear war would be widespread adoption of the concept of defensive defense, stressing defensive as opposed to offensive policies. This change would be reinforced by restructuring strategic forces so as to eliminate apparent first strike systems, particularly fixed-site land-based ballistic missiles, such as the US Minuteman III and MX and the Soviet SS-18 and SS-19. These missiles are each perceived as having offensive first strike characteristics by the other side, and their elimination would be seen as an important step toward defensive defense. Their elimination would also be seen as an initiative that would reduce the incentives toward the development of highly unstable launch-on-warning systems in response to the perceived vulnerability of such weapons.[49] Another reinforcing initiative would be reduced reliance and eventual elimination of forward bases and of short flight time systems.

12. *Establishment of an international early-warning monitoring system.* Currently all nuclear nations rely on their own national monitoring systems. It would be useful to have an international system as a backup, one that would be independent of any national system but which would provide early-warning information to all nuclear powers. Such a system, which could be established and maintained through an international organization or through a group of neutral and nonaligned nations, could play a role for antagon-

---

[49] See Intriligator (1989a) for a specific proposal along these lines. The land-based leg of the triad could then be replaced by mobile and concealable missiles, such as long-range cruise missiles, which have a mission as second strike retaliatory weapons since they are difficult to locate and, at the same time, too slow for use in a first strike.

istic nuclear weapons nations comparable to that played by the United States in providing early-warning monitoring of the border between Israel and Egypt as part of their peace treaty.

5. Conclusion

The risk of accidental nuclear war is a real one and one of growing relative significance. It is a problem that is not confined to the United States and Russia, but applies to all the nuclear weapons states, both overt and covert. Indeed, the end of the Cold War and the dissolution of the Soviet Union suggests that the problem is not only of growing importance but also highly relevant to the newer, smaller, and covert nuclear weapons states. The twelve initiatives presented here could reduce the chance of accidental nuclear war, and it would be useful if they would become part of the arms control agenda for unilateral, bilateral, and multilateral action.

Chapter 14

Political Aspects of Minimizing the Risk of Accidental Nuclear War

Alexander K. Kislov

Humanity is now at a crucial turning point, having a chance of living in a truly new world of positive interaction where genuine peace is a natural state and not just a respite or a pause between periods of military confrontation. Such a world, unfortunately, is far from completion. As it was stressed by many politicians including the presidents of the USA and the former USSR the threat is in the unpredictable march of events and lack of stability.

The powerful processes accompanying the revision of relationships formed by the bipolar military confrontation are indeed largely unpredictable. Old grievances and claims as well as new ambitions crop up everywhere. The 'working order' in the Third World normally includes more than twenty wars and military conflicts, the South/South and the North/South contradictions are growing. Many national states and political movements feel that they are left to their own devices, that new natural allies should be looked for, that new political - and military - arguments are needed. Economic and political differences between rich and poor countries get increasingly bitter; new waves of aggressive nationalism are spreading all over the world; the 'Islamic factor' assumes a new significance in the military sphere; and a growing economic and psychological discomfort is widespread.

In spite of its economic troubles, the Third World has entered a new twist of the arms race spiral. An increasing number of countries try to get up-to-date weaponry, in particular weapons of mass destruction and their vehicles. In several regions, military power unabatedly serves as a practical argument in disputes and a warrant against the instability of the international community and the impredictable behavior of some of its members.

The growing connectedness and interdependence of today's world tend to affect the threat of an accidental nuclear war in two ways. On the one hand, vigorous pressure can be brought to bear on potential military (and, in particular, nuclear) adventurers. One cannot hide explosions of nuclear weapons or disasters in nuclear power plants. Nations can be better informed about each other's intentions, and their behavior and reactions to potential changes can be better predicted.

On the other hand, this interconnectedness may, under unfavorable circumstances, increase the risk of vertical or horizontal military escalation, as well as that of an accidental nuclear war.

This is not a recent problem, having been with us for the last three decades. Notwithstanding the propaganda exercises of the early and mid-1950s, the first meeting of Soviet and American experts on the prevention of surprise attacks was held in November 1958, and gave an important impetus to the formation of the arms control concept in the United States and other Western countries. By including the threat of an accidental nuclear war in its deliberations, it also served to place that problem on the agenda.

The complexity of the problem is demonstrated by its being the subject of discussions even today. In a world that changes, so, inescapably, does the very structure of the problem as well as the relative emphases. Previously insignificant or nonexistent aspects of the problem may thus come to the forefront.

Some experts have maintained, even recently, that an accidental or unauthorized launching of a missile or an explosion of any nuclear charge may result in a nuclear war. Are they right?

Whenever there has been a *real* threat of nuclear war in the post-war period, it did not originate in some accidental or unauthorized acts but in the deliberate political and military actions of Nuclear Powers. The likelihood of a really accidental nuclear war has been diminished by a number of important agreements entered into by the Soviet Union and the Russian Federation. These include the Hot Lines (USA 1963, France 1966, UK 1967); Measures to Reduce the Risk of Outbreak of Nuclear War (including accidental or unauthorized use; USA 1971); and Nuclear Accidents (France 1976, UK 1977). During the period of confrontation, the top political and military leaders of the Nuclear Powers were nevertheless convinced that there was every chance of any nuclear accident developing into a nuclear war; and this belief, on the other hand, has increased the possibility of an accidental war.

Yet in spite of the dozens of serious nuclear accidents, the worst did not happen. This means that the nuclear balance proved an effective deterrent. We can hardly deny that at one stage of the world's political development, including the active 'glacial period' of the Cold War, nuclear weapons served as an insurance factor. On the other hand, the risk that the nuclear weapon might be employed was rather great; but a counterbalance to its 'demonical' force lay precisely in the fear of its being used in a large-scale military conflict.

This effect of the nuclear balance was greatly enhanced in the early 1970s, when both sides recognized the existence of a strategic parity. Never before in human history have two adversaries been equally capable of certainly destroying each other in a retaliatory strike. It was not by accident that one of the most important results of their summit meeting in Geneva in 1985 was the expression by Mr. Gorbachev and Mr. Reagan of the mutual conviction that there can be no victors in a nuclear war.

We should therefore question an assumption that has been widespread for three decades: that a full-scale nuclear war, triggered by an accident or by unauthorized use of nuclear charges, is strongly probable or even fatally inevitable.

Let us consider the conceptual framework of the problem of accidental nuclear war. This book makes a detailed analysis of different unforeseeable and unintentional factors (such as technological faults and breakdowns, individual psychological flaws, organisational lapses, etc.), defining, as it were, the concept 'accidental.' We have, however, virtually - and unduly - ignored the last term: 'war.'

'War' means a major military conflict pursuing some definite goals. It is an armed *struggle* of states, differing from an ordinary armed conflict by its scale and its political goals.

A deliberate nuclear war between East and West is out of the question; but what about a war caused by chance factors? An accidental or unauthorized launching of a missile or even of several missiles (in itself highly improbable) is unlikely to bring about a full-scale *war* when neither side has any incentive for it. We assume a very small probability of a very limited ('automatic' or unauthorized) reaction and a close-to-zero probability of a very limited authorized 'retaliation'; this is the maximal assumption that is possible if we want to remain realistic. There should thus be no question of an accidental East-West nuclear war, today or in a foreseeable future. We may imagine an accidental missile launch or an accidental explosion of some nuclear charge, an accidental nuclear strike or even an accidental nuclear conflict; but an accidental nuclear war for instance between the United States and our country is unimaginable.

The problem of accidental nuclear war cannot, however, be completely removed from our agenda. There is the danger that mankind may get accustomed to nuclear weapons as an instrument of policy, as an inevitable price of security; and the possibility of an accidental nuclear conflict between advanced states will still remain, theoretically, as long as there are nuclear weapons. In addition, there is the possibility of an accidental nuclear war between developing countries, and, to a certain extent, between the developed and the developing nations of the world.

An accidental nuclear war may have various trigger mechanisms, which become more probable with the increasing proliferation of nuclear arms and technology: accidental use of nuclear weapons by a third country, their employment in regional conflicts, or nuclear terrorism.

The risk of a provoked or deliberate use of nuclear weapons is considerably enhanced by the increasing number of such weapons, of their potential users and of vehicles for them. In addition, the weapons themselves may become targets of, e.g., attacks, terrorist acts, or attempts at stealing them.

The global community, and the political and social leaders of the countries of different orientations, must develop a sort of 'atomophobia,' a psychological aversion to nuclear weapons, their possession, their use or the threat of it, in warfare or as an instrument of policy. Most of the quasi-nuclear states are now hostages of their nuclear ambitions. Their policies by no means contribute to their military security, they undermine their political and economic security, they increase regional instability and compound the arms race.

Several factors speak for focusing the problem of an accidental nuclear war on the developing world, rather than on the official members of the nuclear club. First, there is the continuing proliferation of nuclear weapons and quasi-nuclear states in the Third World. Physicists used to represent the likelihood of a nuclear war as a geometrical progression, rising sharply with the number of states possessing nuclear weapons. This forecast fortunately did not prove to be correct; but the probability does obviously increase. Therefore, a strict and effective control over the future diffusion of nuclear weapons, on a multilateral basis and with the mandate and approval of the world community, remains a matter of paramount importance. This includes tightening the control of arms exports, particularly of destabilizing technologies, avoiding, however, discriminatory measures.

There is a still a growing risk that nuclear weapons may be obtained by unstable regimes with revanchist ambitions or a fanatical religious orientation. Another great danger lies in the up-to-date means of delivery that are acceleratingly supplied to developing countries. When armed with nuclear charges, these can rapidly expand any conflict, involve major powers in local conflicts, or even accidentally (without planning or authorization) involve the territory of other states. If these tendencies continue, the probability of a 'chance' nuclear war will increase: one that is 'not planned' and is unexpected for the victimized neighboring nations.

Regional conflicts in the Third World involve a particularly great risk of an accidental nuclear war. In a long-term perspective, the fact that they have been fought with lots of modern armory means that it makes little sense for global powers to try to control their scale, to maintain them at a certain level, or to continue using them as a political instrument of pressure against each other. Such conflicts can detonate in an unexpected and undesired manner, even in the form of a nuclear conflagration. In particular, the Near and Middle East has long caused the anguish and concern of the world community. The march of events in this area has more than once brought mankind to the brink of a global conflict.

Second, we have possible acts of nuclear terrorism. This problem has technological as well as economic and political aspects. The diffusion of knowledge and the miniaturization of nuclear weapons mean that states no longer have a monopoly on the ability to produce nuclear weapons. A small group, or even a malicious man of talent, can now make a nuclear charge within a short time, provided that the necessary materials, technology and equipment are put at their disposal by some interested circles.

It is very difficult to control leakages of raw materials, technologies, equipment or its components. There is no lack of unprincipled and greedy groups or individuals with some vested interests, prepared to supply anything to anyone.

To prevent an accidental nuclear war, we also have to consider the risk of creeping confrontations - even nuclear ones - between

nations, in which one side suspects the other of supporting potential
terrorists or the nuclear ambitions of irresponsible leaders.

Such suspicions are, alas, not always unfounded. It need not even
be government agencies that render support to potential nuclear
terrorists or have an interest in their activity. In practical politics, we
sometimes find a queer symbiosis of forces and movements having
different or even opposite interests, but joining forces to achieve a
specific goal. One link in this 'chain of action' may try to use other
links in its own interests to get political protection, access to
resources, or other opportunities. Such openings may be used by
some irresponsible group or regime in order to get access to nuclear
technology, raw materials, etc.

Let us try to draw the portrait of such an actor (one or more
states, or even a non-state group or organization), potentially capable
of plunging the world into an accidental nuclear war - which may be
undesirable for the world and maybe for the actor himself. Apart
from variations due to specific situations, his essential characteristics
are as follows:

- he possesses nuclear weapons or he can obtain them;
- he assigns a predominant role to the military force as a policy
  instrument;
- he is not restrained from using nuclear weapons by any moral or
  ethical considerations;
- he feels he is cornered, having nothing to lose;
- he feels he is free of control by the world community, being able
  to pursue his policy with impunity; and
- he is unable to assess all the consequences of his action.

What attitude should the world community take to such states,
regimes or movements that feel threatened by changing situations in
various regions of the world?

When one party to a conflict loses its former status, or even
becomes an outcast, it will be worried that the other party may try to
achieve some goals of its own by exploiting its weaknesses and
troubles, which may merely be (believed to be) short-term ones. That
will inevitably define a factor that may provoke a military conflict,
even if this is the intention of neither side. If nuclear weapons are
there, it can provoke an accidental nuclear conflict. A period of
radical changes in political and military structures thus saddles all

parties concerned with a great responsibility in pursuing their policies. The global community should not engage in a definite policy of confrontation against any country or movement. There is no alternative to their incorporation in it, even if that involves some economic and political liabilities for it.

To reduce the possibility of an accidental nuclear conflict (or war), it is important to have a correct idea of the potential and the intentions of the other side. The following factors may complicate this understanding:

- distorted ideas about the policies and intentions of the adversary;
- arbitrary assessments by the military leadership of the potential for a disarming strike that the other side has;
- arbitrary ideas in political and military leaders, based on those false assessments, about the possibility and expediency of a preventive attack; and
- all kinds of wrong moves by the political and military leadership, etc.

Two further aspects of the problem should be emphasized: first, our attitude towards the increasing risks of an accidental nuclear conflict will be more and more influenced by the unchecked development of war technology and by the tendency towards the 'automated battlefield,' including the 'space battlefield.' The 'smart weapons,' which can bring about a qualitatively new fighting capability, are dangerous for both sides. The potential victim of aggression will have a distorted idea of the scale, character and level of the threat; and the automatic and computerized system of the aggressor may make him miscalculate and deliver a first strike. If eventually realized in a few decades, SDI can dramatically upset the strategic balance, thus increasing the risk of an accidental war.

Second, the continuing flow to parts of the Third World of up-to-date armaments - especially long-distance vehicles - can also undermine the balance, substantially destabilize the international situation and enhance the risk of an accidental nuclear war. This is also true of further proliferation of nuclear and other weapons of mass destruction.

Adequate perception - minimizing the gap between estimates and reality - is a condition for avoiding worst-case analysis. This is the essence of the problem of confidence building in the world.

In addition, the course of the liberation processes from the existing and rather rigid bipolar structures also contributes to the growing tension in the world. These processes do bring about a reduced level of war danger and demilitarization; but sometimes they also have a destabilizing effect, when fairly stable structures are removed and leave a vacuum. Military security is only one component of national security in any state; but when a state feels inferior in other respects, it may assume a predominant role in its policies.

In an overall assessment of the risk of accidental nuclear war, we must revise an assumption that only recently appeared indisputable: that there is a direct correlation to the effect that a reduction of the number of weapons means a lessened probability. Conversely, nor is there any simple and direct correlation between the build-up of nuclear weapons and an increasing risk of accidental nuclear war. The reduction of nuclear weapons may thus have the wrong effect, if there is lack of confidence and inadequate mechanisms of ensuring transparency, etc.

To reduce the risks of an accidental nuclear conflict we have to minimize all the (technological, human, organizational, etc.) errors already mentioned; but is not only the war economy and the military policies that must be de-nuclearized, but also military thinking. Einstein's prophetic words come to mind here: one of the contradictions of our time is that between twenty-first century technology and nineteenth-century thinking.

Reducing the risks of an accidental nuclear war simultaneously calls for increased international openness and confidence building, for the political will to control the most dangerous forms of the technological arms race, and for military and technological North/South cooperation. In addition, the advanced states have to join forces to render effective aid to developing countries.

The most important task consists in moving from a confrontation-of-forces mentality to a constructive mentality of cooperation and mutual security.

Chapter 15

Counteracting Accidental Nuclear War

Vladimir Belous

Banning all nuclear weapons and destroying them under strict international control is definitely the only way of removing every risk of a nuclear war occurring against the will of political leaders. Complete nuclear disarmament is an ideal of mankind, and will certainly be achieved, if it wants to remain immortal; but the stern reality of our century cautions against excessive optimism as to when and how.

Yet it is reasonable to assume that the 45 years of peace we have had, in spite of all the contradictions and the Cold War, are partly due to nuclear weapons. Given the present international situation with its arrangement of forces, complex dynamic processes and differential economic development of the different countries, a world without nuclear weapons might be less stable and safe than the present. Some politicians even maintain that 'if humanity loses its nuclear innocence, it'll never manage to return it.' Not sharing this opinion, I still believe that nuclear weapons will long remain in the military arsenals of the leading powers, threatening world civilization.

It is hence necessary to invent and implement a whole complex of measures to prevent a nuclear catastrophe. As indicated elsewhere in this book, they must deal with a wide range of problems: political, military, diplomatic, technical, etc. Historically, the risk of an accidental conflict has been influenced by the state of international relations, especially between the United States and the Soviet Union. We now witness the emergence of several factors that objectively reduce the risks of premeditated as well as accidental war: the end of the Cold War, reduced emphasis on deterrence, accelerated disarmament, and a transition from confrontation to collaboration. The reduction of middle and short range missiles of the USSR and the USA defined a historical turning point. Though only 4-5 percent of nuclear weapons were to be reduced, it was the first and the most difficult step in the process of disarmament. The agreement to cut offensive strategic weapons by 50 percent will increase the security of both Nuclear Powers and of the whole world. It will still be necessary

245

to continue the disarmament process, but the question is how far this will be possible, given the conditions of our modern world.

Moving along the road of disarmament, the CIS and the United States will finally arrive at a mutually agreed level of 'minimal nuclear deterrence,' determined in accordance with military parity and equal security for every country. This calls for retaining the ability to inflict 'unacceptable damage' on an aggressor by a second strike - and for taking into account possible influence from other nuclear states.

We cannot estimate the required minimum of warheads by 'common sense' or by a brainwave; it primarily follows from scenarios for a possible war. Let us thus consider a worst-case scenario for the CIS, based on NATO's doctrine of flexible response. In a crisis between USA and the CIS, there will be military actions with conventional armaments: tanks, artillery, airplanes, helicopters, etc. Simultaneously, American troops will engage in eliminating those CIS strategic forces, in particular ICBMs, that are within range of their air force and cruise missiles.

The initial phase of the war may last several weeks, striking out the number N1 of CIS nuclear war heads. For geographical reasons, the CIS ability to strike out US strategic nuclear forces will be fairly limited. It is then assumed that after this first phase, there will be a sudden counterforce strike, further weakening CIS strategic forces by, say, N2 warheads. In case the SDI program results in a comprehensive ABM system, another N3 warheads will be eliminated from the CIS counterstrike. In order to inflict 'unacceptable damage' on the adversary, NU warheads are required; according to the calculations of Robert MacNamara, this number may be 400-500 warheads of megaton magnitude.

In this scenario, the minimum level required for the CIS side in order to be certainly able to deter a potential adversary is thus

$$N = N1 + N2 + N3 + NU \times CT,$$

where CT, which is greater than 1, is a coefficient, indicating the technical reliability of the missiles. It must be assumed that the corresponding number for the USA will hardly be much lower. Approximate calculations then show that the initial arsenal of each country will contain thousands of warheads, which will also entail a high risk of accidental war.

According to calculations by Soviet and American scientists, already a smaller number of nuclear detonations will lead to irreversible ecological consequences for the planet known as 'nuclear winter,' and in the ultimate case to the extinction of all forms of life on earth.

To remove such a threat, it is necessary to analyze and coordinate the military doctrines of both countries, make them highly defensive, abandon the concept of first strike, abolish the counterforce character of strategic weapons, and abstain from large-scale ABM defense. In this case, we can considerably reduce the level required for minimum nuclear deterrence, and hence the risk of a nuclear catastrophe by accident.

We should also keep in mind that there is presently no common understanding among Nuclear Powers of such fundamental concepts of security policy as 'strategic parity' (especially in asymmetric cases), 'strategic stability,' 'sufficient defense,' 'advantage,' 'military superiority' and so on.

The leading Nuclear Powers often interpret such fundamental notions differently, which complicates negotiations and the coordination of military doctrines. When the German mathematician David Hilbert was arguing why it is utterly important to pay attention to the fundamental premises of theories, he made the point by saying: 'Let me assume that twice two makes five, and I shall prove that witches are flying from the chimney.' It is very important that scientists from the CIS and the USA - and other countries - join efforts in elaborating an agreed concept of how strategic stability is possible, given radical cuts in strategic and conventional forces. It must be mutually acceptable to East and West, and must give a clear orientation in the search for how to continue the disarmament process and strengthen international security.

In April 1990, a delegation of the Soviet Scientists for Peace Committee, headed by Academician Roald Sagdeev, visited the USA to negotiate with the International Institute for Strategic Research at Stanford University, discussing joint scientific research on strategic stability, disarmament, radical reductions of miliary budgets and conversion. We hope that their joint efforts will help to lay the scientific foundations for further promotion of peace and international security.

Such coordinated actions are also urgent, since unilateral peace moves may be counterproductive, thus weakening international stability. For instance, Professor R. Dittman from the University of

California has stated that the strategic imbalance in American favor that would result from a unilateral CIS reduction of strategic forces would affect the strategic stability negatively, giving the USA no net benefit.

As military confrontation recedes, the qualitative characteristics and structure of strategic offensive weapons get even more important, also directly affecting the risk of inadvertent conflicts. Thus silo-based ICBMs have the advantage over other strategic systems that they have fairly stable and reliable control and communication systems with a high degree of redundancy. They are also easier to guard and defend, hence safe from terrorist actions and accidents due to natural phenomena.

Mobile ICBMs have some edge in survivability over silo-based ones, and can be regarded as stabilizing second strike weapons; but they are worse in terms of the risk of inadvertent conflict, also because of being more vulnerable to breakdowns and human errors in their staffs. The future structure of strategic forces should also take into account that MIRVed missiles are destabilizing, tempting their owners to strike first in order to paralyze the strategic triad of the enemy with a minimum of their own missiles.

In moving towards minimum nuclear deterrence, USA and the CIS should thus give priority to single-warhead silo-based ICBMs. The two countries might have largely (quantitatively and qualitatively) symmetrical force structures, consisting of silo-based ICBMs and a number of SLBMs. It stands to reason that all this becomes realizable, provided that both sides give up the creation of a large-scale ABM system.

Under the aegis of the 'International Fund for the Survival and Development of Mankind,' Soviet and American experts prepared several notable concrete proposals on reducing the risk of an accidental nuclear conflict. For example, they considered it necessary to equip all strategic nuclear devices with electronic coded locks, making them operative only by a coded signal from the supreme head-quarters. If terrorists seize one and try to break the code, their attempts will make the warhead inoperative. They also suggest installing on every missile a special mechanism for destroying it by a command from the ground in case of unauthorized or accidental launching.

Another noteworthy proposal is to install special devices, which can be controlled by the other side, in all regions with ICBM bases.

They can be acoustic, seismic, optic or infrared, designed to monitor missile launches in this host region and to notify the other country instantaneously. Such a system could both make the monitoring more reliable and eliminate any first strike advantages, and thereby the temptation for either side to attempt one.

Unauthorized use of tactical nuclear weapons deserves increased attention, their destructive power being comparable with 'Little Boy' in Hiroshima and 'Fat Man' in Nagasaki. They are scattered over many countries - in Europe alone, there are thousands of them - which excludes them from being particularly secure, as their relatively small size makes them easier to steal or hijack. They have no electronic locks, the level of command authorizing their use is low and their combat readiness high, all of which compounds the risk of unauthorized use. To reduce the risk of accidental nuclear conflict, we have to reduce their number in regions where potential adversaries face each other, ban their modernization (in particular where it would increase their range), improve their storage and transportation safety and, finally, restrict them to the national territories of their owners. The Belgian minister of defense, Guy Coëme, made an interesting proposal on short-range (0 - 500 km) nuclear arms, calling for negotiations on reducing nuclear artillery and land-based missiles, covering NATO's Lance (120 km) and WTO's SS-21 (120 km) and Scud (300 km). This proposal was then realized by the Bush and Gorbachev initiatives, which also meant the realization of a nuclear-free corridor in Central Europe, first suggested by the late Swedish Premier Olof Palme. Such a 'zone of confidence' might later be extended to the entire continent. This, of course, presupposes mutual confidence and mutual interest in continued disarmament, all Nuclear Powers being concerned about war prevention and increased global stability.

Among the most important issues of international stability is the improving of the precision and reliability of BMEWS, of the CIS and USA alike, by a variety of measures. A failure in either system entails a risk of apocalyptic consequences, and their interdependence means that their reliability rests on their weakest link. Each side must therefore worry about the BMEWS of the other side as much as about its own. This calls for mandatory advance notification of missile launches and a ban on disturbing the functioning of BMEWS or, even better, a 'BMEWS enhancement regime.' The CIS and USA should enter negotiations about these systems, whose functioning concerns not only them but every country in the world. The present reliability of BMEWS not being very high, the United States and the CIS have to abstain from 'launch on warning' in order to reduce the risk of accidental nuclear war. The global security inter-dependence means that in the nuclear age, security can only be universal or nonexistent. *Tertium non datur.*

The dangers with widespread military use of computers are discussed elsewhere in this volume. They are especially well demonstrated for BMEWS and large-scale ABM systems with space-based elements; and the more hierarchical the computer-based systems, the greater the danger of fatal results. The internal instability inherent in computer systems will grow even more in the future, which limits their use in the military sphere.

Another task of great importance is that of reducing risks of statesmen making erroneous military-political decisions. These risks are correlated with the state of international relations, with the level of military confrontation. When this is intensified, accidental nuclear war grows more likely for several reasons: appraisals of the situation and the intensions of the adversary are blunted by stress, military systems increase their readiness, BMEWS get more sensitive, and the psychological pressure on control operators increases. The perception of the intentions of the opposite side is so biased by random factors, stereotypes of the past, group think and emotional personality factors, that the adequacy of situation appraisals and decision-making becomes dubious.

Dangerous situations are best averted by required political steps, like reducing the levels of international tension and military confrontation, establishing mutual trust and maintaining cooperation based on a shared concern to preserve global peace. These aims are served by strict observation of treaties and agreements between Nuclear Powers on 'hot lines,' early warning of occasional unauthorized missile launches and prevention of dangerous military accidents, as well as by national nuclear danger prevention.

In our present interdependent world, the origins of nuclear conflict may be related to local wars in different parts of the world. Their interests in many regions and treaty obligations to many states could under certain circumstances get the Nuclear Powers unwittingly drawn into armed conflicts, and the step might be small between conventional and nuclear war.

Tomorrow's strategic landscape may be more complicated, poly-chromatic and impredictable. The world is in transition from a habitual and stabilized bipolarity to multipolarity. The correlation of forces is fundamentally changed by the emergence and strengthening of additional large centers with sizable political, economic and military potentials. The stern reality beyond the year 2000 includes a Western Europe with the fresh energy of a united Germany; a Japan uniting Asian and Pacific countries under its aegis, Brazil and Argentina in Latin America, and a struggle among the largest African countries for the domination of their continent.

The emergence of a Common European Home, with multi-faceted integration of its countries and multilateral cooperation, will be a natural result of continental processes that are already unfolding. Its urgency is underlined by the two world wars having been ignited precisely here, and by the two most powerful blocs facing each other, with thousands of nuclear warheads deployed here.

The analysis of these future realities entails an unexpected con-clusion: that the CIS and the United States will have to establish and preserve friendly relations, or even an alliance; not just because somebody wants it, but by historical inevitability. These two main nuclear states do not have the most profound and obstinate types of contradictions we find in the international system: fundamental economic conflicts or incompatible territorial claims. While it only took them one year after World War II to switch from alliance to Cold War, the reversal will be more complicated and time-consuming, taking them roughly ten to fifteen years. This alliance will stabilize peace, promote the role of the United Nations, avert armed conflicts and prevent other nations from using nuclear weapons. The USA and the CIS will play a decisive role in reducing the global arms trade, establishing an international registration of sales, which will limit military confrontation in many regions.

There exists an - erroneous - opinion that our possession of nuc-lear weapons will prompt other countries to manufacture them. No country doing this is likely to have enough to compete with the CIS and the USA within the foreseeable future. Inevitable reprisal would then make it very risky to use nuclear weapons for political or economic aims, and it would make doubtful sense to acquire the new armaments that would lie dead in the arsenals.

In a nuclear free world, on the other hand, clandestine produc-tion of nuclear warheads would make the perpetrator decisively

superior to all other countries and thus able to dictate. This scenario
can as little be ignored as the existence of nuclear weapons. Nor can
the great dangers inherent in horizontal nuclear proliferation, which
is a potential by-product of the development of nuclear energy,
especially in near-nuclear countries. According to the IAEA, the
reserves of plutonium in non-nuclear countries amounted to 155 tons
by 1985. This figure is doubtlessly much higher today. Specialists warn
that the main danger may now lie in near-nuclear countries that lack
modern security systems. Israel has nuclear installations that are not
monitored by the IAEA; so had South Africa until joining the NPT
in 1991.

Academician Vitalii Goldansky has pointed out that the simplest
uranium and plutonium fission bombs can be made secretly without
testing. The type of bomb used in Hiroshima had had no preliminary
test. There are grounds to fear that if one country openly crosses the
nuclear threshold, there may be a chain reaction of proliferation. This
calls for all efforts - at UN, governmental or NGO level - to prevent
it, the most urgent task being to get the near-nuclear states to accede
to the NPT (Non-Proliferation Treaty). We must also improve the
guarantee system of the IAEA and its functioning, intensify its control
of exports of nuclear materials and assist it in taking strong measures
to prevent their embezzlement.

The SDI program in the USA has attracted the attention of the
scientific community for years. In spite of recent considerable revisions of it, its main strategic ideas still arouse anxiety. The deployment of a new strategic defensive component would undermine
military parity and stability. Strategic defensive and offensive weapons
define a unified system in Ludwig Bertalanffy's sense: 'a complex of
elements in interaction with each other.'

Specialist models of the exchange of nuclear strikes when both
sides have large-scale ABM systems with space components have
indicated that strategic stability would be greatly afflected, since
either side might be tempted to obtain the superiority that would
result from combining a counterforce first strike with an ASAT
elimination of ABM space components. Large-scale ABM systems
would undermine the 1972 ABM Treaty, which has reined in the
arms race for almost two decades, and perhaps also the possibility of
an agreement to cut down offensives strategic forces by 50 percent.
That would throw the world into an unrestrained nuclear arms race,

which would diminish strategic stability and considerably increase the risk of war.

The main problem in connection with SDI is the space deployment of attack weapons. Several types of space-based weapons might be used against targets in the air space, at sea or on the ground. At the same time, one may understand American concerns about the possibility of accidental launch targeting US territory or of some third country using nuclear missiles. One discussed project concerns establishing a 'thin' ABM system with 1,000 ground-based missiles deployed in different regions of the United States. Its architects claim that it would provide reliable defense of the entire US territory against a single-missile attack. Such an ABM version appears negotiable between the United States and the CIS, but on one definite condition: a ban on attack weapons in outer space. On that issue there can be no compromise.

Already a brief examination of the problems related to the necessity of lowering the risk of accidental nuclear war shows how serious and multifarious they are. This understanding, however, should not engender despair, but a resolute struggle for the world free of nuclear weapons, for the survival of mankind. This calls for scientists to join forces even more in order to eliminate the impending threat.

Chapter 16

Would Actions to Survive a Nuclear Winter Help Public Opinion See the Urgency of Preventive Measures?

Ingemar Ahlstrand

1. A new situation

During the first years of the 1980s, the high level of East-West tension made the world worry about an intentional nuclear war. The talk in military circles about the possibility of a first strike made the world nervous, as did NATO's flexible defense doctrine with its 'first use' of nuclear weapons.

Many persons active in the peace movement were of the opinion that any use of nuclear weapons would lead to an all out nuclear war with no survivors. Some thought that taking actions to limit the effects of nuclear war might increase the military's readiness to use nuclear weapons.

Today we have an entirely new situation. There is no more talk about possible first strikes or about a massive armored aggression from the Warsaw Pact troops in Europe. But as Professor Joseph Rotblat, president of Pugwash, said as his closing words at the Pugwash annual meeting in Cambridge, Massachusetts in 1989: 'The threat to our civilization of the nuclear arms race is far from over. The danger for nuclear war started inadvertently or accidentally still looms over us.'

For example, one mad submarine crew on a modern submarine would have enough nuclear weapons to have a possibility of starting a nuclear winter (as would a rational crew unable to receive accurate information). Limited nuclear wars, for example in the Middle East, could result in so many nuclear explosions that a nuclear winter would follow.

A nuclear war is here defined as the explosion of so many nuclear devices that there would be a risk for a nuclear winter. According to Professor Carl Sagan (Turco & Sagan, 1989) this

255

number could be as low as 100 nuclear weapons. A nuclear winter could be a mild 'nuclear fall,' but it could also be a severe nuclear winter.

2. Nuclear winter

In 1986, at the initiative of Sweden and Mexico, the UN decided to carry out a thorough investigation of the effects of a nuclear war. Experts from the Soviet Union, the United States and Sweden took part in the work.

The results of this investigation was presented in August 1988 in Stockholm. The joint declaration from the Stockholm conference concluded that a full scale nuclear war could mean that hundreds of millions of people are killed immediately and that billions of people starve to death (*Ambio*, 1989).

Professor Richard Turco from the US said at the conference that according to his best estimate 500 million people would die immediately and 4 billion people would starve to death.

Over the last five years, scientific research has made the estimates of the effects of a nuclear winter much better founded than before. This, however, has only resulted in minor changes in the earlier predictions of effects (Turco et al., 1990).

3. Why the nuclear winter is not discussed

One would have had reason to believe that the nuclear winter and the recent UN report would have been discussed at the Pugwash annual meeting in Cambridge, Massachusetts in 1989. The nuclear winter was, however, hardly mentioned in the discussions.

What was the reason for this strange state of affairs? After a lot of private conversations with participants at this meeting, I found three main explanations.

1. Many scientists resented Professor Carl Sagan for introducing, with ample media coverage, the nuclear winter as something that 'would' happen - rather than as something that 'could' happen - as the result of a nuclear war. The resulting strife within the scientific community made everybody feel uncomfortable about the issue. At the same time, many seemed to deplore the fact that the question had disappeared from the agenda.

Today, all efforts should be made to decrease the risk for the use of nuclear weapons. The disagreement in details between scientists is very unfortunate. Both sides agree that even a nuclear war resulting only in a 'nuclear fall' would have such catastrophic effects that all efforts should be made to prevent the use of nuclear weapons. Professor Carl Sagan has made the following observation (Turco & Sagan, 1989):

> No one has proven or disproved the contention that the human species would become extinct following a nuclear conflict. Even to say that the probability is 'vanishingly small,' for example, implies that it is possible; such statements are subjective and of little analytical use. Indeed, the debate over extinction is misleading because from it one might infer that the environmental effects of nuclear weapons are important only if they bring about human extinction.

2. A second explanation was that Caspar Weinberger, President Ronald Reagan's Secretary for Defense, tried to gain support for the SDI/'Star Wars' by claiming that even if it could not stop an all out nuclear first strike, it would be useful to stop missiles that might be launched by mistake. Thus SDI could even save the world from a nuclear winter. Many scientists are against the SDI, since it is obvious that the system will not work and that it will create new hazards. Discussion of accidental nuclear war and nuclear winter could thus give new arguments for continuing the SDI.

3. The third and most important reason seemed to be that the US, as well as the CIS, would be so severely directly damaged in a major nuclear exchange that the additional damage that the nuclear winter brings is considered to be marginal. According to a study (Office of Technology Assessment, 1979), 88 percent of the US population would die from the direct effects of a nuclear war. The remaining 10-20 percent that would be killed in the 'nuclear winter' are not considered to be worth worrying too much about.

4. The implications for neutral countries

For a neutral country such as Sweden, however, the situation is totally different. Here hardly anybody would die from the direct effects of a nuclear war, whereas 100 percent of the population would starve and freeze to death because of the nuclear winter combined with injuries caused by radiation.

Professor George Rathjens (1985) wrote:

The situation would be radically different for the leadership of those countries that would probably not be directly attacked during a nuclear war between the superpowers. For many, nuclear winter (if severe) could mean the difference between total disaster and survival with little damage. Could they - should they - do anything to avoid or alleviate disaster? Many countries would have the possibility of greatly reducing suffering if they were to stockpile food and fuel and to provide adequate shelter for the population. People do, after all, live through long, cold, dark winters with no great difficulty, if they are prepared.

5. The case of Sweden

What conclusions has the Swedish government drawn from these facts? None - in spite of the fact that a nuclear winter is particularly serious in those northern latitudes where Sweden is situated!

In Sweden's last election campaign in 1988, the risk of nuclear war and the need to prevent such a war were hardly mentioned. Everybody seemed to believe that the danger is over. This is an extremely dangerous belief.

Ironically enough, the Swedish government is prepared to close the twelve Swedish nuclear power plants in order to prevent nuclear accidents from happening. At the same time, it ignores the risk that some of the world's 50,000-60,000 nuclear weapons might explode by mistake.

The cost of the first step of the program to close the power plants, the stopping of one nuclear reactor in 1995 and one in 1996, is estimated at about 30 billion SEK (5 billion dollars) (*Statens energiverk*, 1990). The cost of storing food for a week for a family with two adults and two children in Sweden is estimated to be 650 SEK by the federal agricultural committee (*Statens jordbruksnämnd*). The cost of a one-year food supply for almost 9 million Swedes would amount to about 75 billion SEK. This food would then be used in the household and renewed. This would give no additional cost for later years.

In Sweden, we already incur considerable costs for central storing of food and fuel in preparation for a new war that might result in an isolation of Sweden similar to that in World War II. After the summer harvest, Sweden has food stored for one year. Before the harvest, the stores amount to about half a year. The fuel supply amounts to about four months. The additional cost for Sweden to be prepared to survive a one-year nuclear winter would not be prohibitive.

In Switzerland, there is already a program to decrease the effects of a nuclear war. Families store one month's supply of food. They also have facilities to filter air and water from radioactive particles (Dyson, 1984).

6. Remember human irrationality

In the work to decrease the risks for accidental nuclear war, it is important to see the limits of human rationality.

Professor Georg Klein, a Swedish physician, writes in his memoirs about the reactions of the Jewish population in Budapest in the spring of 1944 (Klein, 1984). They were almost the only Jews left to be killed by the Nazis. Georg Klein got hold of a report from two Jews that had escaped from Auschwitz and he understood that the thorough description of what was happening there was true. He then went to his relatives and friends and told them to go underground and refuse to board the deportation trains. They did not believe a word of what he told them. They preferred to stay in their homes in the vain hope that the Nazis would not come for them.

When the facts add up to something very alarming, but at the same time something that we cannot see directly with our own eyes, human beings often fail to be rational. The easy and dangerous way out is to deny the facts.

Professor Erich Fromm (1976), the American psychologist, wrote:

The almost unbelievable fact is that no serious effort is made to avert what looks like a final decree of fate. While in our private life nobody except a mad person would remain passive in view of a threat to his total existence, those who are in charge of public affairs do practically nothing, and those who have entrusted their fate to them let them continue to do nothing. How is it possible that the strongest of all instincts, that for survival, seems to have ceased to motivate us?

7. What actions would make people understand?

In the new situation, the old thinking that any use of nuclear weapons - intentional or accidental - would lead to a catastrophe without survivors is dangerous. With little hope of improving the situation, the normal human reaction is just to try to forget about the threatening facts - to repress them - to forget about 50,000-60,000 nuclear weapons that can be used at a few minutes' notice and to believe that the danger is over because East-West relations have improved.

To prevent the tendency to repress unpleasant facts, it is important to make the facts vivid and impossible to ignore. Then preventive actions will follow. A number of possible ways to draw attention to the problem are presented below.

1. *Programs to reduce the damage of a nuclear war*
    Programs to survive a nuclear winter would only be meaningful in non-nuclear countries. Such programs would make the general public in non-nuclear as well as in nuclear countries understand the danger. People that are preparing to survive a nuclear winter will put pressure on the politicians to take actions that will prevent the nuclear winter from happening. People in nuclear countries that understand that they are at the mercy of the risk of accidental or intentional nuclear war and that protective measures in their countries are meaningless will pressure their politicians to dismantle the nuclear threat.

2. *Efforts to make the risk conceivable*
    The estimates of the annual risk for inadvertent or accidental nuclear war varies from 'larger than zero' to 10 percent. The vagueness of the risk makes it difficult for politicians and experts in different fields to get started with programs of preventive actions. It is impossible to get a scientifically based figure of the annual risk. Many experts, however, seem to agree that a totally subjective estimate would have an order of magnitude of the annual risk of about 1 percent for a nuclear war during present circumstances. This would include risks such as technical

accidents, human failures, intentional nuclear wars among Third World nations, the developments in Eastern Europe and nuclear terrorism.

My proposal is to agree on an operative subjective estimate that the annual risk for nuclear war is 1 percent until someone can prove that this estimate is too low or too high.

With the help of an estimate it is possible to make social cost-benefit studies of preventive actions as well as of suitable programs to survive a nuclear winter.

3.   *Use of the legal process to draw attention to the problem*
In a democracy it is not acceptable that certain individuals have the right to decide about life and death of whole nations or of the entire world. In the US, the president and 36 submarine commanders have this position. The situation is probably similar in the other four main nuclear powers.

Non-nuclear nations should protest forcefully against this state of affairs. In the nuclear nations, court cases should be filed in order to draw attention to the fact that this is not in accordance with democratic values.

In the US, Dr. Clifford Johnson filed his third lawsuit in this field in May 1989, alleging that the nuclear hair-trigger could be accidentally sprung by computer-related error. He contends that this represents a day-to-day risk to his life, imposed in violation of his constitutional due process rights, because it abrogates both the power of the Congress to declare war and the power of the president to command the armed forces, and because it imposes government by computer.

Professor Elaine Scarry is also preparing a court case that claims that it is unconstitutional that the president of the US and 36 submarine commanders, rather than Congress, can decide on first use of nuclear weapons.

8. Conclusions

Public opinion's lack of rationality has let the new hopes for peace obliterate almost all discussion about the remaining threat. This seems to be a normal human reaction, although it is an irrational and very dangerous one.

The attention is now captured by such environmental hazards - mild in the short run - as the greenhouse effect. The disarming of the nuclear threat must be the number one priority.

The scientists and other members of the world community who see the overriding danger have an obligation to do their best to make the world remember the nuclear threat and to do something about it. The three measures proposed in this paper could be a help in this effort.

The big danger is that we do not see it.

Chapter 17

Multilateral Measures to Prevent Accidental Nuclear War and to Manage Nuclear Crisis

Tapio Kanninen[50]

1. Introduction

The main purpose of this chapter is to discuss how one might implement multilateral proposals to avert accidental nuclear war and to suggest a systematic approach for their implementation. It is not meant to propose new measures. A case could be made that there is no lack of suggestions on what to do, but rather a lack of serious thought on their feasibility in present or future international situations and on how to advance them in different fora. A second purpose is to describe and evaluate, as a case study, a particular proposal to prevent accidental nuclear war originating from the UN Secretary-General.

Michael Intriligator and Dagobert Brito (1988: p. 20) recently articulated nine specific multilateral arms control proposals to reduce the chance of accidental nuclear war (summarized and reorganized in Table 1). Whereas they all merit careful evaluation, the case study described in this paper is primarily concerned with the last one in their list which deals with the establishment of an international early-warning monitoring system that would be independent of any national monitoring system and would provide information to all major powers. The UN Secretary-General's proposal, going somewhat in the same direction as Intriligator's and Brito's, and the support from various quarters to seriously consider Mr. Perez de Cuellar's idea, are an indication of a growing interest in multilateral measures in this field, despite expected political and technical obstacles.

This study does not want to suggest that the implementation of various multilateral proposals discussed, and particularly the

---

[50] The views presented are the author's and do not necessarily reflect those of the United Nations.

'multilateral nuclear alert center' concept proposed by the Secretary-General, is politically, organizationally, technically or financially a realistic opportunity anytime in the near future. However, ideas take root gradually. When international factors suddenly make the implementation of some aspects of the proposals more feasible than before, it helps greatly if serious thinking has already taken place. Being prepared for an occasion makes it easier to take advantage of that occasion when the time arrives.

2. Concepts and methodology

We take a broad definition here of what accidental nuclear war is. Sven Hellman (1990: p. 99) used the term to include any way a nuclear war could start in response to false signals, incorrect or misinterpreted information, or in response to an unauthorized, accidental or terrorist launch, or due to uncontrolled escalation of a limited conflict. Similarly, Herbert Abrams (1988: p. 48) saw that accidental nuclear war had genuine meaning primarily in the context of a crisis. The narrower definition of accidental nuclear war relates to technical or human-technical failure. But, according to him, the term 'accidental' also serves as a contrast to the intent of all nations to avoid this kind of event. The accidental nuclear war is undesigned, unforeseen, occurs by chance; is unintended, unexpected, unpremeditated.

A number of proposals - unilateral, bilateral and multilateral - have been made over the years for preventing accidental nuclear war. It is argued that it would be most helpful at this time not necessarily to propose an array of new proposals, but rather to study the previous ones carefully, especially those which have been successfully implemented. In that way we can identify the right conditions: a) to make a useful proposal; b) to study its merits in a credible and representative manner; c) to promote it among strategically important interest groups; and d) to implement it successfully. This chapter reaches a somewhat dim conclusion that only a major crisis - although perhaps a geographically limited one - could change the initial reluctance to a proposal to establish truly multilateral nuclear crisis prevention and control mechanisms. But even a crisis cannot do this if adequate proposals have not been: a) made at an appropriate time; b) studied and discussed carefully; and c) promoted vigorously. The history of the hot line is a good example to support this argument

(Ury, 1985: pp. 142-148; Bracken, 1988: p. 5), and will be discussed shortly.

A systematic framework to assess the merits and weaknesses of each proposal to prevent accidental nuclear war can direct our efforts to areas which have the greatest likelihood of success, and keep momentum in areas which, in peaceful conditions, are not taken seriously. The following categories could be a useful start for such a framework:

1. *What is the substance of the proposal; does it make sense?* The proposal should address a concrete need and be feasible to implement in proper circumstances. But this is usually not really the issue since most proposals are sensible and there is a need for their implementation. The next steps are, therefore, more critical in terms of practical results.

2. *Who initiates the idea and how is the groundwork done?* This might be a critical phase because it determines whether the proposal is taken seriously. If the original proponent does not have a sufficiently high status, enough credibility or access to decision-makers, another proponent might be identified to complement the original one.

3. *Who makes the public or formal proposal?* Sometimes the side from which the proposal comes is critical. An initial proposal from a 'wrong' source can kill an excellent effort. Typical initiators are: either one of the Superpowers, an alliance, a grouping in the UN General Assembly, a state, the UN Secretary-General, a non-governmental organization, a conference or a seminar, a scholar, a journalist or a respected individual.

4. *What is the forum to study the proposal and who are the participants in the discussions?* Usually proposals are studied in scholarly conferences and publications. A critical question is to what extent governmental and military officials, as well as politicians from major countries, participate in these debates since they often are able to influence the very start of the implementation process.

5. *What is the forum for serious discussions on implementation?* Usual fora are bilateral talks between the US and Russia, but discussions could also begin in the UN Conference on Disarmament, regional conferences (e.g. CSCE related talks) or other kind of international meetings. Each proposal might require its own initial discussion forum.

6. *What are the major difficulties encountered: political, financial, technical, organizational, etc.?* It is important to identify major problems prior to discussion, and modify the proposals accordingly. During the discussions and implementation process proposals are vulnerable to a number of skeptical comments which must be addressed on merit.

7. *What are the options to overcome obstacles?*
   - Political: would a major crisis change attitudes, or breakdown of old alliances and coalitions, etc?
   - Financial: could financing from private sources be possible if funds from governmental sources were not available, etc?
   - Technical: should a feasibility study be conducted to solve technical problems involved, etc?
   - Organizational: would a change of supporting agents be necessary to make the proposal more palatable to skeptical decision-makers?

William Ury has given an illustration of a success story in implementing a bilateral agreement - the *history of the hot line agreement* (Ury, 1985: pp. 142-148). This case provides elements to identify what might be a successful combination of measures to implement any multilateral initiative as well (the categories defined above are broadly followed in the following presentation):

1. *Did it make sense?* The idea made a lot of sense: 'Must the world be lost for want of a telephone call?' as one originator put it.

2. *Initiative.* The initiative came from a scholar (Thomas Schelling) who got a staff member in the US State Department's Policy Planning Staff (Henry Owen) and its Director (Gerard Smith) interested, and separately from a magazine editor (Jess Gorkin),

who made background checks on the feasibility of the idea through his friend at the Pentagon before making it public.

3. *Formal proposal.* Gorkin published an open letter to President Eisenhower and Premier Khrushchev in *Parade* magazine proposing an emergency communication link for preventing accidental nuclear war. The proposal got an enthusiastic reply from the readers and the letter was subsequently published in *Izvestia* and *Pravda* in the USSR, where it also received a favorable response.

4. *Promoting and discussing the idea.* In spite of great initial political and bureaucratic reluctance to the idea, Gorkin and Owen continued promoting the idea, including talks with high-level officials, US presidential candidates - even with Nikita Khrushchev when he visited the UN - and through letter-writing campaigns in the press.

5. *Start of the implementation process.* The US Government finally accepted the idea and proposed an emergency link to the Soviets at the UN Conference on Disarmament, in Geneva, in April 1962. Although the Soviets agreed to discuss it, progress was minimal because the proposal became tangled with other general disarmament proposals.

6. *Momentum.* The Cuban missile crisis provided a strong ultimate impetus to conclude the agreement. With the prodding of other nations at the UN disarmament talks, the US-Soviet negotiators reached a separate agreement, and on 31 August 1963 the Hot line went into operation.

Before discussing the proposal by the UN Secretary-General to establish a multilateral nuclear alert center, let us first review other multilateral proposals for preventing accidental nuclear war.

3. Review of some multilateral proposals to prevent accidental nuclear war

While not trying to be exhaustive, the following section refers to some proposals made earlier, mainly by scholars, to prevent accidental nuclear war through multilateral means. This review approaches the question of preventing and managing accidental nuclear incidents at three levels: the developments taking place in current *international relations*; the necessity of providing adequate *information and analyses* to prevent incidents of this nature; and the *communication and mediation* requirements for managing any actual event.

Level 1 (international relations): Rapidly changing international and regional situations, nowadays especially in Europe, the Middle East and South Asia, pose new challenges for security concepts and frameworks. New types of diplomatic and technical arrangements and political coalitions are needed to make the world a more secure place. Stable relations among nuclear states prevent extreme tension when peacetime safeguards of using nuclear weapons might be lifted. Stability also discourages desperate efforts by nuclear terrorists. A question of nuclear command stability (who controls the weapons) in the face of internal disruptions in a major or minor nuclear state also has to be addressed in this context.

As a special confidence building measure, proposals have been put forward to establish one or more 'regional war risk reduction centers' within an overall framework of existing or planned regional security arrangements and with possible links to present bilateral nuclear risk reduction centers and to a proposed global center. After the UN Secretary-General's proposal in 1986 for a 'multilateral nuclear alert centre' (see Ch. 4) a number of variations of the concept has been presented. For instance, the Polish Government, in June 1988, suggested establishing a system of 'hot lines' between the highest state authorities and military high commands including study visits and multilateral working meetings (United Nations, 1988a: paragraph 28). In July 1988 a joint working group of the Socialist Unity Party of Germany (SED) in the GDR and the Social Democratic Party of Germany (SDP) in the FRG submitted a proposal for a Zone of Confidence and Security in Central Europe, including the establishment of confidence building centers in all states involved, and possibly, a joint center being furnished with the same technical equipment and directly communicating with other centers (Müller, 1988; Grundmann, 1988). Also in July 1988, General Secretary Mikhail Gorbachev proposed a 'European Center to reduce the danger of war, as a place for co-operation between NATO and Warsaw Pact' (*Arms Control Reporter*, 1988: p. 54).

After the events in 1989 and 1990 in Eastern Europe and moves towards German unification, proposals for a European Center became more commonplace. For instance, in the Winter 1990 issue of *The Washington Quarterly* Jonathan Dean, former US head of Mutual and Balanced Force Reduction talks in Vienna, proposed a NATO-Warsaw Pact risk reduction center (Dean, 1990: p. 183). Hans-Dietrich Genscher, Minister for Foreign Affairs in the FRG, proposed in March 1990 the creation of a 'European Verification Agency' and a 'Center for the Settlement of Conflicts' within the CSCE framework (Genscher, 1990: p. 8). Later in June 1990 came a Czech-Polish-GDR proposal, promoted especially by Czech President Vaclav Havel and Foreign Minister Jiri Dienstbier, for a Confidence-Building, Arms Control and Verification Center to be established in Berlin. In July 1990, came a breakthrough in terms of NATO support. The NATO Summit declaration in London recommended that CSCE governments establish a 'CSCE Center for the Prevention of Conflict' that might serve as a forum of exchanges of military information, discussion of unusual military activities and the conciliation of disputes involving CSCE member states (*New York Times* 7 July 1990: p. 5).

At one level, in terms of exchange of views of military doctrines among the highest military commands, these and similar proposals (like Daniel Frei's in 1982, see Table 1) have seen their first implementation when, for three weeks beginning 16 January 1990, the highest military representatives of the Warsaw Treaty Organization, NATO and Europe's neutral and non-aligned countries participated in the Seminar of Military Doctrine at Vienna's Hofburg Palace (for summary of the talks, see Almquist, 1990).

But the need for regional CBM arrangements goes beyond Europe. Michael Klare, director of the Five College Program in Peace and World Security Studies in Amherst, Massachusetts, would expand similar proposals to the Third World: 'More so than in Europe, there is a need for secure "hot line" communications between the leaders of rival Powers, for reliable intelligence of remote border skirmishes, and for establishment of demilitarized zones and "risk reduction centers"' (Klare, 1990: p. 12). Reference could be also made to a broader proposal by William Ury and Richard Smoke to hold regional congresses early in any regional crisis, as was done often by the nineteenth-century Great Powers, in order to head off a Superpower entry (Ury & Smoke, 1984: pp. 73-74).

Level II (information and analysis): In a more multipolar and multinuclear world there is also a growing need to establish a global focal point to gather information on any threats to international security, especially on such potential conflicts or incidents which could reach a nuclear level. Coordination of urgent multilateral action would also be needed and should start early enough.

In this line Ury and Smoke proposed a UN 'situation room' or crisis center to serve as a clearinghouse of information about a developing crisis, verifying and updating information, eventually to be provided with resources for gathering its own information in the crisis region (Ury & Smoke, 1984: p. 75). Thomas Boudreau similarly proposed a UN centralized computer data set - data bank - that will deal specifically with conflict prevention (Boudreau, 1984: p. 27). An important start for these types of operations at the UN was the creation of the Secretary-General's Office for Research and Collection of Information (ORCI), which was mandated to provide early warning and otherwise to serve the Secretary-General in his conflict prevention and resolution functions (see United Nations, 1987). The proposal by Intriligator and Brito to establish an international early warning monitoring system (Intriligator & Brito, 1988: p. 20) and the French 1978 proposal to create an international satellite monitoring agency, also having early warning functions, stress the importance of timely information for efforts to prevent nuclear crisis.

In addition, a proposal has been made to establish a UN Multilateral War Risk Reduction Center for related analytical and information collection tasks (including the gathering of information on social and economic root causes of conflicts and with a liaison to the UN peace keeping office to use UN troops as peace assurance). To maintain its executive efficiency it has been proposed to establish it under the direct authority of the UN Secretary-General, who would also have the political mandate to initiate necessary action, on the basis of information received from the Center, with the states concerned and with the Security Council and other relevant UN agencies and bodies, as appropriate (see Sutterlin 1988 & 1989; (the idea has in principle been supported by the Soviet Deputy Foreign Minister) see Petrovsky, 1988).

Level III (communication and mediation): If accidents or incidents involving nuclear weapons happen, or appear about to happen, rapid communication and dissemination of impartial information on the circumstances are of crucial importance. The key is to prevent military escalation and to contain any dramatic ramifications of a political and humanitarian nature. Ury's and Smoke's, as well as Intriligator's and Brito's, proposals for crisis centers address this issue. Boudreau, concerned about the inability of the UN's present communication systems to serve rapid communication needs in nuclear or other international crises, proposed a satellite-based communication system for the UN. This would also include electronic linkages between the Security Council and the Office of the Secretary-General and designated electronic offices for all Council members - big or small, permanent or non-permanent members - close to the Council chamber, thus facilitating extraordinary communication needs during the crisis (Boudreau, 1984). Finally, the proposal to establish a 'Multilateral Nuclear Alert Center' also addresses this issue, and will be discussed in detail later.

Another aspect of a crisis approaching the nuclear level is the rapid initiation of unilateral, bilateral and multilateral mediation, crisis management and control activities. Among the multilateral measures proposed one which deserves special mention is Ury's and Smoke's 'international mediation service,' by which a core of respected individuals would offer their services during a crisis (outside Superpowers' veto rights) and a 'rapid-deployment peace-keeping force,' standing multinational peace keeping force (UN Guard), would be dispatched to head off a potential nuclear crisis (Ury & Smoke, 1984: p. 75-76).

To summarize, the above views might all be divided into the following three categories:

1. *Creating security regimes and building confidence*. This approach means creating in advance safety mechanisms, procedures and rules for stable and predictable relations among States, and preventing any 'situational variables' (such as threats to regional interests of states or escalation of conventional war to nuclear war, see Abrams, 1988: pp. 48-49) from getting out of control.

2. *Early warning*. The purpose is to prevent any sudden international situation or expected incident from taking place or getting worse by being able to identify well in advance the dangerous trends and risks involved, and by proposing measures that decision-makers would be able to use in order to avert a disaster.

3. *Managing, controlling and terminating actual crises.* When a nuclear crisis has started it has to be controlled and terminated as soon as possible. Certain mechanisms and rules set up in advance might facilitate this crucial function.

Table 1 employs the above three categories and summarizes three sets of comprehensive proposals for multilateral measures to prevent accidental nuclear war.

4. Case study: proposal by the UN Secretary-General to establish a multilateral nuclear alert center

4.1 Initial proposals for multilateral nuclear alert and war risk reduction centers
Several important agreements have been reached over the years between the two Superpowers to avert nuclear war. Among the most recent ones is the 1987 agreement between the United States and the Soviet Union to establish bilateral nuclear risk reduction centers in Washington and Moscow. The prevention of escalating tensions to a nuclear level is not, however, only a bilateral concern, as it was often thought in the midst of the Cold War. It is a global concern. A prototype scenario of the 1990s and later might, in fact, be a chain of events involving, along with (or without) the Superpowers, disputing regional parties, Nuclear Powers other than the US and Russia, or, increasingly, nuclear terrorists. This scary multinuclear scene would be beyond the direct control of the Superpowers regardless of the improvements achieved in their bilateral relations. Preventing accidental nuclear war is thus a responsibility for the whole international community, now more than ever.

Aware of a gloomy picture of nuclear incidents of this nature in the future, the UN Secretary-General proposed in his 1986 Annual Report that:

...consideration be given to the establishment of a multilateral nuclear alert center to reduce the risk of fatal misinterpretation of unintentional nuclear launchings or, in the future, the chilling possibility of isolated launchings by those who may clandestinely gain access to nuclear devices. (United Nations, 1986: p. 4)

Table 1.
*Multilateral measures proposed to avert
accidental nuclear war*

	1. Towards Creating Security Regimes and Building Confidence	2. Towards Early Warning	3. Towards Managing, Controlling and Terminating Actual Crises
Daniel Frei (1982: pp. 111-112)	-discussions about 'conventions of crises' toward agreeing on minimum standards of behavior when using force -talks on strategic doctrines of major powers -satisfaction of legitimate security needs of threshold countries -coping with arms race instability -priority for regional arms control measures		-quick and efficient communication between opponents in case of crisis
Ury & Smoke (1984)	-regional congresses to head off Superpower entry	-UN 'situation room' or crisis center -multilateral crisis analysis center	-international crisis mediation service -rapid-deployment peacekeeping force ('UN Guard')
Intri-ligator & Brito (1988)	-agreements in advance on how to deal with accidents and nuclear threats -strengthening of non-proliferation regimes -prenotification of major military exercises and missile flight tests	-international early warning monitoring system -extension of the Agreement of the Prevention of Nuclear War (multilateral consultations if there is the risk of nuclear conflict) -notification of accidents involving nuclear weapons	-upgrading of the 'hot lines' among nuclear weapons states -agreement not to interfere in C^3I systems -sharing Permission Action Links and command/destruct technology and inclusion in all nuclear weapons -limiting/eliminating vulnerable nuclear weapons and short flight time systems -multilateral agreement not to deploy ASAT systems

This was not the first time some variation of multilateral center idea has been mentioned. The US Congress directed in 1982 the secretary for defense to conduct a full and complete study and evaluation of possible initiatives for improving the containment and control of the use of nuclear weapons, particularly during crises (Section 1123 (a) of Public Law 97-252, 8 September 1983). It also specified, as a first item, that the report should address: 'Establishment of a multinational military crisis control center for monitoring and containing the use or potential use of nuclear weapons by third parties or terrorist groups' (Blechman, 1985: p. 173). William Ury and Richard Smoke note that Secretary for Defense Caspar Weinberger's April 1983 report rejected the concept of multilateral centers as impractical. While acknowledging that the utility of such centers might decline as the number of participants rose, Ury and Smoke, however, maintain that as the nuclear hazard becomes more multilateral through nuclear weapons proliferation, some forum of multilateral or multilaterally sponsored crisis analysis center may still be useful (Ury & Smoke, 1984: p. 75).

The Secretary-General's proposal reflected, in any case, the following, already quite generally recognized concerns:

1. The increasingly multilateral character of both potential future conflicts, or any incidents having the possibility to escalate to a nuclear war, and an increasingly multilateral nature of any solution for this threat to peace.

2. The gradual establishment by the Superpowers of extremely complex nuclear command, control, communication and intelligence systems (C^3I) without sufficient consideration being given to military, political and diplomatic ways of controlling the automatic escalation of alert status of nuclear forces in a severe nuclear crisis (Bracken, 1983). Furthermore, the problems of potential escalation of multinuclear alerts, involving other Nuclear Powers, have not received much attention.

3. The potential inability of the UN system to carry out its functions as a facilitator of communication or as a last face-saving resort in a nuclear crisis. During the Cuban crisis, U Thant's letter to Khrushchev of 24 October 1962 offered a face-saving device for the Soviet leader to accept U Thant's proposal not to escalate the

conflict. According to the latest information, U Thant was also considered as a final resort for a face-saving solution by President Kennedy. But this might no longer be the case. Due to technological advances in weapons systems and C³I and to the inability of the present UN communications system to track rapidly the escalating developments in the field and to enable the Secretary-General to communicate with the Security Council members in time, a conflict might escalate to a nuclear level too rapidly.

The Secretary-General's proposal received immediate high-level support. General Secretary Gorbachev supported the idea of preventing conflicts increasingly within a multilateral context, rather than only bilaterally. When he spoke before the Indian Parliament in November 1986, he said, referring to the United Nations and the Secretary-General's proposal:

> ...The Soviet Union wants the potential of this universal international organization to be used more effectively than in the past, which must be achieved, *inter alia*, by making its proceedings and its main bodies more democratic. Specifically, we support the proposal of the UN Secretary-General to set up within the Organization a multilateral center for reducing the risk of war. ... (Gorbachev, 1986)

However, Mr. Gorbachev omitted in this speech the explicit nuclear dimension of the original proposal. But in his article appearing in *Pravda* and *Izvestia* on 17 September 1987, he stressed the importance of rapid communication, evidently to make the role of the Secretary-General more credible in a modern-day conflict management situation, whether nuclear or non-nuclear:

> ...At the same time the world community cannot stay away from inter-state conflicts. Here it could be possible to begin by fulfilling the proposal made by the United Nations Secretary-General to set up under the United Nations Organization a multilateral center for lessening the danger of war. Evidently, it would be feasible to consider the expediency of setting up a direct communication line between the United Nations Headquarters and the capitals of the countries that are

permanent members of the Security Council and the location of
the Chairman of the Nonaligned Movement. (Gorbachev, 1987)

After discussing the Center concept General Secretary Gorbachev
continued that it could be possible to set up within the United
Nations a mechanism for extensive international verification of
compliance with agreements to lessen international tension, limit
armaments and for monitoring the military situations in conflict
areas, using various forms and methods of monitoring to collect
information and promptly submit it to the United Nations. Finally, in
July 1988, he proposed a new variation, a European Center to reduce
the danger of war, as was already discussed in Ch. 3.

4.2 Further development of the original concepts
After their first presentation, the specific concepts relating to
multilateral prevention and management of nuclear war or incidents
referred above underwent critical scholarly examination. The Harvard
Nuclear Negotiation Project, in spring 1987, did an evaluation of the
original 'center' concept presented by the UN Secretary-General. A
number of high-level expert interviews were conducted in the US by
the project staff. (The following is based on the material submitted
by the Harvard Project to the UN Secretary-General.)

Some of those interviewed favored operational activities as the
functions of the Center: monitoring nuclear threats (to be a clearing
house for satellite data collection), or carrying out multilateral
nuclear crisis prevention and management activities, including coordination of responses. Others thought that the focus should rather
be in the study, training and analysis of the multitude of unforeseen
problems related to nuclear accidents and nuclear terrorists (what to
do in case of a nuclear accident in terms of notification, clean-up,
emergency medical and economic help, how to deal with long-term
consequences, etc.). Some saw the center as providing a negotiation
forum and offering the best potential for a confidence-building
measure in a regional context.

The main problem mentioned in the interviews conducted by the
Harvard Project concerning the establishment of a multilateral
Center, was the lack of high political demand to set one up, which
took into account the financial difficulties the idea would most likely
face. Other concerns dealt with potential leaks, the expected
reluctance of one or many nuclear states to share sensitive

information with any multilateral entity, and how efficient international staff would be to act quickly in a nuclear emergency. One respondent thought that a way of proceeding with the idea would be to start with a broad, nebulous mandate within which there would be plenty of room to grow, especially after successes in some specific functions assigned to the Center. Financing could also start first through independent means and then, gradually, the Center could expand its activities through governmental funding.

Later in 1988-89, the multilateral Center concepts were discussed in a number of seminars sponsored by the Yale Program for International Security and Arms Control: in Kingston, Canada (together with the Canadian Institute for International Peace and Security), in Warsaw, Poland (together with the Polish Peace Research Council), and Kiev, in the USSR (jointly with UN Disarmament Campaign). The results of these discussions can be crystallized in the following conceptual distinctions:

1. The concept 'Multilateral War Risk Reduction Center' was thought to best be limited to analytical and early warning functions related to regional conflicts and security threats of both a politico-military and socio-economic nature, and to have only an indirect link to nuclear war or nuclear weapon incidents.

2. Establishing a 'Regional War Risk Reduction Center' was generally considered to be an innovative way to promote confidence building as a part of various regional security arrangements (for instance, in Europe, as part of the CSCE-process).

3. A distinct concept from those above, a 'Multilateral Nuclear Alert Center' (see next section) was seen as related to early warning and rapid communication and coordination requirements in case of a potential nuclear weapon incident or accident, and promising as a forum for discussions of strategic and other issues pertaining to military affairs.

The idea of eventually integrating global, bilateral and regional war risk reduction centers - whether they are dealing with nuclear or conventional crises or both - was discussed in the conference in Canada in October 1988 (Kanninen, 1988). Whether a European center, which NATO came to support in principle in July 1990, should and would be integrated to other centers is still an open question. The representative of Belarus stated, however, already in fall 1988 in the General Assembly debate (United Nations, 1988b: p. 4) that the idea of the European center was in consonance with the proposal by the Secretary-General to set up a United Nations multilateral nuclear-risk reduction center, and that such a multilateral center at the United Nations should be linked by a modern communication system with a network of regional military-risk reduction centers. This approach implicitly supported the idea of an eventual integration of all kinds of risk reduction centers. Only time will tell whether this will be implemented in practice.

4.3 Multilateral nuclear alert center

James Sutterlin, who in the early 1970s headed the Office of Central European Affairs and served briefly as Director of Policy Planning Staff in the US State Department, elaborated in a recent paper the concept of a multilateral nuclear alert center (Sutterlin, 1989). Since, in the 1980s, Sutterlin was also one of the key aides and speech-writers for the UN Secretary-General - when Mr. Perez de Cuellar made his proposal in 1986 - one could take his elaboration as somewhat authoritative on the original proposal. (The following comments are based on Sutterlin's paper and later discussions with him.)

Although the US and the CIS have crisis centers and agreements in place which offer some assurance against automatic nuclear counter-launching or escalation of the alert status of nuclear forces beyond control in case of any nuclear weapon incident of either of the two States, no such assurance exists, according to Sutterlin, against the nuclear counter-launch of other Nuclear Powers or triggering of the alert systems of Superpowers by nuclear events of unclear identity or intent. Present hot line facilities do not involve the constant presence of experts able to interpret nuclear weapons-related developments and to maintain a continuing contact to avoid any misinterpretation. China is not included in any hot line arrangement, nor are several other countries with the capability of producing nuclear weapons and launching systems. Since integrated parts of the Superpower nuclear C^3I systems are located in or monitoring these volatile regions, any action from an outside party which might rightly or wrongly be interpreted as a nuclear launch could lead to catastrophic consequences, including almost automatic triggering of the escalating nuclear alerts by the Superpowers' nuclear forces, unless the original action were subject to immediate clarification.

On the other hand, outside an imminent crisis situation, there is also a possibility that countries without the domestic capacity to produce nuclear weapons might be able to purchase various components and seek to gain a nuclear capability. As this becomes known, the need for instant communication among other technologically competent, influential or threatened countries would be important. Finally, in case of nuclear terrorists, instantaneous communication and consultation among Powers with the technological capacity to interpret any seemingly threatening action and agree quickly on countermeasures would be urgently needed as well.

Sutterlin lists the following objectives which the Center should pursue in particular:

1. Receive and circulate information provided by states, on a voluntary basis, on any action pertaining to nuclear weapons (interpreted as destabilizing or peace threatening);

2. Receive and assess information from all available sources, including an eventual UN satellite, on indications of unusual or threatening nuclear activity;

3. Seek urgent clarification of any threatening nuclear event;

4. Inform participating states and the UN Secretary-General, the Security Council and Member States (as needed by the urgency of the situation) of such events, with the assessment of their implications, and advice on appropriate countermeasures;

5. Obtain, on a continuing basis, information from the International Atomic Energy Agency (IAEA) on any diversion of nuclear fuel from peaceful energy installations and seek to determine the reason for the diversion;

6. Advise the UN Secretary-General on the significance of any new activity involving nuclear weapons;

7. Develop a data bank on nuclear arms, nuclear capacities and nuclear components that would be of assistance in interpreting incoming information, and reports on known or suspected activities related to nuclear weapons; and finally (and possibly)

8. Monitor compliance with treaties on the reduction or limitation of nuclear weapons should the United Nations be given this responsibility in the future.

As a structure for the Center, Sutterlin proposes that an Alert Center be established by the decision of the General Assembly as part of the United Nations Organization or, alternatively, by an international conference as a semi-independent agency closely linked to the United Nations but with its own budget and financial support. Physically the Center would best be located in Vienna, close to IAEA. It would consist of a small staff of technically qualified international civil servants headed by an executive director appointed by the UN Secretary-General. It would also have a consultative council made up of qualified representatives of the five nuclear weapon states and representatives of non-nuclear states rotating on an established schedule. The council would meet regularly to review developments, consider reports and analyses provided by the Center staff, and give guidance on the Center's operation. The Center would have an advanced communication system giving it access to the UN Secretary-General, the Security Council, and the capitals of the members of the advisory council.

4.4 Evaluation and discussion of the proposal for a multilateral nuclear alert center

In 1978, France presented at the First UN Special Session of Disarmament a somewhat similar proposal (although lacking an immediate nuclear connection) to establish an international satellite monitoring agency (ISMA) with two functions: to monitor compliance with arms control agreements, and to keep a close eye on global trouble spots and provide early warning of impending crises. Although the Group of Experts, appointed by the Secretary-General at the request of the General Assembly, concluded in 1981 that an ISMA was technically, legally and financially feasible, the idea did not survive Superpower objections at that time and was dropped (see, e.g., Florini, 1988: pp. 114-115; (the CIS appears now to be ready to discuss this again) see Petrovsky, 1988).

It is possible to think that a nuclear alert center could be established, at least in the first instance, in a regional context. A natural starting point is Europe. Any monumental political change in the area as a whole or rapid events in its parts - as happened in 1989 - have potential implications on the command and control of nuclear weapons in Europe. A multilateral crisis center of some sort might provide a forum for discussion of necessary short or long-term safeguard measures against unknown dangers of this kind, most naturally within the framework of the CSCE process (see the Helsinki and Stockholm documents). A number of proposals have been, in fact, made to establish such a center in Europe as was discussed before. (One could also refer to the proposal made by British-based scholars Jasani, Prins and Rees to set up an independent multilateral satellite agency for Europe; they cite as their starting point Chancellor Helmut Kohl's hope that the Europeans could 'monitor compliance with arms control agreements using our own resources'; Jasani et al., 1990: pp. 15-16.) The European center (or any UN-linked center) would not necessarily need its own satellite since most relevant data could be acquired from commercial sources, especially from the French SPOT satellite (Florini, 1988: pp. 102-103).

In practice, the establishment of a global center would need the concurrence of the five permanent members of the Security Council, which are formally the states of the world that possess nuclear weapons. At the moment such a development does not appear likely. But the events leading to an extraordinarily quick agreement on IAEA notification and assistance conventions in case of nuclear accidents provide an illustration of how the international atmosphere could change quite rapidly.

Only a major disaster gave the necessary impetus to conclude the IAEA conventions, although earlier accidents, such as those at the Windscale fuel processing plant and at Three Mile Island, paved the way for the final acceptance of necessary multilateral measures mitigating the effects of this kind of modern danger. The Chairman of the Group of Governmental Experts which drafted the Conventions, Ambassador L.H.J.B. van Gorkom of the Netherlands, stated:

Within four months after the Chernobyl nuclear accident the two conventions were drafted by consensus; within five months they were adopted and signed by over 50 states; within six months the Convention of early Notification entered into force; and within ten months the Convention on Mutual Assistance entered into force. All of this was accomplished under the impact of the disaster. (Adede, 1989: p. xiii)

This case also showed how the positions of the major nuclear power states were changing on a question whether to include nuclear weapons in multilateral agreement of this kind. According to A.O. Adede, legal adviser to IAEA during the negotiations, the majority of experts, including some from important nuclear weapon states, were in favor from the start of a so-called 'full scope' agreement which would cover any accident or emergency resulting in a transboundary radiological release, irrespective of the nature of the activity involved; i.e. the notification should apply to such releases from accidents relating to nuclear weapons as well. In the words of Adede:

It is important to note also that it was during the discussion of the proposal set out above that certain nuclear weapon States (France and the United Kingdom, later joined by China) expressed a willingness to negotiate an agreement which covers nuclear accidents in both civilian and military activities in the territory of a State or in areas under its jurisdiction or control. The other nuclear weapon States (the United States and the Soviet Union) both remained reluctant and cautious until the package solution was formulated towards the very end of the negotiation... (Adede, 1989: pp. 21-22)

This tendency of regimes or organizations to change only after a major crisis, in order to meet the requirements of the time, is well documented. The UN is no exception. As an illustration one can refer to the creation of an early warning machinery for the UN Secretary-General in 1987 (the establishment of ORCI). It was only possible to make this reform in the aftermath of the UN financial crisis, although the reform was preceded by thinking and elaborate blueprints for a modern early warning and data management system at the UN, proposed both by insiders and outsiders. The crisis provided the impetus and opportunity to put any tentative plans into action.

Although a nuclear alert center of some sort could be implemented in Europe in the present political situation when solutions for an emerging security regime are negotiated, that might not easily be the case in other regions. The participants in the UN meeting on confidence building measures in the Asia-Pacific region, for instance, in Kathmandu, Nepal (29-31 January 1990) felt that the European experience had value but clearly could not be adopted in its entirety. Premature timing should be avoided. Different security perceptions and asymmetrical impacts of some CBMs on different countries were cited as possible difficulties, as was the claim that some measures might undermine deterrence and thus increase the risk of war. An incremental, step-by-step approach was considered more feasible than an all-embracing one. The meeting noted that a broad value-sharing process that had been instituted in Europe through the Helsinki Final Act and the Stockholm document had no region-wide counterpart in the Asia-Pacific region (United Nations Disarmament Newsletter, 1990: p. 14).

Recent regional developments outside Europe have given some urgency to thinking about new regional measures, or global ones in case regional ones are not viable, to prevent accidental nuclear war. For instance, in the Middle East the continuous arms race, including ballistic missiles, and subsequent deepening distrust among regional powers emphasizes the need for preventive machinery. In South Asia, a region with a number of nuclear states, the question of Kashmir between India and Pakistan is of considerable concern to many observers. The overt and covert hostilities make the initiation of regional CBM measures, including the establishment of a nuclear alert center, a very difficult task indeed. Therefore, a global nuclear alert center is an option to consider even in the regional context. Another reason for a global center is the global integration of C^3I systems of both Superpowers, which makes any distinction between regional and global nuclear crises a tenuous one.

The proposal for a global nuclear alert center, as elaborated by James Sutterlin, was discussed in Kiev in a seminar in September 1989, as referred to earlier (the following is based on an unofficial transcript of discussions). The participants thought the proposal timely, but they also indicated a number of problems involved:

- the center would be too expensive in the UN context if it has to operate with a 24-hour watch, and if the center would need to acquire and use its own UN satellite;
- how could efficiency and impartiality be guaranteed in a multilateral environment when urgent action was needed (a commonly asked question in terms of any UN operation);
- who will evaluate the information, and how? This query relates to the credibility problem of an international team of experts.

The following suggestions were made offering possible solutions to these concerns:

- the center could be mainly a strategic rather than tactical or technical center with the purpose of sharing ideas, discussing nuclear security and strategy issues, etc.;
- costs could be substantially reduced if the UN could use commercial satellites or, in case of its own satellite, use it for other purposes as well;
- it would perhaps be advisable to separate verification from other functions of the center to make it less expensive.

5. Conclusions

Turning back to the categories designated at the beginning of this paper when assessing multilateral proposals to avert accidental nuclear war, the initiative to seriously consider a multilateral nuclear crisis center seems to have advanced to a stage of discussion, elaboration and some tentative processes towards implementation (in Europe). No one has yet seriously questioned the need for a multinational center, although a number of observers have had doubts about its practicability and financial, political and technical viability (as was the case about the proposals for the hot line in the 1950s and early 1960s). Our case study showed that Americans were involved in initiating the discussion, the UN Secretary-General made the formal proposal, and the Soviets were first to welcome the initiative. The question looms large, however, whether or not a crisis of some sort is needed to push the idea to an active implementation phase beyond partial experiments taking place in Europe.

In conclusion, it seems that it is not very realistic to expect that the proposal to establish a Multilateral Nuclear Alert Center, or a variation of some kind, for global early warning and monitoring functions, would be accepted by the major nuclear weapon powers at this time. There is a great reluctance by the Superpowers and other nuclear power states to share with any multilateral entity sensitive information related to nuclear weapons or nuclear terrorists. However, if one accepts the premise that the threat of nuclear incidents has increased in a world which has become more multipolar and more interdependent and where nuclear technology has spread and become more advanced, then the situation might suddenly change if accidents or incidents really happen where multilateral preventive measures or availability of effective international communication links would have made a difference.

Small steps could be taken towards a multilateral center. A privately or semi-privately funded center or institute with high-credibility research and watch functions, to be recognized by political decision-makers as an impartial and credible organization with a multinational staff, could be established to deal specifically with the questions on preventing accidental nuclear war and, possibly, with the threats of use of chemical and biological weapons - the poor man's atomic bombs. One can mention as organizational models for a center of this kind SIPRI in Stockholm, and IISS in London, in the fields of arms control and strategic studies; and the Worldwatch Institute in Washington, DC in environmental monitoring and research. The center(s) when set up might provide information to the UN Secretary-General and issue public documents to the research community and media. Gradually, as a respondent suggested to the Harvard Nuclear Negotiation project staff (see section 4.2 above), a center's mandate could grow after initial experience and successes. Later it could be more closely related to official multilateral arrangements which, once established, would enhance the avoidance and management of potential or real nuclear incidents in the future, one of the most urgent tasks of our generation.

Appendix A

THE STOCKHOLM DECLARATION
ON PREVENTING ACCIDENTAL NUCLEAR WAR

Vastly improved East-West relations during the last years have created better prospects for common security and arms control agreements than ever before in the post world war era. Regional conflicts, however, at present constitute severe threats.

An intentional war between the major nuclear-weapon states seems unlikely today. Nevertheless, technological developments, dangerous military doctrines, and nuclear weapon proliferation to additional countries create dangers for an accidental nuclear war. An initiative now against these dangers would seem both urgent and promising.

It is responsibility of the global community to work for the complete elimination of nuclear arms everywhere, in a manner which handles security matters so as to avoid the re-emergence of nuclear weapons. This is the only way to totally eliminate the risks of accidental nuclear war.

In order for humankind to survive, it is necessary in the meantime to reduce the danger of this type of war. Primary responsibility for avoiding nuclear war lies with the nuclear-weapon states, but all nations have a vital interest in measures for the prevention of nuclear war, in view of the catastrophic consequences that such a war would have for humankind.

Representatives of all six political parties in the Swedish Parliament and nine Swedish professional organizations against nuclear arms, organized an international conference in Stockholm, Sweden, November 14 -16, 1990, to design an Action Program for the Prevention of Accidental Nuclear War. Some thirty experts from different countries contributed to these efforts as consultants.[51]

The Action Program recommends that all governments should work for the adoption of several preventive measures. A summary of these follows below.

---

[51] The consutants provided expert advice, and presented various proposals to the Board of the Swedish Initiative for the Prevention of Accidental Nuclear War. The Declaration and the Action Program were finally formulated by the Swedish Board.

Nuclear weapons should be removed from any plans for the conduct of war. Political developments in Europe, and emerging changes in military doctrines, now make it clear that tactical nuclear weapons could be eliminated.

'No first-use' policies should be adopted by all nuclear-weapon states. Tactical nuclear weapons, ground, air and sea-based, should be abolished. No new tactical nuclear weapons such as air-to-surface missiles (TASM) should be introduced.

Acknowledging the human factor in accidents.
Most accidents are caused by the human factor. Since humans are not infallible, there will always be risks while nuclear weapons exist. In order to minimize the consequences of human fallibility, the following measures are recommended: monitor all nuclear weapons personnel; train decision-makers in crisis management; educate all those involved in the limitations of human performances under stress.

Launch-on-warning plans should be eliminated.
Operational capability for quick response is dangerous because of the stress it puts on the man-machine systems involved. As long as strategic deterrence remains, these dangers should be reduced by phasing out such capabilities. The most destabilizing weapons, especially missiles with many warheads, should be eliminated. Further developments in the accuracy and capabilities of nuclear weapons and delivery vehicles should be avoided, as well as space-based weaponry. A main route towards this goal would be a ban on nuclear weapon testing and limitations on missile flight testing.

Strengthen the political control of nuclear weapons.
All nuclear weapons, including those at sea, should be protected by electronic locks in order to strengthen the political control. Further important steps include the provision of all strategic nuclear missiles with command/destruct devices.

Risk of break-down in central goverment control poses problems for countries that possess nuclear weapons. To reduce such risks, nuclear weapons should be withdrawn from any areas where central government control might be jeopardized.

Risks of nuclear terrorism can be reduced by increased control of nuclear weapons, technical devices, and by control of fissionable material.

Reduce incentives for nuclear weapon proliferation.
The proliferation of nuclear weapon capabilities among additional international actors poses extra threats to international security. Efforts to solve the underlying conflicts in certain areas can only be undertaken on a regional basis.

Substantial reductions in the existing nuclear arsenals, and a comprehensive ban forbidding all nuclear testing would contribute fundamentally to the viability of the present non-proliferation regime. Only in the context of a decreased role for nuclear weapons is there a chance of eliminating all weapons of mass destruction.

Increase openness on existing nuclear arsenals.
A further transition from confrontation to cooperation and trust would be promoted by increased openness on existing nuclear arsenals. Measures such as prenotification of missile launches, reports on arms restructuring, and nuclear accidents are recommended. Nuclear risk reduction centers could provide avenues for exchange of information contributing to confidence-building.

Increased negotiation efforts.
Every opportunity should be taken in order to make the UN an effective international negotiation forum. Efforts by the nuclear-weapon states and by the Conference on Security and Cooperation in Europe to reduce the risk of accidental war are welcomed. International legal regimes should also be strengthened. If necessary a new forum for accidental nuclear war prevention should be established.

Alert the general public.
Information to alert the general public on the continued risk posed by nuclear weapons is essential, especially in a situation where awareness of these dangers is diminishing. All information campaigns should involve the young, and educational programs should be encouraged. Recent developments in East Europe remove the concern that such information might act asymmetrically in different societies, thereby creating a security risk.

Appendix B - Abbrevations

ABM	Anti-Ballistic Missile
ASAT	Anti-Satellite Weapons
ASW	Anti-Submarine Warfare
AT&T	American Telephone and Telegraph Company
B-1	A type of US bomber aircraft
B-52	A type of US bomber aircraft
BMEWS	Ballistic Missile Early Warning System
C^3	Command, Control, Communications
C^3I	Command, Control, Communications, Intelligence
CBM	Confidence-Building Measure
CFE	Conventional Armed Forces in Europe
CIA	Central Intelligence Agency
CIS	Commonwealth of Independent States
CSBM	Confidence and Security Building Measures
CSCE	Conference on Security and Cooperation in Europe
D-5	Type of missile (on Trident II submarine)
DR	Defense Ratio
DSB	Department of State Bulletin
ELF	Extremely Low Frequency
EMP	Electromagnetic Pulse
F-14	A type of US fighter aircraft
HUMINT	Human Intelligence
I&W	Indications and Warning system
IAEA	International Atomic Energy Agency
ICBM	Intercontinental Ballistic Missile
IHE	Insensitive High Explosives
INF	Intermediate-Range Nuclear Forces
ISMA	International Satellite Monitoring Agency
KGB	Komitet Gosudarstvennoj Bezopasnosti (Committee for State Security)
LOW	Launch-On-Warning
MAC	Missile Attack Conference
MAD	Mutual Assured Destruction
MDC	Missile Display Conference
MHV	Miniature Homing (Intercept) Vehicle
MIRV	Multiple Independently Targetable Reentry Vehicle
NATO	North Atlantic Treaty Organization
NGO	Non-Governmental Organization

NORAD	North American Aerospace Defense Command
NPT	Non-Proliferation Treaty
NTM, NTMV	National Technical Means of Verification
ORCI	Office for Research and the Collection of Information
PAL	Permissive Action Link
PRP	Nuclear Weapons Personnel Reliability Program
PWR	Pressurized Water Reactor
RAF	Royal Air Force
RC-135	A type of US reconnaissance aircraft
RV	Reentry Vehicles
SAC	Strategic Air Command
SDI	Strategic Defense Initiative
SALT-II	Strategic Arms Limitation Talks
SED	Sozialistische Einheitspartei Deutschlands (The government party of former East Germany)
SLBM	Sea-Launched Ballistic Missile
SLCM	Sea-Launched Cruise Missile
SPD	Sozialdemokratische Partei Deutschlands (The Social Democrat party of former West Germany)
SS-13	Surface-to-surface missile
SS-19	Surface-to-surface missile
SS-N-21	Cruise missile
SS-24	Surface-to-surface missile
SS-25	Surface-to-surface missile
SSBN	Strategic Submarine, Ballistic, Nuclear
START	Strategic Arms Reduction Talks
TAC	Threat Assessment Conference
TEC	Threat Evaluation Conference
U-2	A type of US reconnaissance aircraft
USS	United States Ship
WTO	Warsaw Treaty Organization

Appendix C - Bibliography

Abrams, Herbert L. 1986. 'Sources of Human Instability in the Handling of Nuclear Weapons', in Fredric Soloman & Robert Q. Marston, eds., *The Medical Implications of Nuclear War*, pp. 491-528. Washington, DC: National Academy Press.

Abrams, Herbert L. 1987. 'The Problem of Accidental or Inadvertent Nuclear War', *Preventive Medicine*, vol. 16, May, pp. 319-333.

Abrams, Herbert L. 1988. 'Inescapable Risk: Human Disability and Accidental Nuclear War', *Current Research on Peace and Violence*, vol. 11, no. 1-2, pp. 48-60. Tampere: Tampere Peace Research Institute.

Abrams, Herbert L. 1990. 'Disabled Leaders, Cognition and Crisis Decision-Making', in Paul, Intriligator & Smoker, eds., *Accidental Nuclear War*, pp. 136-149. Toronto: Science for Peace / Samuel Stevens.

Adede, A. O. 1987. *The IAEA Notification and Assistance Conventions in Case of a Nuclear Accident*. London: Graham & Trotman/Martinus Nijhoff.

Albright, David & Mark Hibbs 1991a. 'Iraq and the bomb: Were they even close?', *The Bulletin of Atomic Scientists*. March.

Albright, David & Mark Hibbs 1991b. 'Iraq's nuclear hide-and-seek', *The Bulletin of Atomic Scientists*, September.

Allison, Graham 1971. *Essence of Decision*. Boston: Little, Brown.

Allison, Graham T. & William L. Ury 1989. *Windows of Opportunity: From Cold War to Peaceful Competition on US-Soviet Relations*. Cambridge, MA: Ballinger.

Almquist, Peter 1990. 'The Vienna Military Doctrine Seminar: Flexible Response vs. Defensive Sufficiency', *Arms Control Today*, April, pp. 21-25.

Ambio 1989. 'Statement from a Conference on the Environmental Consequences of Nuclear War', vol. 18, no. 7, pp. 1.

Anderson, H. R., R. S. MacNair & J. D. Ramsey 1985. 'Deaths from Abuse of Volatile Substances: A National Epidemiological Study', *British Medical Journal*, vol. 290, January 26.

Angell, Norman 1908. *The Great Illusion*. London.

Apter, David E. 1967. 'The Politics of Modernization'. Chicago: University of Chicago Press.

Arkin, William M. & Richard W. Fieldhouse 1985. *Nuclear Battlefields: Global Links in the Arms Race*. Cambridge, MA: Ballinger.

Arms Control Reporter, 1988. 'NATO-WTO Stability/Reduction Talks - Chronology 1988.', September, pp. 53-56.

Asch, Solomon 1956. *Studies of Independence and Conformity: A Minority of One against a Unanimous Majority*. Psychological Monographs, 70(9).

Åslund, Anders 1989. *Gorbachev's Struggle for Economic Reform*. Ithaca: Cornell University Press.

Associated Press, 1984. 'Demonstrators Criticize Security at Missile Plant', *New York Times*, April 24.

Associated Press, 1989. 'Bangor Marine Apparent Suicide,' *The Bremerton Sun*, January 16, p. B5.

Avenhaus, Rudolf, Steven J. Brams, John Fichtner & D. Marc Kilgour 1989. 'The Probability of Nuclear War', *Journal of Peace Research*, vol. 26, no. 1, pp. 91-100.

Azar, Edward E. & John W. Burton 1986. *International Conflict Resolution. Theory and Practice*. Brighton: Wheatsheaf.

Babst, Dean, ed. *International Accidental Nuclear War Prevention Newsletter*. Nuclear Age Peace Foundation, 1187 Coast Village Road, Suite 123, Santa Barbara, CA 93108, USA.

Babst, Dean & Robert Aldridge 1986. 'Summary of the Nuclear Time Bomb', May. Santa Barbara: Nuclear Age Peace Foundation.

Babst, Dean 1989. 'Accidental Nuclear Weapon Explosion?' *International Accidental Nuclear War Prevention Bulletin*, December.

Babst, Dean 1990. *Global Security Study*, no. 9, Nuclear Age Peace Foundation.

Ball, Desmond 1981. 'Can Nuclear War be Controlled?' *Adelphi Papers* No. 169. London: International Institute of Strategic Studies, p. 4.

Ball, Desmond 1988. *Pine Gap*. London: Pinter.

Barber, Michael A. 1990. 'Probers Piece Together Triple-Slaying Jigsaw', *Seattle Post-Intelligencer*, January 19, p. B1.

Barlow, Richard E. & Frank Proschan 1975. 'Importance of System Components and Fault Tree Events', *Stochastic Processes and their Applications*, vol. 3, pp. 153-173.

Barlow, Richard E. & Frank Proschan 1981. *Statistical Theory of Reliability. Probability Models*. Silver Spring: To Begin With.

Beeston, Nicholas 1986. 'Armed Forces Recruits Face Drug Tests', *The Times*, July 4, p. 1.

Belous, Vladimir 1988. *Star Wars and Star Peace*. New Delhi: Allied Publishers Private Ltd.

Berlyne, Donald E. 1970. 'Novelty, Complexity, and Hedonic Value', *Perception and Psychophysics*, vol. 8, pp. 279-286.

Beukel, Erik 1989. *American Perceptions of the Soviet Union as a Nuclear Adversary*. London: Pinter.

Berger, James O. 1985. *Statistical Decision Theory and Bayesian Analysis*. New York: Springer Verlag.

Betts, Richard 1982. *Surprise Attack*. Washington, DC: The Brookings Institution.

Betts, Richard 1985. 'A Joint Nuclear Risk Control Center,' in Barry Blechman, ed., *Preventing Nuclear War*. Bloomington: Indiana University Press.

Bialer, Seweryn 1989. 'Rethinking Foreign Policy' in Allison & Ury, *Windows of Opportunity*. Cambridge, MA: Ballinger.

Blair, Bruce G. 1985. *Strategic Command and Control: Redefining the Nuclear Threat*. Washington, DC: The Brookings Institution.

Blair, Bruce G. 1993. *The Logic of Accidental Nuclear War*. Washington, DC: The Brookings Institution.

Blake, Nigel & Kay Pole, eds. 1983. *Dangers of Deterrence. Philosophers on Nuclear Strategy*. London: Routledge & Kegan Paul.

Blake, Nigel & Kay Pole, eds. 1984. *Objections to Nuclear Defence: Philosophers on Deterrence*. London: Routledge & Kegan Paul.

Blechman, Barry 1985. *Preventing Nuclear War*. Bloomington: Indiana University Press.

Bodrov, V. A. 1984. 'Basic Principles of the Development of a System for the Occupational Psychological Selection of Servicemen and its Performance,' *Voenno-meditsinskii zhurnal*, vol. 9, pp. 41-43.

Borning, Alan 1985. 'Computer System Reliability and Nuclear War', *Technical Report*, October, no. 85-10-01. Seattle: Department of Computer Science, University of Washington.

Boudreau, Thomas 1984. *The Secretary-General and Satellite Diplomacy: An Analysis of the Present and Potential Role of the United Nations Secretary-General in the Maintenance of International Peace and Security*. New York: Council on Religion and International Affairs.

Bracken, Paul 1983. *The Command and Control of Nuclear Forces*. New Haven: Yale University Press.

Bracken, Paul 1988. 'Some Thoughts on Multilateral Nuclear Worlds'. Paper presented at the Conference on War-Risk Reduction through Multilateral Means, Kingston, Ontario, organized by the Canadian Institute for International Peace and Security, 7 - 8 October 1988.

Bracken, Paul 1990. *High Command: the Theory and Politics of National Security Organization*. Cambridge, MA: Cambridge University Press.

Bradley, Morris 1986a. 'Psychological Distortion of the Nature of the Risk of Unintentional Nuclear War'. Paper given at the Conference of the International Peace Research Association, Sussex University.

Bradley, Morris 1986b. 'Psychological Processes Increasing the Risks of Accidental Nuclear War'. *Proceedings of the International European Psychologists for Peace Conference*, Helsinki.

Bradley, Morris 1987a. 'Psychological Processes that Make Accidental Nuclear War More Probable', *Technical Report*, no. 8. Santa Barbara: Nuclear Age Peace Foundation.

Bradley, Morris 1987b. 'The Application of Systems Theory to the Psychology of the Arms Race'. Paper for Seventh International Congress of Cybernetics and Systems, London University.

Bradley, Morris 1987c. 'The Dynamics of Nuclear Confrontation and Conflict Resolution'. Paper given at the Conference on Accidental Nuclear War, Lancaster University.

Bradley, Morris 1987d. 'Attitudes to Nuclear War: A Psychological Survey'. Paper given at the Fourth European Conference of the International Society for Research on Aggression, University of Sevilla.

Bradley, Morris 1988a. 'The Application of Psychology to Problems of Nuclear Confrontation and the Risk of Accidental Nuclear War', *Current Research on Peace and Violence*, vol. 11, no. 1-2, pp. 61-71.

Bradley, Morris 1988b. 'Accidental Nuclear War: An Imperative for Disarmament'. Conference on Accidental Nuclear War, Edinburgh Peace Festival.

Bradley, Morris 1989a. 'Conflict Dynamics and Conflict Resolution' in Barnett, L. & I. Lee, eds., *The Nuclear Mentality*. London: Pluto Press.

Bradley, Morris 1989b. 'Problems of Methodology and Interpretation in Psychological Research'. Paper given at the International Conference on the Psychology of Nuclear War, Rome University.

Bradley, Morris 1990. 'The Implications of Accidental Nuclear War: Identifying and Surmounting the Psychological Barriers to Cooperation' in Paul, Intriligator & Smoker eds., *Accidental Nuclear War*. Toronto: Science for Peace / Samuel Stevens.

Bradley, Morris & Paul Smoker 1988. 'Logical Implications of the Risk of Accidental Nuclear War and Concomitant Psychological Factors', *Current Research on Peace and Violence*, vol. 11, no. 1-2, pp. 72-79.

Braithwaite, R. B. 1955. *Theory of Games as a Tool for the Moral Philosopher*. Cambridge: Cambridge University Press.

Brams, Steven J. 1985. *Superpower Games: Applying Game Theory to Superpower Conflict*. New Haven & London: Yale University Press.

Brante, Thomas 1989. 'Empirical and epistemological issues in scientists' explanations of scientific stances: a critical synthesis', *Social Epistemology*, vol. 3, no. 4, pp. 281-295.

Bray, Robert M., Mary E. Marsden, L. Lynn Guess, Sara C. Wheeless, D. K. Pate, G. H. Dunteman & V. G. Iannacchione 1986. *1985 Worldwide Survey of Alcohol and Nonmedical Drug Use Among Military Personnel*. Research Triangle Park: Research Triangle Institute.

Bray, Robert M., Mary E. Marsden, L. Lynn Guess, Sara C. Wheeless, V. G. Iannacchione & S. Randall Keesling 1989. *Highlights of the 1988 Worldwide Survey of Substance Abuse and Health Behaviors*

Among Military Personnel. Research Triangle Park: Research Triangle Institute.

Bray, Robert M., Mary E. Marsden & Sara C. Wheeless 1989. *Military/Civilian Comparisons of Alcohol, Drug and Tobacco Use*. Research Triangle Park: Research Triangle Institute.

Brehmer, Berndt & Robert Allard 1985. *Dynamic Decision Making: A General Paradigm and Some Experimental Results*. Manuscript, Uppsala: Uppsala University, Dept. of Psychology.

Brehmer, Berndt 1987. 'Systems Design and the Psychology of Complex Systems' in Jens Rasmussen & Pranas Zunde, eds. *Empirical Foundations of Information and Software Science, III*. New York: Plenum Publ. Corp, pp. 21-32.

Broad, William J. 1990. 'Specter is Raised of Nuclear Theft', *New York Times*, January 28, p. 7.

Brunson, Nils 1985. *The Irrational Organization*. Chichester: John Wiley & Sons.

Broadbent, Donald & Ben Aston 1978. 'Human Control of a Simulated Economic System' in E. De Corte et al., eds., *Learning and Instruction*. Amsterdam: North Holland.

Brook-Shepherd, Gordon 1988. *The Storm Birds*. London: Weidenfeld and Nicolson.

Burt, Marvin R. 1982. 'Prevalence and Consequences of Drug Abuse Among US Military Personnel: 1980,' *American Journal of Drug and Alcohol Abuse*, vol. 8, no. 4, pp. 419-439.

Bunn, Matthew & Kosta Tsipis 1983. 'The Uncertainties of a Preemptive Nuclear Attack', *Scientific American*, November.

Buzan, Barry 1983. *Peoples, States and Fear: The National Security Problem in International Relations*. Brighton: Wheatsheaf.

Caldwell, Dan 1986. 'Permissive Action Links (PAL): A Description and Proposal', paper based on presentations made to the project on 'Alternative Approaches to Arms Control' at UCLA, December 3, 1985, and the Conference on Assuring Control of Nuclear Weapons sponsored by the Center for Science and International Affairs, Harvard University, February 7-8, 1986.

Caldwell, Dan & Peter D. Zimmerman 1989. 'Reducing the Risk of Nuclear War With Permissive Action Links', in Barry M. Blechman, ed., *Technology and the Limitation of International Conflict*, pp. 151-175. Washington, DC: John Hopkins Foreign Policy Institute.

Carter, Ashton B. 1987. 'Assessing Command System Vulnerability' in Ashton B. Carter, John Steinbruner & Charles Zraket, eds., *Managing Nuclear Operations*. Washington, DC: The Brookings Institution, pp. 555-610.

Carter, Don 1989. 'Nuclear Sub Sailor Held in Death of 2', *Seattle Post-Intelligencer*, July 4, p. B1.

Chauvistré, Eric 1993. 'Nuclear Ambiguity: (2) North Korea', *Pacific Research*, vol. 6, no. 2, June, pp. 5-8.

Chen, Edwin & Ronald J. Ostrow 1990. 'A-Bomb Triggers For Iraq Seized in London', *New York Times*, March 29, p. 1.

Child, James W. 1986. *Nuclear War: The Moral Dimension*. London & New Brunswick: Transaction Books.

Christian, Shirley 1990. 'Argentina and Brazil Renounce Atomic Weapons,' *New York Times*, November 29, p. 1, A-11.

Christmas-Møller, Wilhelm 1985. *Niels Bohr og atomvåbnet* ('Niels Bohr and the Atomic Weapon'). Copenhagen: Vindrose.

Cochran, Thomas B., William M. Arkin, Robert S. Norris & Jeffrey I. Sands 1989. *Soviet Nuclear Weapons, Nuclear Weapons Databook Vol. IV*. New York: Harper & Row.

Cockburn, Andrew 1983. *The Threat: Inside the Soviet Military Machine*. New York: Random House.

Committee on Government Operations 1982. 'NORAD Computer Systems Are Dangerously Obsolete', 23rd report, 97th Congress, 2nd session, March 8. Washington, DC: US Government Printing Office.

Cooper, Nancy & Steven Strassner 1986. 'We Closed Our Eyes To It', *Newsweek*, October 6.

Council for Science and Society 1977. *The Acceptability of Risks*. London: Barry Rose.

Cowen Karp, Regina 1992. 'The START Treaty and the future of nuclear arms control', Ch. 1 in *SIPRI Yearbook 1992: World Armaments and Disarmament*. Oxford: Oxford University Press.

Davis, Robert B. 1985. 'Alcohol Abuse and the Soviet Military', *Armed Forces and Society*, vol. 11, no. 3, Spring, pp. 403-404.

Dean, Jonathan 1990. 'CFE Negotiations', *The Washington Quarterly*, Winter 1990, p. 183.

Defense Intelligence Agency, 1989. *A Guide to Foreign Tactical Nuclear Weapon Systems Under the Control of Ground Force Commanders*, DST-1040S-541-89, September 18, 1989.

Degrais, D. 1971. 'Les Critères de la Selection des Engagés Dans la Marine', *Revue des Corps de Santé des Armées*, vol. XII, no. 3, June, pp. 271-282.

Demchuk, Andrea, ed. 1987. *The Risk of Accidental Nuclear War*. Proceedings of the Conference on the Risk of Accidental Nuclear War, Vancouver, 26-30 May 1986. The Canadian Institute for International Peace and Security, 307 Gilmour Street, Ottawa, Ontario K2P 0P7, Canada.

Department of the Army, 1978, 1979, 1980, 1981, 1982, 1983, 1984, 1985, 1986, 1987, 1988, 1989. 'Annual Status Report, Nuclear Weapon

Personnel Reliability Program', RCS DD-COMP(A) 1403, Year Ending Dec

Department of the Army, 1985. 'Disposition and Incidence Rates, Active Duty Army Personnel, Psychiatric Cases, Worldwide, CY 80-84'. Washington, DC: US Army Patient Administration Systems and Biostatistics Activity.

Department of the Army, 1990. 'Number of Dispositions of Psychiatric Principal Diagnoses, Worldwide, CY 85-89.' Washington, DC: US Army Patient Administration Systems and Biostatistics Activity.

Department of Defense, 1975, 1976, 1977. 'Annual Disqualification Report, Nuclear Weapon Personnel Reliability Program', Office of the Secretary of Defense, RCS DD-COMP(A) 1403, Calendar Year Ending December 31.

Department of Defense, 1978, 1979, 1980, 1981a, 1982, 1983, 1984, 1985, 1986, 1987, 1988, 1989. 'Annual Status, Nuclear Weapon Personnel Reliability Program', RCS DD-POL(A) 1403, Year Ending December 31.

Department of Defense, 1981b. 'Nuclear Weapon Personnel Reliability Program', Directive Number 5210.42, April 23.

Department of Defense, 1985b. 'Nuclear Weapon Personnel Reliability Program', Directive Number 5210.42, December 6.

Department of the Navy, 1990. Distribution of Psychiatric Diagnoses in the US Navy (1980-1989). Bethesda, MD: Naval Medical Data Services Center, August 2.

Deutsch, Karl W. et al. 1957. *Political Community and the North Atlantic Area*. Princeton: Princeton University Press.

Dickerson, Marc, John Hinchy & John Fabre 1987. 'Chasing, Arousal and Sensation Seeking', in Off-Course Gamblers, *British Journal of Addiction*, 82, pp. 673-80.

Dickerson, Marc 1984. *Compulsive Gamblers*. London: Longman.

Dixon, Norman 1976. *On the Psychology of Military Incompetence*. London: Jonathan Cape.

Dixon, Norman 1987. *Our Own Worst Enemy*. London: Jonathan Cape.

Dougherty, James E. 1984. *The Bishops and Nuclear Weapons*. Handen, CT: Archon Books.

Douglas, Mary 1986. *Risk Acceptability According to the Social Sciences*. London: Routledge & Kegan Paul.

Dumas, Lloyd J., 1980. 'Human Fallibility and Weapons', *The Bulletin of the Atomic Scientists*, November, pp. 15-20.

Drell, Sidney D., Phillip J. Farley & David Holloway 1984. *The Reagan Strategic Defense Initative: A Technical, Political and Arms Control Assessment*, A Special Report of the Center for International Security and Arms Control, July. Stanford University.

Dyson, Freeman 1984. *Weapons and Hope*. New York: Harper and Row.

Dörner, Dietrich 1980. 'On the Problems People Have in Dealing with Complexity', *Simulation and Games*, vol. 11, pp. 87-106.

Easterbrook, Gregg 1983. 'Try an MX Missile', *The New York Times*, February 18, p. A31.

Easterbrook, J. A. 1959. 'The Effects of Emotions on Cue Utilization and the Organization of Behaviour'. *Psychological Review*, vol. 66, pp. 183-201.

Ekéus, Rolf 1992. 'The United Nations Special Commission on Iraq', Ch. 13 in *SIPRI Yearbook 1992: World Armaments and Disarmament*. Oxford: Oxford University Press.

Elliott, Harvey & Stephen Lynas 1984. 'Forces Drug Test Plan', *Daily Mail*, September 8.

Evans, Richard 1984. 'Military Bases Security Criticized', *The Times*, July 27, p. 1.

Evans, Richard 1985. 'Tighter Security at Nuclear Weapons Bases Disclosed', *The Times*, June 18, p. 5.

FBIS, 1990. *Foreign Broadcast Information Service Daily Report*, China, April 11, p. 48.

Fieldhouse, Richard 1992. 'Nuclear weapons developments and unilateral reduction initiatives', Ch. 2 in *SIPRI Yearbook 1992: World Armaments and Disarmament*. Oxford: Oxford University Press.

Fletcher, James C. 1984. *Report on the Study on Eliminating the Threat Posed by Nuclear Ballistic Missiles, Volume V: Battle Management, Communications and Data Processing*. Washington, DC: US Department of Defense.

Florini, Ann 1988. 'The Opening Skies: Third Party Imaging Satellites and US Security', *International Security*, vol. 13, no. 2, pp. 91-123.

Fox, M. & L. Groarke, eds. 1985. *Nuclear War: Philosophical Perspectives*. New York: Peter Lang.

Fox, Robert 1990. 'Soviet Nuclear Civil War Feared', *Washington Times*, March 29, p. 1.

Frank, Jerome 1986. 'Pre Nuclear Age Leaders and the Nuclear Arms Race' in Fenton, I., ed. *The Psychology of Nuclear Conflict*. London: Conventure.

Frankel, Sherman 1990. 'Stopping Accidents After They've Happened,' *Bulletin of the Atomic Scientists*, November, pp. 39-41.

Frankenhaeuser, Marianne 1985. 'To Err is Human: Psychological and Biological Aspects of Human Functioning' in Hellman ed., *Nuclear War by Mistake - Inevitable or Preventable?* Report from an International Conference in Stockholm, Sweden, 15-16 February, pp. 42-48

Frankenhaeuser, Marianne 1988. 'To Err is Human: Nuclear War by Mistake?' pp. 53-60 in Gromyko & Hellman eds., *Breakthrough - Emerging New Thinking*. New York: Walker & Co.

Frei, Daniel 1982. 'Escalation: Assessing the Risk of Unintentional Nuclear War' in Frei, Daniel ed., *Managing International Crises*. Beverly Hills: Sage, pp. 97-112.

Frei, Daniel & Christian Catrina 1983. *Risks of Unintentional Nuclear War*, United Nations Institute for Disarmament Research. Totowa, NJ: Rowman and Allandheld.

Freudenberg, William R. 1988. 'Perceived Risk, Real Risk: Social Science and the Art of Probabilistic Risk Assessment', *Science*, vol. 242, no. 4875 (7 October), pp. 44-49.

Fromm, Erich 1976. *To Have Or To Be - A New Blueprint for Mankind*, pp. 224. London: Abacus.

Gabriel, Richard A. 1980. *The New Red Legions: An Attitudinal Portrait of the Soviet Soldier*. Westport: Greenwood Press.

Garwin, Richard L. 1979. 'Launch Under Attack to Redress Minuteman Vulnerability?' *International Security*, vol. 4, no. 3, Winter.

Garwin, Richard L. 1985. 'Star Wars Shield or Threat?', *Journal of International Affairs*, vol. 39, no. 1, Summer.

Garwin, Richard L. & John Pike 1984. 'Space Weapons: History and Current Debate', *Bulletin of the Atomic Scientists*, vol 40, no. 5, May.

Genscher, Hans-Dietrich 1990. 'German Unification as a Contribution to European Stability.' Text of a speech of the Minister of Foreign Affairs of the Federal Republic of Germany delivered at the Special Session of the WEU Assembly, Luxembourg, 23 March 1990. New York: Permanent Mission of the FRG to the UN, Press Release No. 04/90.

George, Alexander L. 1986. 'The Impact of Crisis-Induced Stress on Decision Making' in Fredric Solomon & Robert Q. Marston, eds.,

The Medical Implications of Nuclear War. Washington, DC: National Academy Press.

Gertz, Bill 1990a. 'Soviet Arms Safe From Civil Strife, CIA Director Says', *Washington Times*, January 28, p. 1.

Gertz, Bill 1990b. 'Soviet Rebels Storm an A-Bomb Facility', *Washington Times*, February 19, p. 1.

Glaser, Charles L. 1985. ' Star Wars Bad Even if it Works', *Bulletin of the Atomic Scientists*, vol. 41, no. 3, March.

Goldblat, Jozef 1989. 'Nuclear Non-Proliferation: A Balance Sheet of Conflicting Trends', *Bulletin of Peace Proposals*, vol. 20, no. 4, pp. 369-387.

Goldblat, Jozef 1990. *Twenty Years of the Non-Proliferation Treaty: Implementations and Prospects*. Oslo: International Peace Research Institute.

Golden, Maj. 1985. 'Physical Security for Remote and Mobile Nuclear Weapon System', *The Inspector General Brief*, no. 37, February, pp. 14-15.

Goldwater, Barry & Gary Hart 1980. 'Report on Recent False Alerts in the Nation's Missile Attack System'. Report to the Committee on Armed Services, United States Senate, Washington, DC: US Government Printing Office.

Goodwin, Geoffrey, ed. 1982. *Ethics and Nuclear Deterrence*. London: Croom Helm.

Gorbachev, Mikhael 1986. Speech before the Indian Parliament. Mission of Union of Soviet Socialist Republics to the United Nations. New York: Press Release No. 176, November 27.

Gorbachev, Mikhael 1987. 'Reality and safeguards for a secure world', *Pravda* and *Izvestia*, 17 September 1987; reprinted in United Nations General Assembly document A/42/574 and S/19143, 18 September 1987.

Gordon, Michael R. 1990. 'A Nuclear Deal is Reported Between Romania and India', *New York Times*, April 30, p. 7.

Gorokhov, A. 1985. 'Behind the Controls of the Strategic Missiles', *Pravda*, May 29, p. 6.

Gottfried, Karl & Bruce G. Blair 1988: *Crisis Stability and Nuclear War*. Oxford: Oxford University Press.

Gray, Colin S. 1977. 'The Future of Land-Based Missile Forces', *Adelphi Papers*, no. 140. London: The International Institute for Strategic Studies.

Gregory, Shaun 1986. *The Command and Control of British Nuclear Weapons*. September. Bradford: University of Bradford School of Peace Studies, Peace Research Report Number 13.

Gregory, Shaun & Alistair Edwards 1988. *A Handbook of Nuclear Weapons Accidents*. Bradford: University of Bradford School of Peace Studies, Peace Research Report No. 20.

Gregory, Shaun & Alistair Edwards 1989. 'The Hidden Cost of Deterrence: Nuclear Weapons Accidents 1950-1988', *Bulletin of Peace Proposals*, vol. 20, no. 1, pp. 3-26.

Gromyko, Anatolij & Martin Hellman, eds.-in-chief; Craig Barnes & Alexander Nikitin, executive eds. 1988. *Breakthrough - Emerging New Thinking*. New York: Walker & Co., pp. 45-52.

Grundmann, Wilhelm 1988. 'For More Confidence and Security in Europe'. Paper presented at the Conference on War-Risk Reduction through Multilateral Means, Kingston, Ontario, organized by the Canadian Institute for International Peace and Security, 7 - 8 October.

Halliday, Fred 1989. *Cold War, Third World*. London: Hutchinson.

Hansen, Chuck 1990. '1,000 More Accidents Declassified', *Bulletin of the Atomic Scientists*, June, p. 9.

Hart, Gary 1981. Statement before a hearing of the US Congress, Committee on Foreign Affairs, on 'IAEA Program and Safeguards', 97th Congress, 1st Session, December 2, p. 9.

Held, David 1987. *Models of Democracy.* Cambridge: Polity Press.

Hellman, Sven, ed. 1985a. *Nuclear War by Mistake - Inevitable or Preventable?* Report from an International Conference in Stockholm, Sweden, 15-16 February 1985. Swedish Physicians Against Nuclear Arms, Repslagargatan 18 C, S-951 35 Luleå, Sweden.

Hellman, Sven 1985b. 'Risks of Nuclear War by Mistake - an Overview', pp. 10-20 in Hellman, *Nuclear War by Mistake - Inevitable or Preventable?* Report from an International Conference in Stockholm, Sweden, 15-16 February.

Hellman, Sven 1990. 'The Risks of Accidental Nuclear War'. *Bulletin of Peace Proposals*, vol. 21, no. 1, pp. 99-103.

Hellman, Sven ed. 1992. 'Towards a Nuclear Weapon-Free World'. Final document from the conference 'Swedish Initiative for the Prevention of Nuclear Proliferation Risks and Non Nuclear Threats', Stockholm November 18-21, 1992. Stockholm: Swedish Initiative (ISBN 91-630-1627-3).

Henricson-Cullberg, Marta 1989. *Human Destructiveness and Its Global Consequences - A Psychological Perspective.* Manuscript, Stockholm: Psychologists against Nuclear Arms.

Heradstveit, Daniel 1981. *The Arab-Israeli Conflict: Psychological Obstacles to Peace.* Oslo: Universitetsforlaget.

Herek, Gregory M., Irving L. Janis & Paul Huth 1987. 'Decision-Making During International Crisis', *Journal of Conflict Resolution*, vol. 31:2, pp. 203-226.

Hersh, Seymour 1986. *The Target is Destroyed.* New York: Random House.

Hiles, F. M. J. 1980. 'The Prevention and Treatment of Alcoholism in the Royal Navy - 1. A Policy', *Journal of the Royal Naval Medical Service*, vol. 3, pp. 180-185.

Hiles, F. M. J. 1981. 'The Prevention and Treatment of Alcoholism in the Royal Navy - 3. Preliminary Report on a Pilot Study of Naval Alcoholics', *Journal of the Royal Naval Medical Service*, vol. 2, pp. 70-76.

Holsti, Ole R. 1972. *Crisis, Escalation, War*. Montreal: McGraw-Queens University Press.

Intriligator, Michael D. 1975. 'Strategic Considerations in the Richardson Model of Arms Races', *Journal of Political Economy*, vol. 83, no. 2, pp. 339-353.

Intriligator, Michael D. 1989a. 'A Better Alternative for START', *Bulletin of Peace Proposals*, vol. 20, no. 2, pp. 225-227.

Intriligator, Michael D. 1989b. 'On the Nature and Scope of Defence Economics', *Defence Economics*, vol. 1, no. 1, pp. 3-11.

Intriligator, Michael D. 1992. 'Prospects for Arms Control: Bilateral, Unilateral, and Multilateral' in Jurgen Brauer & Manas Chatterji, eds., *Economic Issues of Disarmament*. New York: New York University Press.

Intriligator, Michael D. & Dagobert L. Brito 1984. 'Can Arms Races Lead to the Outbreak of War?', *Journal of Conflict Resolution*, vol. 28, no. 1, pp. 63-84.

Intriligator, Michael D. & Dagobert L. Brito 1986. 'Arms Races and Instability', *Journal of Strategic Studies*, vol. 9, no. 4, pp. 113-131.

Intriligator, Michael D. & Dagobert L. Brito 1987a. 'Arms Control: Problems and Prospects'. IGCC Research Paper No. 2, La Jolla: University of California Institute on Global Conflict and Cooperation, University of California, San Diego.

Intriligator, Michael D. & Dagobert L. Brito 1987b. 'The Stability of Mutual Deterrence' in Kugler, J. & F. C. Zagare, eds. *Exploring the Stability of Deterrence*. Denver: University of Denver School of International Studies Monograph Series in World Affairs.

Intriligator, Michael D. & Dagobert L. Brito 1988. 'Accidental Nuclear War: A Significant Issue for Arms Control', *Current Research on Peace and Violence*, vol. 11, no. 1-2, pp. 14-23.

Intriligator, Michael D. & Dagobert L. Brito 1989. 'Arms Control' in Kolodziej, Edward A. & Patrick M. Morgan, eds. *Security and Arms Control*, vol. 1. Westport, Connecticut: Greenwood Press.

Intriligator, Michael D. & Dagobert L. Brito 1990a. 'Accidental Nuclear War: An Important Issue for Arms Control' in Paul, Intriligator & Smoker eds., *Accidental Nuclear War*. Proceedings of the Eighteenth Pugwash Workshop on Nuclear Forces, pp. 6-30. Toronto: Science for Peace/Samuel Stevens.

Intriligator, Michael D. & Dagobert L. Brito 1990b. 'Arms Race Modeling: A Reconsideration', in Nils Petter Gleditsch & Olav Njølstad, eds.: *Arms Races: Technological and Political Dynamics*, pp. 58-77. London, Newbury Park & New Delhi: Sage.

Intriligator, Michael D. & Dagobert L. Brito 1993. 'The Economic and Political Incentives to Acquire Nuclear Weapons' forthcoming in *Security Studies*.

Janis, Irving L. 1972. *Victims of Group Think*. Boston: Houghton Mifflin.

Janis, Irving L. & Leon Mann 1977. *Decision-Making: A Psychological Analysis of Conflict. Choice and Commitment*. New York: Free Press.

Japuncic, Katharine-Mary, John Forge & Sverre Myhra 1993. 'Nuclear Ambiguity: (1) India', *Pacific Research*, vol. 6, no. 2, June, pp. 3-5.

Jasani, Bhupendra & Christopher Lee, 1984. *Countdown to Space War*. London: Taylor & Francis.

Jasani, Bhupendra 1984. 'Part I. The Arms Control Dilemma - An Overview.' in Jasani, Bhupendra ed., *Space Weapons - The Arms Control Dilemma*. London: Taylor & Francis.

Jasani, Bhupendra, Gwyn Prins & Martin Rees 1990. 'Share Satellite Surveillance', *The Bulletin of the Atomic Scientists*, March 1990, pp. 15-16.

Jervis, Robert 1976. *Perception and Misperception in International Politics*. Princeton: Princeton University Press.

Jervis, Robert 1982. 'Security Regimes'. *International Organization*. No. 2.

Jervis, Robert 1984. *The Illogic of American Nuclear Strategy*. Ithaca, NY: Cornell University Press.

Jervis, Robert, Ned Lebow & J.G. Stein 1985. *Psychology and Deterrence*. Baltimore, MD: John Hopkins Univ. Press.

Johnson, Gerald W. 1989. 'Safety, Security and Control of Nuclear Weapons' in Barry M. Blechman, ed., *Technology and the Limitation of International Conflict*. Massachusetts: John Hopkins Foreign Policy Institute, pp. 137-150.

Jones, Rodney W. 1984. *Small Nuclear Forces*, The Washington Papers, vol. XI, no. 103. Washington, DC: Praeger.

Julian, Thomas A. 1987. 'Nuclear Weapons Security and Control' in Paul Leventhal & Yonah Alexander, eds., *Preventing Nuclear Terrorism*, pp. 169-190. Lexington: Lexington Books.

Kahn, Herman 1965. *On Escalation: Metaphors and Scenarios*. New York, Washington & London: Praeger.

Kanninen, Tapio 1989. *Frameworks for the Monitoring of Emergent and Ongoing Conflicts*. ISA paper, April 1989.

Kanninen, Tapio 1990. 'Towards Effective War Risk Reduction within the United Nations Framework'. Paper presented at the Conference on War-Risk Reduction through Multilateral Means, Kingston, Ontario, organized by the Canadian Institute for International Peace and Security, 7 - 8 October 1988.

Kelleher, Catherine McArdle 1987. 'NATO Nuclear Operations' in Ashton B. Carter, John Steinbruner & Charles Zraket, eds., *Managing Nuclear Operations*, pp. 445-469. Washington, DC: The Brookings Institution.

Kellen, Konrad 1987. 'The Potential For Nuclear Terrorism: a Discussion' in Paul Leventhal and Yonah Alexander, eds., *Preventing Nuclear Terrorism*, pp. 104-133. Lexington: Lexington Books.

Keohane, Robert O. 1986. *Neorealism and its Critics*. New York: Columbia University Press.

Kerr, Donald 1984. 'Implications of Anti-Satellite Weapons for ABM Issues' in Jasani, Bhupendra, ed. *Space Weapons - The Arms Control Dilemma*. London: Taylor & Francis.

Klare, Michael 1990. 'An Arms Control Agenda for the Third World', *Arms Control Today*, April 1990, pp. 8-12.

Klein, Georg 1984. ... *i stället för hemland*. Stockholm: Bonniers.

Kleinmuntz, Donald N. 1985. 'Cognitive Heuristics and Feedback in a Dynamic Decision Environment' in *Management Science*, 31, pp. 680-702.

Kluwe, Rainer H., Carlo Misiak & Holger Reiman 1984. *Lernvorgänge beim Umgang mit Systemen*. Technical Report 7, Hamburg: Hochschule der Bundeswehr, Fachbereich Pädagogik.

Kohl, Wilfred 1971. *French Nuclear Diplomacy*. Princeton: Princeton University Press.

Kramer, John M. 1988. 'Drug Abuse in the Soviet Union', *Problems of Communism*, March-April, pp. 30-36.

Kringlen, Einar 1985. 'The Myth of Rationality in Situations of Crisis' in Hellman ed., *Nuclear War by Mistake - Inevitable or Preventable?* Report from an International Conference in Stockholm, Sweden, 15-16 February 1985, pp. 49-57.

Kull, Steven 1988. *Minds at War: Nuclear Reality and the Inner Conflicts of Defense Policy Makers.* New York: Basic Books.

Laaksonen, Jukka 1986. 'The Accident at the Chernobyl Nuclear Power Plant', Society of Reliability Engineers, Scandinavian Chapter-Symposium, Otaniemi, Finland, 14-16 October 1986. Technical Research Centre of Finland, Electrical Engineering Laboratory, Otakaari 7 B, SF-02150 Espoo, Finland.

Laffin, Art 1984. 'Direct Disarmament: Plowshares Actions 1980-1985', *Resistance News*, no. 18, August 1.

Larus, Joel 1970. 'Safing the Nukes: the Human Reliability Problem'. Stockholm: Stockholm International Peace Research Institute.

Lazarev, P. L. 1986. 'Opyt profilatiki p'janstva i alkogolizma', *Voenno-meditsinskii zhurnal*, November, pp. 55-57.

Lebow, Richard Ned 1987. *Nuclear Crisis Management: A Dangerous Illusion.* Ithaca, NY: Cornell University Press.

LeFebvre, P. 1981. 'Les Conduites Toxicophiles dans les Armées Francaises', *Annales Medico-Psychologiques*, Paris, June, p. 669.

Leurdijk, J. H. 1974. 'From International to Transnational Politics: A Change of Paradigms', *International Social Science Journal*, vol. 26, no. 1.

Leventhal, Paul & Yonah Alexander, eds. 1987. *Preventing Nuclear Terrorism.* Lexington: Lexington Books.

Lewis, Harald W. et al. 1978. *Risk Assessment Review Group Report to the US Nuclear Regulatory Commission.* Washington DC: Nuclear Regulatory Commission.

Lewy, Guenter 1970. 'Superior Orders, Nuclear Warfare, and the Dictates of Conscience', in Richard A. Wasserstrom, ed., *War and Morality*. Belmont, CA: Wadsworth, pp. 115-134.

Lifton, Robert J. 1986. *The Nazi Doctors - A Study of the Psychology of Evil*. London: Macmillan.

Lijphardt, Arend 1974. 'International Relations Theory: Great Debates and Lesser Debates', *International Social Science Journal*, vol. 26, no. 1.

Lin, Chong-Pin 1988. *China's Nuclear Weapons Strategy: Tradition Within Evolution*. Lexington: Lexington Books.

Longo, James 1990. 'Murders Spark Nuclear Safety Review', *Navy Times*, February 5, p. 2.

Los Angeles Times, 1990. 'Britain Seizes Huge Gun Barrel Near Iraqi Ship', April 12, p. 5.

Luce, R. Duncan & Howard Raiffa 1957. *Games and Decisions*. New York: Wiley.

Luttwak, Edward N. 1987. *Strategy: The Logic of War and Peace*. London & Cambridge, MA: Belknap.

Lynch, Lt. Col. P. 1987. 'Alcohol Associated Deaths in British Soldiers', *Journal of the Royal Army Medical Corps*, vol. 133, no. 1, February, pp. 34-36.

Mark, J. Carson, Theodore Taylor, Eugene Eyster, William Maraman & Jacob Wechsler 1987. 'Can Terrorists Build Nuclear Weapons?' in Paul Leventhal & Yonah Alexander, *Preventing Nuclear Terrorism*, pp. 55-65. Lexington: Lexington Books.

Markoff John, 'Superhuman Failure', *The New York Times*, January 17, p. A14.

Marsh, Gerald E. 1985. 'SDI: The Stability Question', *Bulletin of the Atomic Scientists*, vol. 41, no. 9, October.

Martin, Michael L. 1981. *Warriors to Managers: the French Military Establishment Since 1945.* Chapel Hill: University of North Carolina Press.

Mastrangelo, Eugene 1987. 'Terrorist Activities By Region' in Paul Leventhal & Yonah Alexander, *Preventing Nuclear Terrorism*, pp. 134-145. Lexington: Lexington Books.

Masters, Dexter 1985. *The Accident.* New York: Knopf. As cited in Gregory & Edwards, *A Handbook of Nuclear Weapons Accidents*, p. 15. Bradford: University of Bradford School of Peace Studies.

McLean, Scilla ed. 1986. *How Nuclear Weapons Decisions Are Made.* London: Macmillan.

McNamara, Robert 1987. *Blundering Into Disaster.* New York: Pantheon.

Merrill, Mike 1989. 'Slaying Sends Shock Waves Through Tri-Cities', *Seattle Post-Intelligencer*, August 3, p. A1.

Meyer, L. 1984. 'Fail-Safe and Subs: Should We Trust the Navy to Trust Itself?' *The Washington Post Magazine*, September 30.

Meyer, Stephen M. 1987. 'Soviet Nuclear Operations' in Ashton B. Carter, John Steinbruner & Charles Zraket, eds., *Managing Nuclear Operations*, pp. 470-534. Washington, DC: The Brookings Institution.

Milgram, Stanley 1968. 'Some Conditions of Obedience and Disobedience to Authority'. *International Journal of Psychiatry*, vol. 6, pp. 259-276.

Morgenthau, Hans J. 1954. *Politics Among Nations.* New York: Alfred Knopf

Morgenthau, Hans 1976. 'The Fallacy of Thinking Conventionally about Nuclear Weapons' in Carlton, David & Carlo Schaerf, eds. *Arms Control and Technological Innovation*, pp. 256-260. New York: Wiley.

Müller, Harald 1992. 'The nuclear non-proliferation regime beyond the Persian Gulf War and the dissolution of the Soviet Union', Ch. 3 in *SIPRI Yearbook 1992: World Armaments and Disarmament*. Oxford: Oxford University Press.

Müller, Manfred 1988. 'Prevention of Conflicts through Confidence-building Measures and Co-operative Security Structures'. Paper presented at the Conference on War-Risk Reduction through Multilateral Means, Kingston, Ontario, organized by the Canadian Institute for International Peace and Security, 7 - 8 October 1988.

Nature, 1986. 'Near-Catastrophe at Le Bugey', vol. 321, 29 May, p. 462.

Natvig, Bent, 1979. 'Litt om Bruk og Manglende Bruk av Pålitelighet-steori i Kjernekraftutvalgets Innstilling (On the Use and Misuse of Reliability Theory in the Report of the Nuclear Power Commission)'. Oslo: The Faculty of Science, University of Oslo.

Natvig, Bent 1985a. 'New Light on Measures of Importance of System Components', *Scandinavian Journal of Statistics*, vol. 12, pp. 43-54.

Natvig, Bent 1985b. 'Multistate Coherent Systems' in Johnson, Norman L. & Samuel Kotz, eds. *Encyclopedia of Statistical Sciences*, vol. 5, pp. 732-735. New York: Wiley.

Natvig, Bent 1988. 'Nuclear Disarmament and Accidental Nuclear War' in *Proceedings of the Thirty-Eighth Pugwash Conference on Science and World Affairs*, Dagomys, USSR, 29 August - 3 September 1988. Pugwash Office, Flat A, 63 A Great Russell Street, London WC1B 3BG, England, pp. 207-210.

Natvig, Bent 1989. 'Nuclear Disarmament and Accidental Nuclear War', *Bulletin of Peace Proposals*, vol. 20, no. 2, pp. 219-223.

Natvig, Bent & Henriette Eide 1987. 'Bayesian Estimation of System Reliability', *Scandinavian Journal of Statistics*, vol. 14, pp. 319-327.

Navari, Cornelia 1989. 'The Great Illusion Revisited', *Review of International Studies*, vol. 15, no. 4, pp. 341-58.

Navlakha, Gautam 1991. 'Kuwaitkrisen og den Tredje verden' ('The Kuwait Crisis and the Third World'), *Vandkunsten* (Copenhagen), no. 5, pp. 68-72.

Nelson, Gregg & David Redell 1986. 'Could We Trust the SDI Software?', Chapter 5 submitted to the Union of Concerned Scientists, April 10.

New York Times, 1990. 'Text of the Declaration After the NATO Talks', 7 July, p. 5, col. 1.

National Institute on Drug Abuse, 1988. *National Household Survey on Drug Abuse: Main Findings 1985*. Rockville: National Institute on Drug Abuse.

Nisbeth, Richard E & Lee Ross 1980. *Human Inference: Strategies and Shortcomings of Social Judgement*. Englewood, NJ: Prentice Hall.

Nolan, Janne E. 1990. 'Missile Mania', *Bulletin of the Atomic Scientists*, May, pp. 27-29.

Norman, Colin 1990. 'Satellite Killers', *Science*, vol. 247, March 16.

Office of Technology Assessment, 1979. *The Effects of Nuclear War*, Washington DC: Government Printing Office.

Office of Technology Assessment 1983. 'Launch Under Attack', *Scientific American*, vol. 250, no. 1, January.

Office of Technology Assessment 1986. *Strategic Defenses: Ballistic Missile Defense Technologies*. Princeton: Princeton University Press.

Offley, Ed 1990a. 'Checkup Ordered at Bangor', *Seattle Post-Intelligencer*, January 23.

Offley, Ed 1990b. 'N-Sub Crew Program Under Review', *Seattle Post-Intelligencer*, February 23.

Offley, Ed 1990c. 'Co-Workers Failed to Report Marine, Navy Probe Finds', *Seattle Post-Intelligencer*, January 24.

Offley, Ed 1990d. 'Bangor Killings: is Suspect Victim?' *Seattle Post-Intelligencer*, February 6, p. 6.

Offley, Ed 1990e. 'Navy Screening Under Fire', *Seattle Post-Intelligencer*, February 15.

Ogunbadejo, Oye 1989. 'Nuclear Nonproliferation in Africa: The Challenge Ahead', *Arms Control*, vol. 10, no. 1, May, p. 69.

Panel on Nuclear Weapons Safety 1990. *Nuclear Weapons Safety*. Report of the Panel on Nuclear Weapons Safety of the Committee on Armed Services, House of Representatives. Washington: US Government Printing Office.

Parhomov, A. F. et al. 1986. 'Opyt provedeniia alkogol'nykh meropriiatii v aviatsionnikh', *Voenno-meditsinskii zhurnal*, November, pp. 55-57.

Paul, Derek, Michael D. Intriligator & Paul Smoker, eds. 1990. *Accidental Nuclear War*. Proceedings of the Eighteenth Pugwash Workshop on Nuclear Forces. Toronto: Science for Peace/Samuel Stevens.

Perry, William J. 1980. Hearings before the Committee on Armed Services, US Senate, part 5, p. 2936.

Perry, William J. 1989. *Defense Investment: A Strategy for the 1990s*. Stanford University: Center for International Security and Arms Control.

Petersen, Ib Damgaard 1987. 'Cybernetics and the Study of War'. Paper for Seventh International Congress of Cybernetics and Systems. Copenhagen: Working Paper,Institut for samfundsfag og forvaltning.

Petersen, Ib Damgaard & Paul Smoker 1989a. *The Fear Trap*. Christchurch, New Zealand: Department of Sociology, University of Canterbury.

Petersen, Ib Damgaard & Paul Smoker 1989b. *The International Tension Monitor*. Sydney: CPACS, University of Sydney.

Petrovsky, Vladimir 1988. 'From Crisis to Preventive Diplomacy in the United Nations'. Text of the speech of the USSR Deputy Foreign Minister delivered at the Conference on War-Risk Reduction through Multilateral Means, Kingston, Ontario, organized by the Canadian Institute for International Peace and Security, 7 - 8 October 1988.

Plag, John A., Ransom J. Arthur & Jerry M. Goffmann 1970. 'Dimensions of Psychiatric Illness Among First-term Enlistees in the United States Navy,' *Military Medicine*, vol. 135, pp. 665-673.

Pringle, Peter & William Arkin 1983. *SIOP, Nuclear War from the Inside*. London: Sphere Books.

Pry, Peter 1984. *Israel's Nuclear Arsenal*. Boulder: Westview Press.

RAF News, 1983. September 9, p. 11. As quoted in Gregory, *The Command and Control of British Nuclear Weapons*, p. 88. Bradford: University of Bradford School of Peace Studies.

Rapoport, Anatol 1960. *Fights, Games and Debates*. Ann Arbor: The University of Michigan Press.

Rapoport, Anatol 1964. *Strategy and Conscience*. New York, Evanston & London: Harper & Row.

Rathjens, George 1985. 'Nuclear Winter: Strategic Significance', Issues in *Science and Technology*, p. 6. The National Academy of Sciences.

Rauschenbach, Boris V. 1987: 'Unbeabsichtige Kernwaffenkonflikte nicht ausgeschlossen', *Wissenschaft und Fortschritt*, nos. 10 and 12.

Reactor Safety Study, 1975. *An Assessment of Accident Risks in US Commercial Nuclear Power Plants*. WASH-1400. Washington DC: Nuclear Regulatory Commission.

Rebane, Karl 1978. 'Energia, entroopia, elukeskkond' ('Energy, Entropy, Environment'). Tallinn: Valgus. (Also published in Russian as Rebane 1980)

Rebane, Karl 1980. 'Energiya, entropiya, sreda obitaniya', Tallinn: Valgus.

Rebane, Karl 1990. 'Energia, entroopia, elukeskkond: Miks on keskonna kaitse ka objektivselt raske?' ('Energy, entropy, environment: Why is protection of environment really difficult?'), *Akadeemia*, vol. 2, no. 3, pp. 451-468.

Redman, R. A. & L. J. Walter, Jr. 1985. *Suicide Among Active Duty Military Personnel*. Washington, DC: Health Studies Task Force, Office of the Assistant Secretary of Defense.

Richter, Horst E. 1981. *Alle Redeten vom Frieden*. Reinbeck: Rowohlt.

Rodley, Gordon ed. 1989. *Beyond Deterrence*. Sydney: Centre for Peace and Conflict Research, University of Sydney.

Rogers, Rita R. 1990. 'The Kaleidoscope of International Decision Making' in Paul, Intriligator & Smoker eds., *Accidental Nuclear War*, pp. 97-107. Proceedings of the Eighteenth Pugwash Workshop on Nuclear Forces. Toronto: Science for Peace/Samuel Stevens.

Ross, Lee & Craig Anderson 1982. 'Shortcomings in the Attribution Process' in Daniel Kahneman, Paul Slovic & Amos Tversky, eds. *Judgement under Uncertainty: Heuristics and Biases*, pp. 129-152. Cambridge: Cambridge Univ. Press.

Rothberg, Joseph M., Nicholas L. Rock & Franklin Del Jones 1984. 'Suicide in United States Army Personnel, 1981-1982', *Military Medicine*, vol. 149, no. 10, pp. 537-541.

Rowen, Henry & Fred Hoffman 1991. 'Soviet Weapons: How Much of a Problem?', *International Herald Tribune*, 2 September.

Russell, Bertrand 1959. *Common Sense and Nuclear Warfare*. New York: Simon & Schuster.

Sacramento Bee, 1987. 'N-Bomb Parts 'Stolen' in Mock Raid', February 12, p. B4.

San Jose Mercury News, 1990. 'China Seeks to Quell Unrest Near Soviet Border', April 10.

Sanders, Ben 1991. 'North Korea, South Africa ready to tell all?', *The Bulletin of Atomic Scientists*. September.

Satloff, A., 1967. 'Psychiatry and the Nuclear Submarine,' *American Journal of Psychiatry*, vol. 124, no. 4, pp. 547-551.

Scheer, Robert 1982. *With Enough Shovels*. New York: Random House.

Schell, Jonathan 1982. *The Fate of the Earth*. New York: Avon.

Schelling, Thomas C. 1963. *The Strategy of Conflict*. New York: Oxford University Press.

Segal, Gerald 1984. 'Nuclear Forces' in Gerald Segal & William T. Tow, eds., *Chinese Defence Policy*, pp. 99-113. Chicago: University of Illinois Press.

Sennott, Linn I. 1986. 'Distributions Arising in the Study of False Alarms in the Early Warning System', Department of Mathematics, Illinois State University, Normal, IL 61761.

Shambaugh, David L. 1989. 'The Fourth and Fifth Plenary Sessions of the 13th CCP Central Committee', *The China Quarterly*, no. 120, December, pp. 856-862.

Shapely, Deborah 1984, 'Strategic Doctrines, the Militarization and the 'Semi-militarization' of Space' in Bhupendra Jasani, ed., *Space Weapons - The Arms Control Dilemma*, pp. 57-70. London: Taylor & Francis.

Shiels, Frederick 1990. *Preventable Disasters: Why Governments Fail.* Savage, MD: Rowman and Littlefield.

Sims, Clavin 1990. 'Disruption of Phone Service Is Laid to Computer Program', *The New York Times*, January 17, pp. 1 and A14.

SIPRI, 1972. *SIPRI Yearbook 1972: World Armaments and Disarmament*. Stockholm International Peace Research Institute. Stockholm: Almqvist & Wiksell; New York: Humanities Press; and London: Paul Elek.

SIPRI, 1989. *SIPRI Yearbook 1989*. Stockholm International Peace Research Institute. New York: Oxford University Press.

Solov'ev, A. D., M. S. Liaskovskit & G. I. Cychev 1971. 'Experimental-Psychological Observations of Pilots Admitting Erroneous Actions', *Voenno-meditsinskii zhurnal*, vol. 9, pp. 66-68.

Spector, Leonard 1987. *Going Nuclear*. Cambridge, MA: Ballinger.

Spector, Leonard 1988. *The Undeclared Bomb: The Spread of Nuclear Weapons 1987-1988*. Cambridge, MA: Ballinger.

Spector, Leonard S. & Jaqueline R. Smith 1990. *Nuclear Ambitions: The Spread of Nuclear Weapons 1989-1990*. Boulder, San Francisco & Oxford: Westview Press.

Statens energiverk, 1990. *Reaktoravveckling 1995/96 - Konsekvenser och samhällsekonomiska kostnader*. Stockholm.

Stein, Peter & Peter Feaver 1987. *Assuring Control of Nuclear Weapons: The Evolution of Permissive Action Links*. Lanham: University Press of America.

Strekozov, V. G. 1990. 'The Law on Defense', *Red Star*, April 29.

Sulzberger, A. O. jr. 1979. 'Error Alerts US Forces to a False Missile Attack', *New York Times*, November 11, p. 30.

Sutterlin, James 1988. 'The Desirability of a War-Risk Reduction Center Within the Framework of the United Nations'. Paper presented at the Conference on War-Risk Reduction through Multilateral Means, Kingston, Ontario, organized by the Canadian Institute for International Peace and Security, 7 - 8 October 1988.

Sutterlin, James 1989a. 'A Multilateral Nuclear Alert Centre: Objectives, Utility and Structure'. Paper presented at the Seminar on Multilateral Confidence-building and the Prevention of War, Kiev, 4 - 7 September 1989.

Sutterlin, James 1989b. 'The Objectives, Requirements and Structure of a War Risk Reduction Centre within the United Nations'.Paper presented at the Conference on the Establishment of Multilateral War Risk Reduction Centres, Warsaw, 24 - 25 April 1989

Tansey, W. A., J. A. Wilson & K. E. Schaefer 1979. 'Analysis of Health Data From 10 Years of Polaris Submarine Patrols', *Undersea Biomedical Research*, vol. 6, pp. S217-S246.

Tarasulo, Y. 1985. 'A Profile of the Soviet Soldier,' *Armed Forces and Society*, vol. 11, no. 2, pp. 221-234.

Tetlock, Philip E. & Charles McGuire 1986. 'Cognitive Perspectives on Foreign Policy', in Ralf K. White, ed., *Psychology and the Prevention of Nuclear War*, pp. 255-273. New York: University Press.

Thompson, James 1985. *The Psychology of Nuclear War*. London: Wiley.

Thompson, M. 1980. 'The Aesthetics of Risk: Culture or Contest.' in R. C. Schwing & W. H. Albers, eds., *Societal Risk Assessment: How Safe is Safe Enough?* New York: Plenum.

Thompson, M. 1983. 'Postscript: A Cultural Basis for Comparison.' in H. Kunreuther & J. Linnerooth, eds., *Risk Analysis and Decision Processes*. Berlin: Springer-Verlag.

Time, 1976. 'How Israel Got the Bomb', vol. 107, April 12. As quoted in Pry, *Israel's Nuclear Arsenal*, pp. 80-81. Boulder: Westview Presspp.

The Times 1986. 'Drug Tests for Army Next Year', September 29, p. 1.

Travis, Larry & Daniel Stock et al. 1983. 'Computer Unreliability and Nuclear War'. Originally prepared for a workshop at a symposium on the Medical Consequences of Nuclear War held on October 15, at Madison, WI. Available from: Computer Professionals for Social Responsibility, P.O. Box 717, Palo Alto, CA 94301, USA.

Tuchman, Barbara W. 1984. *The March of Folly. From Troy to Vietnam*. London: Michael Joseph.

Tunander, Ola 1989. 'Avskräckningens logik' in Wiberg ed., *Farväl till avskräckningen? (Good-bye to Deterrence?)*. Lund: Lund University Press.

Turco, Richard & Carl Sagan 1989. 'Policy Implications of Nuclear Winter', *Ambio*, vol. 18, no. 7, pp. 7.

Turco Richard, O. Toon, T. Ackerman, J. Pollack & Carl Sagan 1990. 'Climate and Smoke: An Appraisal of Nuclear Winter', *Science*, Vol. 247, 12 January, p. 11.

Turner, Stansfield & Thomas Davies 1990. 'Plutonium Terror on the High Seas', *New York Times*, April 28, p. 15.

United Nations, 1986. Report of the Secretary-General on the Work of the Organization. A/41/1, September 1989.

United Nations, 1987. 'Secretary-General's Bulletin: Office for Research and the Collection of Information'. ST/SGB/225, 1 March 1987, New York.

United Nations, 1988a. Forty-third Session of the General Assembly. 'General and Complete Disarmament: Letter dated 17 June 1988 from the Permanent Representative of Poland to the United Nations Addressed to the Secretary-General', 17 June 1988, A/43/411, New York.

United Nations, 1988b. Forty-Third Session of the General Assembly. 'General Debate on Disarmament Continues in First Committee.' DPI Press Release, 31 October 1988, GA/PS/2716, New York.

United Nations, 1990. Department for Disarmament Affairs. *Disarmament Newsletter*, vol. 8, no. 2, April.

Ury, William 1985. *Beyond the Hotline: How Crisis Control Can Prevent Nuclear War*. Boston: Houghton Mifflin.

Ury, William L. 1984. *Beyond the Hot-line - Controlling a Nuclear Crisis.* Cambridge, MA.

US Congress, 1975. 'Authority to Order the Use of Nuclear Weapons (United States, United Kingdom, Soviet Union, People's Republic of China),' House of Representatives Committee on International Relations, Subcommittee on International Security and Scientific Affairs, December 1.

US Congress, 1976. 'Second Annual Report to the US Congress by the Joint Committee on Atomic Energy', June 30, pp. 30-31. As quoted in Stein & Feaver, *Assuring Control of Nuclear Weapons: The Evolution of Permissive Action Links*, pp. 60-61. Lanham: University Press of America.

US Congress, 1977. *Nuclear Proliferation and Safeguards*. Office of Technology Assessment. New York: Praeger.

US Congress, 1978. 'Security of Nuclear and Chemical Weapons Storage'. Hearings before the House Subcommittee on Military Construction Appropriations, 95th Congress, 2nd Session, Part 2, pp. 137-336. Washington, DC: Government Printing Office.

US Congress 1981. 'Failures of the North American Aerospace Defense Command's (NORAD) Attack Warning System', Hearings before a Subcommittee of the Committee on Government Operations, House of Representatives, 97th Congress, 1st session, May 19 and 20. Washington, DC: US Government Printing Office.

US Congress, 1984. 'Security of US Bases Overseas', House Subcommittee on Military Construction Appropriations, 98th Congress, 1st Session, December 2.

US General Accounting Office 1981. *NORAD's Missile Warning System: What Went Wrong?*, Report to the Chariman, Committee on Government Operations, House of Representatives, by the Comptroller General of the United States, MASAD-81-30, May 15.

Vauterin, C. L. 1970. 'Problemes Posés par les Mutilations Volontaires dans l'Armée', *Revue des Corps de Santé des Armeés*, vol. XI, no. 4, August, p. 455.

Von Neumann, John & Oscar Morgenstern 1944. *Theory of Games and Economic Behavior*. Princeton: Princeton University Press.

Wallace, Michael D., Brian L. Crissey & Linn I. Sennott 1986. 'Accidental Nuclear War: a Risk Assessment', *Journal of Peace Research*, vol. 23, no. 1, March, pp. 9-27.

Waller, Bruce, James Bruce & Douglas Cook 1986. *SDI: Progress and Challenges*, Staff Report Submitted to Senator William Proxmire; Senator J. Bennett Johnson & Senator Lawton Chilles, March 17.

Walters, Ronald W. 1987. *South Africa and the Bomb*. Lexington: Lexington Books.

Washington Times, 1990. 'Soviet Nuclear Civil War Feared', March 29, p. 1.

Wedar, Carin Atterling, Peeter Vares & Michael D. Intriligator, eds. 1992. *Implications of the Dissolution af the Soviet Union for Accidental/Inadvertent Usre of Weapons of Mass Destruction*. Tallinn: Estonian Academy of Science.

Wedge, Bryant 1986. 'Psychology of the Self in Social Conflict' in Edward Azar & John Burton, eds., *International Conflict Resolution: Theory and Practice*, pp. 56-62. Brighton: Wheatsheaf Books.

Wiberg, Håkan ed. 1989. *Farväl till avskräckningen? (Good-bye to Deterrence?)*. Lund: Lund University Press.

Willrich, Mason & Theodore Taylor 1974. *Nuclear Theft: Risks and Safeguards*. Cambridge, MA: Ballinger.

Wilentz, Amy 1986. 'Scientific Hurdles: From Sensor to Software, the Needs are Daunting', *Time*, June 23.

Wimbush, E. 1981. 'The Red Army', PBS TV documentary, May 6. As cited in Cockburn, 1983, *The Threat: Inside the Soviet Military Machine*, p. 62. New York: Random House.

Wohlstetter, Roberta 1962. *Pearl Harbor: Warning and Decision.* Stanford: Stanford.

Wood, P. J. 1980. 'Alcoholism in the Army: A Demographic Survey of an Inpatient Population', *British Journal of Addiction*, vol. 75, pp. 375-380.

Wooldridge, Chris, Nigel Draper & Tom Hunter 1980. *The Systems Approach to Safety: Risk and Rationality.* Milton Keynes: Open University Press.

Wæver, Ole 1989. *Hele Europa.* Copenhagen: SNU.

Zimmerman, Peter D. 1989. 'Navy Says No PALs for US,' *Bulletin of the Atomic Scientists*, November, p. 37.

Zuckerman, Mark 1971. 'Dimensions of Sensation Seeking', *Journal of Consulting and Clinical Psychology*, 36, pp. 45-52.

Zuckerman, Mark, Sybil B. G. Eysenk & Hans K. Eysenk 1978. 'Sensation-seeking in England and America: Cross Cultural, Age and Sex Comparisons.' in *Journal of Consulting and Clinical Psychology*, 46, pp. 139-49.

Zuckerman, Mark 1979. 'Sensation Seeking and Risk-taking' in Izard, C. E., ed. *'Emotions in Personality and Psychopathology'.* London: Plenum.

Zuev, V. S. & Karl K. Rebane 1990. 'Opticheski zamok' ('Optical lock'). Moscow: Physical Institute of the Academy of Sciences of the USSR, Preprint no. 102.